George Salmon

Non-miraculous Christianity and other sermons

Second Edition

George Salmon

Non-miraculous Christianity and other sermons
Second Edition

ISBN/EAN: 9783337085766

Printed in Europe, USA, Canada, Australia, Japan

Cover: Foto ©Lupo / pixelio.de

More available books at **www.hansebooks.com**

NON-MIRACULOUS CHRISTIANITY

And other Sermons

PREACHED IN

THE CHAPEL OF TRINITY COLLEGE
DUBLIN

BY

GEORGE SALMON, D.D.

CHANCELLOR OF ST. PATRICK'S CATHEDRAL, AND REGIUS PROFESSOR OF
DIVINITY IN THE UNIVERSITY OF DUBLIN

SECOND EDITION

London
MACMILLAN AND CO.
AND NEW YORK
1887

All rights reserved

CONTENTS

I

Non-Miraculous Christianity

[Preached in Cambridge, May 23, 1880.]

St. Matthew xi. 2-5.—*Now when John had heard in the prison the works of Christ, he sent two of his disciples and said unto Him, Art thou He that should come, or do we look for another? Jesus answered and said unto them, Go and show John again those things which ye do hear and see: the blind receive their sight, and the lame walk, the lepers are cleansed, and the deaf hear, the dead are raised up, and the poor have the gospel preached to them* . . . . Page 1

II

The Name Christian.—I

Acts xi. 26.—*And the disciples were called Christians first in Antioch* 31

III

The Name Christian.—II

1 Corinthians i. 12.—*Every one of you saith, I am of Paul; and I of Cephas; and I of Apollos; and I of Christ* . 50

IV

A Scientific Test applied to Atheistic Theories of Religion
[Preached in Belfast, December 1875.]

ST. JOHN vi. 67, 68.—*Then said Jesus unto the twelve, Will ye also go away? Then Simon Peter answered Him, Lord, to whom shall we go? Thou hast the words of eternal life*

Page 72

V

Theism and Modern Science.—I

ROMANS i. 20.—*The invisible things of Him from the creation of the world are clearly seen, being understood by the things that are made, even His eternal power and Godhead* . 95

VI

Theism and Modern Science.—II

ROMANS i. 20.—*The invisible things of Him from the creation of the world are clearly seen; being understood by the things that are made, even His eternal power and Godhead* . 121

VII

Evolution

ST. MARK vi. 26-29.—*And He said, So is the kingdom of God, as if a man should cast seed into the ground; and should sleep and rise night and day, and the seed should spring and grow up, he knoweth not how. For the earth bringeth forth fruit of herself; first the blade, then the ear, after that the full corn in the ear. But when the fruit is brought forth, immediately he putteth in the sickle, because the harvest is come* . . 155

VIII
The Evidential Value of the Eucharistic Rite
[Reprinted here from Series of Sermons published in 1873.]

St. Matthew xxvi. 26-28.—*And as they were eating, Jesus took bread, and blessed it, and brake it, and gave it to the disciples, and said, Take, eat; this is My body. And He took the cup, and gave thanks, and gave it to them, saying, Drink ye all of it: for this is My blood of the new testament, which is shed for many for the remission of sins* . . . Page 174

IX
The Parable of the Sower

St. Matthew xiii. 3-9.—*Behold, a sower went forth to sow; and when he sowed, some seeds fell by the wayside, and the fowls came and devoured them up: some fell upon stony places, where they had not much earth; and forthwith they sprung up, because they had no deepness of earth, and when the sun was up, they were scorched; and because they had no root, they withered away. And some fell among thorns: and the thorns sprung up, and choked them: but other fell into good ground, and brought forth fruit, some an hundredfold, some sixtyfold, some thirtyfold. Who hath ears to hear, let him hear* . . . 195

X
Leaning on Man's own Understanding

Proverbs iii. 5.—*Trust in the Lord with all thine heart, and lean not unto thine own understanding. In all thy ways acknowledge Him, and He shall direct thy paths.*
Proverbs xxvii. 1.—*Boast not thyself of to-morrow; for thou knowest not what a day may bring forth* . 218

XI
Wisdom

Job xxviii. 28.—*Unto man He said, Behold, the fear of the Lord that is wisdom, and to depart from evil is understanding* 241

XII
Self-Righteousness

St. Luke xviii. 14.—*I tell you this man went down to his house justified rather than the other* . . Page 261

XIII
The Slavery of Sin

St. John viii. 33-36.—*They answered Him, We be Abraham's seed, and were never in bondage to any man: how sayest Thou, Ye shall be made free? Jesus answered them, Verily, verily, I say unto you, Whosoever committeth sin is the servant of sin. And the servant abideth not in the house for ever: but the Son abideth ever. If the Son therefore shall make you free, ye shall be free indeed* 285

XIV
Progress

St. Matthew xix. 30.—*But many that are first shall be last, and the last shall be first* 307

XV
Truthfulness

Ephesians iv. 25.—*Putting away lying, speak every man truth with his neighbour, for we are members one of another* . 328

XVI
The Sin of Mutilating the Gospel Message

Hebrews vi. 1, 2.—*Therefore leaving the principles of the doctrine of Christ, let us go on unto perfection; not laying again the foundation of repentance from dead works, and of faith towards God, of the doctrine of baptisms, and of laying on of hands, and of resurrection of the dead, and of eternal judgment* . 351

I
NON-MIRACULOUS CHRISTIANITY

> "Now when John had heard in the prison the works of Christ, he sent two of his disciples and said unto Him, Art thou He that should come, or do we look for another? Jesus answered and said unto them, Go and show John again those things which ye do hear and see: the blind receive their sight, and the lame walk, the lepers are cleansed, and the deaf hear, the dead are raised up, and the poor have the gospel preached to them."—
> ST. MATTHEW xi. 2-5.

ALTHOUGH the celebration of this day[1] is a comparatively modern appendix to the feasts of the Christian year, it is very fitting that an opportunity should be given us to ask ourselves what conclusion ought we to draw from the facts we have commemorated; what is the only theory which will make these things credible. We have commemorated the day of the birth and the day of the death of the Founder of our religion; and in this there is nothing to be ashamed of, whatever theory we hold about Him; for all must allow that He was one of the world's greatest benefactors, and filled

[1] Preached at Great St. Mary's, Cambridge, on Trinity Sunday, 1880.

a place in its history such as scarcely any other has occupied: and that therefore those who bear His name may rightly strive that His life and death should not be forgotten. But we preceded our commemoration of His birth by a season of preparation, and we thereby signified our belief that His appearance in the world had been no chance birth of time, but an event long prepared in the Divine counsels, prefigured in the ceremonies of the Mosaic law, announced beforehand by the Jewish prophets in predictions which, as the time of His coming drew near, became more numerous and more distinct. In a special festival we celebrated His Conception as an exception to the laws of human generation. In commemorating His Nativity we acknowledged it as signalised by miracle, and in our glad hymns we echoed the strains in which the shepherds keeping watch over their flocks heard the heavenly host welcome the glad tidings of great joy. We not only commemorated His death, but, three days after, we declared our belief that death had not been able to hold Him captive. On this belief we found our own hopes for future reunion with those we have loved; for (in the Apostle's words) if we believe that Jesus died and rose again, even so them also which sleep in Jesus will God bring with Him. We celebrated His glorious Ascension into heaven, and last Sunday testified our gratitude for that, when He departed from this world, He did not leave His people orphans, but gave them another Comforter, who should abide with them for ever.

And now the question comes—What mean we by all this service? Did the facts which we commemorate really happen? If not, why do we commemorate them? Then, indeed, have we cause to be ashamed, not for ourselves only, but for the whole Christian Church throughout the world, and from nearly the apostles' times to our own, that the true history of Him by whose name we are called has been so overlaid with fable, and that it is with the fabulous part we have all been almost exclusively taught to occupy our minds, and thereon to rest our hopes. On the other hand, if these facts did happen, things are true of Jesus of Nazareth which are true of no one else that ever lived in the world. He is a unique person in the world's history. And the more we think on the matter, the less can we be satisfied in ascribing to Him any dignity short of Divine. It seems to me, then, that the answer to the question, Have we a right to call ourselves Christians? depends on our answer to two questions which really reduce themselves to one: Are the things commemorated in the feasts of the Christian year true, and was Jesus of Nazareth a unique person?

I. There were among the Socinians of a former generation those who rejected the doctrine of our Lord's Divinity, but who yet felt no difficulty in admitting the truth of some, if not all, of the supernatural facts of the Gospel history, and in ascribing to the New Testament books a Divine inspiration distinct in kind from any which can be attributed to the best of human productions. It may be safely said that the times in which such an attitude of mind was possible have passed away never to return. Any difficulties which are felt now relate to the belief in supernatural facts, not to the acceptance of the doctrinal inferences which such facts once admitted suggest. Nay, it will be found that the admission of the doctrine in which we this day profess our belief sweeps away at once the most formidable difficulties which now stand in the way of the acknowledgment of the supernatural facts.

There has been a tendency of recent years to sneer at the evidential school of the last century, as if Lardner, Paley, and the rest had failed in the task they set themselves, and as if their failure did not much matter to us who have a more sure foundation for our faith. Such sneers indicate a complete failure to apprehend that ours is a historical religion, the cardinal tenet of which is that some eighteen centuries ago there was in this world One who was like no one else who ever lived in the world, and who then did a work for the benefit of the world which none but He could have accomplished. All those celebrations of the Christian year of which I spoke are nothing but an expanded expression of our faith in the articles of the baptismal creed. Without such faith I do not see how any one can rightly call himself a Christian.

If we can imagine ourselves asking any of the ancient teachers whom the Church has honoured, What must a man do before you can acknowledge him as a Christian? he would no doubt answer, He must be baptized. And what is necessary before he can be baptized? He must believe. And what is the belief of which you require him to make public profession? "I believe in God the Father Almighty, and in Jesus Christ His only Son our Lord; who was born of the Holy Ghost and the Virgin Mary, was crucified under Pontius Pilate and was buried, and the third day rose again from the dead, who ascended into heaven, and sitteth on the right hand of the Father, whence He cometh to judge the quick and the dead; and I believe in the Holy Ghost, in the Holy Church, the forgiveness of sins, and the resurrection of the flesh."[1] For almost the entire, if not the entire, of the duration of the Christian Church no one was recognised as a member of it without some such profession of belief as I have read; and you will have observed that the articles of that profession are, for the most part, exactly those which the feasts of the Christian year successively present to us for our meditation. But several of these articles relate to historical facts, and our belief in these must be obtained by evidence of the same nature as that on which we believe other historical facts. Our belief that our Lord suffered under Pontius Pilate must be justified by the same kind of evidence as that on which we believe that there was such a person as Pontius Pilate. Our belief that our Lord rose again on the third day must be justified by the same kind of evidence as that on which we believe that He was crucified and was buried. It is impossible to evolve a historical fact out of our internal consciousness, or to have any real belief that anything took place 1800 years ago, merely because we wish it did, and

---

[1] The form here translated is the baptismal creed of the early Roman Church. On the proof of its great antiquity, see Caspari, *Quellen zur Geschichte des Taufsymbols und der Glaubensregel*, part iii.; Gebhardt and Harnack's *Apostolic Fathers*, fasc. i., 2, p. 115, or an article which I contributed to the *Contemporary Review*, August 1878.

because we find such a belief comforting and consolatory. Writers on evidences, then, have undertaken no needless task when they have set themselves to inquire whether our belief in the facts of the Christian creed can be justified by the ordinary rules of historical investigation. If they have failed in what they tried to establish, we must be forced to admit that the faith which the Christian Church has always held rests on no solid foundation.

It must be owned, however, that times have changed since the natural course of a defender of Christianity was accounted to be that he should establish the occurrence of certain miracles, and offer these as credentials of a divine revelation. Nowadays instead of regarding the miraculous part of Christianity as the foundation on which the remaining part rests, many look on this miraculous part as the overburdening weight under which, if it cannot be cleared away, the whole fabric must sink. Only get rid of this and we may still have, we are told, a very noble religion. If we will but surrender the Christian miracles we may still have our Christ. No honours will be too great for Him, no language too lofty to describe the services He has rendered humanity.

II. But is such a compromise possible? In the

first place, if our Lord be worthy of all the reverence which we are permitted to pay Him, we cannot in judging of His miracles leave out the consideration how did He judge of them Himself? How did He teach others to judge of them? I do not dwell on the fact that in the fourth Gospel His mighty works are always represented as *signs* wrought by Him to testify a divine commission; it suffices to refer to that story the account of which I read as recorded in the text. It is common to two of the Synoptic Evangelists, Matthew and Luke. If we are to discriminate the records of our Saviour's sayings into more or less trustworthy, this story must be regarded as belonging to one of the earliest forms in which sayings of His were committed to writing. And the substance of it is, that when He was asked if it was He of whom the prophets of the nation had spoken, He on whom the expectations of the nation were fixed, He appealed to His miracles, or rather perhaps to the correspondence of those mighty works with what the prophets had told concerning Him—"The blind receive their sight, the lame walk, the lepers are cleansed, the deaf hear, the dead are raised up, and the poor have the gospel preached to them." If the wonders related of Him are to be reduced to exaggeration, misconception, natural occurrences falsely attributed to supernatural causes, we must say that the mistake which His Church has made was made in His own lifetime, and was shared by Himself.

In one of the earliest attempts made in this century to write a non-miraculous life of Jesus, the method of accepting the Gospel narratives as in their substance true, but depriving them of their supernatural character, was fairly worked out *ad absurdum*.[1] Our Lord had been believed to walk upon the water, but this was because He had been seen walking on rising ground close to the lake, and by a precipitate judgment of the disciples had been imagined to walk on the surface of the water: the story that He had been transfigured arose out of the fact that the disciples had seen the beams of the morning sun brilliantly reflected from His garments: the story that He had miraculously multiplied the food of the 5000 arose out of the fact that the multitude had been influenced by the examples of Himself and His disciples, each to bring out his private store and share it with his neighbours, so that all ate and were satisfied. I need not repeat in detail how improbability is heaped upon improbability, until the explanation how Jesus of Nazareth came to be

---

[1] The reference is to Paulus, whose *Commentary on the Gospels* appeared in the very first years of the century. His *Life of Jesus* came out in 1828.

regarded as a miracle-worker presents us with a story quite as inconsistent with human experience as that He actually wrought the wonderful works attributed to Him. No one can treat this method of naturalistic interpretation with more scorn than does Strauss, who declares that if the Gospels be once admitted as historical records, it is impossible to eliminate miracle from the life of Jesus.[1]

But what if giving up the historical character of the Gospels as we have them now, we transfer our allegiance to a supposed original Gospel, from untrustworthy enlargement of which our present Gospels took their rise? May it not then be possible for criticism to reduce the Gospel narrative to a form, in which the method of naturalistic interpretation shall not be inapplicable? Some of the more refractory miracles will have been cleared away, and the total number so greatly reduced that the calculus of probabilities will no longer present so appalling a result, when, in order to measure the probability of the non-miraculous life of Jesus, we multiply together the chances against the truth of each particular explanation. I am far from denying the possibility that criticism may be able in the texts of our present Gospels to distinguish, with more or less confidence, material derived from an earlier document. That the task

[1] *Das Leben Jesu* (1864), p. 18.

is enormously difficult may be inferred from the want of agreement between the able men who have attempted to perform it: that it is impossible I do not venture to say. But two things I think we may safely say. One that this task, if ever it is performed, cannot be accomplished by any mere mechanical process. For instance, it may be a very important step, in the process of ascertaining the facts with which criticism must deal, to take out the words common to the three Synoptic Gospels.[1] But it would be clearly irrational if we were to imagine that criticism had then finished its work, and that we might jump to the conclusion that in these common words, and these only, we had the original document. Such a process involves the assumption (the unreasonableness of which is seen the moment the assumption is put into words) that, on the supposition that such a document existed, and that it was made use of by three subsequent compilers, each of these compilers was bound to incorporate every particular of it in his work, so that an omission by any one of them condemns the part left out as no portion of the original Gospel. So far is this from being true, that I very confidently believe that if such a document existed there are things which we

---

[1] This work has been carefully done by Mr. Rushbrooke in his *Synopticon*, published by Macmillan.

now find in no Gospel but St. Mark's which certainly formed part of it. And if in our search for the original document the concurrence of the three witnesses is not necessary, neither again is it sufficient. Unless we can say with certainty that none of the Evangelists made use of the work of another, we cannot be certain that all the things they have in common were independently taken from their common source.

But I think it more important to express my belief, in the second place, that in this matter criticism will not do its work successfully unless it is single-minded and works without any *arrière pensée*. If the investigation is prompted by the hope or dominated by the expectation that the discovered residuum of the Gospels will be non-miraculous, it must end in failure. For it will be in vain to have got rid of all other miracles if we are forced to leave behind the miracle of our Lord's resurrection, and what can we imagine to have been the date of a Gospel which did not contain this miracle? It must certainly have been earlier than any of the Epistles of St. Paul, in whose mind our Lord's resurrection is one of the most certain of facts—a fact so certain that a doctrine is convicted of falsity if it involves the denial of the resurrection. " If there be no resurrection of the dead then is Christ not risen, and if Christ be not risen, then is our preaching vain, and your faith is also vain. Yea, and we are found false witnesses of God, because we have testified of God that He raised up Christ, whom He raised not up, if so be that the dead rise not. And if Christ be not raised, your faith is vain; ye are yet in your sins. Then they also which are fallen asleep in Christ have perished."

But we need not come down so late as Paul. Those who believe and those who disbelieve in our Lord's resurrection can at least have no difficulty in agreeing as to the date at which such a belief arose. If a year had elapsed, if six months had elapsed, from the time at which our Lord had died on the cross the death of shame, and if during all that time no sign had clouded over the completeness of the triumph of His enemies, if His followers had for so long a time been forced to acquiesce in the conviction that He who had saved others had been unable to save Himself, we may say with certainty that it would have been impossible to revive their crushed expectations, and that one who should then first come to them with the story of a resurrection would find them in no state of mind to give it credence.

Or take the thing another way. They who, denying a real resurrection of Jesus, attempt to explain the rise of a belief in it, appeal to the fact that there often remains on the mental retina the image of a luminous object after the object itself has been withdrawn. The face long familiar and long loved refuses to vanish from our mental vision, or is ever starting up unbidden. So the minds of those to whom Jesus was inexpressibly dear, and who had built on Him all their hopes, could not let His image go. Their prophet could not die. Thus whether or not Jesus of Nazareth actually did rise again, it was inevitable that His followers should believe that He did. I shall not discuss whether or not this explanation is sufficient, but it is evident that the exaltation of mind which it assumes on the part of our Lord's disciples only belongs to the time when their loss was still fresh. It is not conceivable after the time when the first poignancy of grief, which refuses to realise its loss, is succeeded by that dull pain which confesses that life has got to be lived on after all that made it dear has gone. Thus, if we are forbidden to hold the article of our creed, On the third day He rose again from the dead, we shall be forced to substitute, On or about the third day it came to be believed that He rose again from the dead. It follows that our chronology can find no place for a non-miraculous Gospel. At the very earliest date that we can imagine the history of our Lord's life put into writing, the story of the resurrection must have come to form an essential part of it. Criticism, then, can give us no help to eliminate this miracle from the record. A gospel which does not tell of a resurrection from the dead is an impossibility. If any critic imagine that he has arrived at such a gospel, the result condemns the method he has employed. If in this part of the history the authorities to which we have access exhibit greater variety than elsewhere, we must not infer that each had to supplement from his own resources an original narrative defective in this part, but rather that it was for this part of the story materials were so abundant that selection became necessary.

In sum, then, a non-miraculous Christianity is as much a contradiction in terms as a quadrangular circle; when you have taken away the supernatural, what is left behind is not Christianity. It is not the religion which the apostles preached; it is not that into which converts were baptized; it is not that for which martyrs gave their lives. There might be differences of enumeration if we were asked to state what were the supernatural facts which we should pronounce essential to Christianity; but on this point we can be agreed that Christianity requires faith in a supernatural person. For any one who tries to clear away the supernatural from Christianity has got to deal with the question, What think you of Christ? Did He differ from other men in degree or in kind? Was He, however pre-eminent above His fellows, a man who possibly may in other ages or other parts of the world have had His equals, and as time goes on, for all we know, may have His superior? Or was He a person altogether unique in the history of humanity? Certain it is that nothing less than this is what His Church has always claimed for Him. From the earliest times Christians refused to acknowledge as belonging to their body those who admitted with Jesus sharers in His honour. There were those who set up images of Christ along with those of Pythagoras, Plato, Aristotle, and others,[1] but such obtained no recognition as fellow-disciples from the Christian body. And if it was thought a degradation to Christ to place Him on a level with philosophers, still more distasteful to Christians was the project attributed to the eclectic liberality of a half-converted emperor to find room for their master in a pantheon of heathen divinities.[2] He was not one who could share His glory with another.

[1] So Irenæus tells of the Carpocratians (*Hær.* i. 25).

[2] "Christo templum facere voluit, eumque inter deos recipere, quod et Hadrianus cogitasse fertur, qui templa in omnibus civitatibus sine simulacris jusserat fieri. Quæ hodieque idcirco quia non habent numina dicuntur Hadriani, quæ ille ad hoc parasse dicebatur, sed

III. This honour of having a place in a pantheon with others is what will now be readily accorded Jesus by students of comparative theology. They recognise the historical claims of Christianity to consideration as one of the world's great religions, and they are prepared to investigate its contents;—on the assumption, however, that this religion is not to be favoured by any specialty of treatment: that its Founder is to be regarded from the outset as fairly comparable with the originator of any other religion that comes under review, and that we are at once to set aside, as undeserving of examination, any wonders told of Him to which we should refuse credence if told of the founder of Buddhist or Brahminical religion. It is evident what must be the result of an investigation into the truth of Christianity which starts with the assumption that the fundamental doctrine of Christianity is false. You cannot expect to arrive by any process of sound reasoning at a conclusion in direct contradiction to the premisses with which you set out, and so the Christian will not be much flattered at hearing that the result of the exami-

prohibitus est ab his qui consulentes sacra reppererant omnes Christianos futuros, si id primum fecisset, et templa reliqua deserenda" (Lamprid. *in vit. Alex. Sever.*, c. 43). Lampridius also has a story (c. 29) that this emperor had in the private chapel where he used to offer his morning devotions effigies not only of the chief gods, but also of Apollonius, Christ, Abraham, Orpheus, and others.

nation has been to ascertain that there are precepts of their Master more noble than anything taught by Gotama or Confucius, if the question whether Jesus does not stand on an altogether different level from them is rejected as not worthy to come under discussion at all.

On the other hand, if that be once conceded, or even admitted as possible, which our faith asserts, namely, that our Blessed Lord was a unique person, distinct in nature from ordinary men, all difficulties about the admission of what would otherwise be accounted supernatural facts at once disappear. There is in Christianity but one miracle, the appearance in the world of a supernatural Person. We may believe most thoroughly in the uniformity of nature, and be fully persuaded that from like antecedents like consequences will follow, but if the antecedents be not like we shall not expect uniformity of result. It is contrary to experience that a man should be able to give sight to the blind, that at his word the dead should return to life, that he himself should die and be buried, and rise again the third day. But if He of whom these things are asserted be more than man, our experience has nothing to say. Once on a time it was received as a proposition universally true that all metals are heavy, and a man who should report that he had seen a metal floating in water might be regarded as asserting what was contrary to experience; but if he explained that his assertion did not relate to any of the known metals, but to one unlike them in character and properties, his announcement, though surprising, ceased to have any opposing experience to encounter. Thus the Christian miracles form a connected system; it is idle to reject one unless you reject the whole. If one be admitted all the rest are credible. If the proof of one be unassailable it avails nothing to raise difficulties about others. If, for instance, it be not denied that Jesus rose from the dead, it is but time wasted to attempt to show that the story of the miraculous conception is later in date. If in His death He was not subject to the ordinary laws of mortality, it is quite as likely as not that He differed from other men in the manner of His birth.

Not merely is it the Christian doctrine that Christ is a unique person, but also that He came to do a unique work. We might think perhaps that His work as a teacher would sufficiently justify His mission. Principles of pure morality for which we may search with more or less success in the speculations of philosophers before Him were converted by Him into the practical rule of life of multitudes. It is of little consequence whether those have succeeded who have tried to find in the writings of an earlier age anything resembling the maxim, "Do unto all men as you would they should do unto you." If such a maxim can be found (and it is singular how a principle which seems to us so obvious should have been so missed and so imperfectly enunciated), yet it was at best but the lofty thought of one or two individuals. Christ made it the professed rule of practice of hundreds of thousands. Those hopes of a future life, which before His time had been but a shadowy dream disputed of by men of speculation, were made by Christ fixed articles of popular belief. We can tell how great a change Christ wrought if we think of those commonplace words of consolation, which naturally present themselves when we come in contact with any bereaved sufferer: of that sure and certain hope which robs sorrow of its bitterness, and enables us without excessive grief to commit to the grave the remains of beloved friends, and if we compare with our feelings at such times those with which Pagans parted from their dead; the broken column, the cropped flower, which represented that death had destroyed all of existence, the cheerless creed which only told of a night that all must sleep, that it must be our fate to descend whither Æneas and Tullus and Ancus have fallen, thenceforward to be but dust and shadow.¹ Still more did Christ benefit the world by raising men's conceptions of the character of God, and so making morality a part of religion. What help could theology give religion when the gods were represented as likely to be indulgent to human vices because they had practised them themselves.² Christ taught His people to believe in a God of infinite holiness and purity, who hates sin, and yet who may be loved with most trusting confidence: a Heavenly Father, to be whose especial children is the best reward of the peacemakers, to see whose face is the highest hope of the pure in heart; who is ever at hand to strengthen His true worshippers; to whom is due our heartiest love, our humblest submission; whose most acceptable worship is a holy heart; in whose constant presence our life is passed; to whose merciful disposal we are resigned by death. If this were all He did, who shall say that Christ's mission to the world had not been justified. But the Scriptures give us to understand that the main object of His coming was not to add certainty to the conjectures of natural religion; not even to communicate some new truths unattainable by human reason, but that it was to atone for the sins of mankind, and effect the redemption of a lost world. This work is truly unique. And

---

[1] Hor., *Od.* iv. 7.   [2] Ovid, *Trist.* ii. 387.

so it will not seem strange that we do not find in everyday experience instances of wondrous works like those ascribed to Him, if we believe that He was not only different from ordinary men, but was sent to do a work quite different from anything that has taken place before or since. If this be true, it is to be expected that the works which He did and the signs which prepared the way for Him should be different from anything which falls within the range of our daily experience.

What has been said applies also to the whole system of prophecy, and to the relation of Christianity to the Jewish dispensation. Once accept the Church's doctrine as to the Person and work of Christ, and it immediately becomes credible that He did not burst on the world without preparation. Christ's mission is by hypothesis an event unparalleled in the world's history, and of infinite importance to the human race. If a theist finds no difficulty in believing that while yet this earth was unpeopled by living creatures, it was through God's providence being prepared to be the future abode of man, still more easily can a Christian regard the advent of Christ as the consummation of the purposes of God, for which all earlier dispensations had been designed to prepare the way. It follows from what has been said, that the doctrines of the Church's creed are so connected together, that if you remove the article of our Lord's Divinity the remaining articles become not more but less credible.

IV. Before I conclude I wish to say something on the question, whether if you remove the doctrine of our Lord's Divinity our religion will be the nobler. I believe the contrary to be so much the case that, if we cease to worship Christ as God, I doubt if we shall do well to call ourselves by His name at all. The question is, in short, whether our souls are more likely to be elevated by the worship of God, or by creature worship. It is notorious how a man's character is moulded by that of the being whom he worships, and in whom is embodied his highest notions of perfection. I had already occasion to glance at the injury done to Pagan morality by the worship of gods, who could not be imagined to hate vices to which they had been themselves addicted. Even under the Christian dispensation, when creature cult has been practised under the most favourable circumstances, the effect has not been favourable to morality. One has been made the object of worship who has been indeed acknowledged to be a creature, but in whom men's highest ideal of purity, tenderness, and self-denial has been embodied. Yet as her mercy was supposed to be not limited by justice, she was regarded as one not hating sin as God hates it, one likely to be indulgent to human frailty and to forgive it on easier terms than the Supreme; and so her office has been looked on as that of shielding the sinner on any terms from punishment, of enabling him to continue in sin with a prospect of escaping with ultimate impunity; and bandits and assassins have found themselves able to continue their trade while paying her the warmest devotion. If God has forbidden us idolatry, it is because the most effectual instrument of our moral renovation is communion with Him who is known to be of spotless purity. It is by contact with God's spirit that man's spirit is sanctified; and we do our souls an infinite injury if, shrinking from God's perfect holiness, we fancy we have found some being higher than man but lower than God, who can shield the soul conscious of guilt from the painful sense of God's immediate presence. The worship of Christ has done the Church no harm, simply because she has *not* looked upon Him as a creature. If it be the perfection of the Christian life to set Christ ever before us, to live as in His sight, to strive to be like Him, to consider how by our actions we shall best please Him, when we say Christ we mean God. We have set before us the very loftiest ideal our minds are able to form, we do not bate a single attribute from infinite perfection. But if by Christ we mean man, the case is different. It might be natural that His followers, in the exuberance of their love and gratitude to Him who had taught them the best lessons they had ever learned, should exceed the limits of sober reason in the honours they paid Him. Perhaps, indeed, we might be obliged to own that in this matter their Master had led them astray, and by the emphasis with which He insisted on personal allegiance to Himself detracted from His merits as a true teacher of humanity. But why should we, if we have learned better, repeat the mistakes of the first disciples? The history of any science, however interesting it may be, is a thing wholly unnecessary to the knowledge of the science. If we know the truths which Archimedes or Sir Isaac Newton discovered, it is needless for us to discuss which of the two were the greater mathematician—needless to inquire whether there may not hereafter arise a mathematician greater than either—unnecessary even to know that such men existed at all. So, in like manner, for the science of religion, if Jesus be no more than the teacher who brought certain truths to light, the vital matter is that we should keep hold of the truths, but the name of the teacher might be forgotten. In short, the teacher who leads us from nature to Christ does us infinite service if by Christ we mean God—if we have been made to feel that in this world we are not the helpless sport of blind forces which toss us about as chance may order, for evil or for good, but the objects of the love of a Heavenly Father, who has not merely shown His love in our creation and preservation, but who has " so loved the world, that He gave His only begotten Son, that whosoever believeth on Him should not perish, but have everlasting life." But if Christ be man, to lead us to Christ is a miserable halting-place. Then to lead us to Christ means this :—to arrest the growth of the science of religion at the point at which it arrived eighteen centuries ago, to throw our thoughts on the past instead of on the future, and to say that at the end of a period when the human intellect has been exerted with unexampled activity, when literature and science have been cultivated as they never have been before, we are to be content to sit at the feet of a highly gifted Jewish teacher who died two thousand years ago.

V. And surely this affords a simple test whether or not we have claimed too much for our Master. If He were only man, He was *ex vi termini* fallible and imperfect. He belonged to a nation far below our own in culture and education ; and the fact that He lived so many years ago implies that

He was in ignorance of all that the accumulated experience of eighteen centuries since His time has added to human knowledge. Unless the science of religion be incapable of progress, it is inevitable but that we shall find in His teaching errors to correct, false conceptions to rectify, half views to enlarge. Yet it is not mere respect for the prejudices of society which induces many who reject His supernatural claims to call themselves by His name. It is because they have really been unable to find any better teacher—any whose lessons so commend themselves to their hearts and consciences.

And what of those who disdain His teaching altogether? Have they improved on it? I believe many of themselves would be the first to own that it is not that they can give better solutions than He of the problems which have perplexed thoughtful men of every age, but that in rejecting His solutions they think such problems ought to be abandoned in despair. I suppose the keynote to our Lord's discourses may be said to be the doctrine that we have a Father in heaven. No other utterance recurs so often, or is made the basis of so many deductions. His disciples' daily prayer was to begin, "Our Father which art in heaven." The sense of their sonship was to be the governing principle of their conduct. They were to do good works, letting their light shine before men that they might glorify their Father which is in heaven. Yet not in order to gain the praise of men or to be seen of men, "otherwise ye have no reward of your Father which is in heaven." To be like their Heavenly Father, perfect like Him, was to be the aim of all who called themselves His children. As He sends His rain, and makes His sun to shine on the evil and the good, so were they to love their enemies, and not grudge to bestow their benefits on the unthankful and the evil. To His love they might safely trust. All corroding cares might be dismissed by the thought, —your Heavenly Father knoweth ye have need of these things. He feeds the fowls of the air; are not ye much better than they? None of you would refuse good gifts to your children, neither will your Heavenly Father refuse good gifts to them that ask Him.

We inquire whether the philosophy of the nineteenth century will endorse this teaching. Is it true that the power to which we owe our being is a Person who loves us, who regards our conduct, whose attributes we may strive to imitate, in whom we can safely trust? Some will tell us that they do not know whether or not we can ascribe anything like personality to that ever-present force, that stream of, on the whole, beneficial tendency which pervades the universe. Others tell us that we have no experience of thought without an organised brain, and that as we know that no such mighty, all-pervading organisation exists, we can safely say that the force which everywhere shows itself is directed by no conscious intelligence. And does this force love us?—Well, the individual certainly not. The laws by which that force works are undoubtedly beneficial on the whole; but the general action of these laws is never modified in the slightest, no matter how cruelly they may affect individuals.—Then this power may be said in a sense to love, if not individuals, at least the race?—Well no, neither can we say this either. Species, like individuals, make progress to a certain point, and then decay and die: this world itself, once incapable of sustaining life, then by degrees decking itself with myriad forms of beauty and vigour, will in all probability again become incapable of sustaining life, and will be borne round through space a burnt-out cinder.—And will no memory anywhere remain of those who during its season of life have on this earth thought and worked and loved?—It is to be feared none.—And those whom we have loved here, and who have gone from us, do they not live?—Oh yes, they live :—in your recollections. Cherish those recollections as best you can, for it is all you will ever know of them.

If this be progress, it is such progress as is predicted for the world we live in—progress to a state when its sun shall have been burnt out, its life departed, its heat evaporated, when it shall have been frozen into a lump of ice. Thanks be to God, our sun has not been quenched. "Jesus lives" was the watchword of our Easter Day—lives not merely in the memory of the lessons He taught—not merely in the admiration of those who have read the history of His life—but lives in power and glory, sitting at the right hand of God, guiding, ruling, defending His Church, daily fulfilling His promise, "I will be with you alway, even to the end of the world"—present with it by His Spirit, which He promised to give us as an abiding Comforter, in the Unity of which Spirit with the Father He lives and reigns ever one God, to whom be ascribed all might, majesty, glory, dominion, and power, now and for ever. Amen.

II

THE NAME CHRISTIAN.—I

"And the disciples were called Christians first in Antioch."—
ACTS xi. 26.

I THINK this remark may be counted a note of the early date of the book of the Acts of the Apostles. The author of the book can remember the time when that which eventually became the recognised appellation of the believers in Jesus of Nazareth was but a local title current in only one city. Whether or not we are to identify the author with the Lucius of Cyrene, who, in the beginning of the 13th chapter, is enumerated as one of the prophets or teachers of the Church at Antioch, ecclesiastical tradition[1] appears to have had good reason for connecting the author of the Acts with that city. We may count it as a sign that he wrote from real knowledge of early facts that he does not ascribe the evangelisation of the

---

[1] Eusebius, *H.E.* iv. 4. In Codex D a "we" introduced at Acts xi. 27 is made to intimate that St. Luke was present at the prophesying of Agabus. The reading is recognised by St. Augustine, *On the Sermon on the Mount*, ii. 57, vol. III., ii. 223.

city to any Apostle, although in quite early times St. Peter was claimed as the first bishop; but the planting of the Gospel in the city is stated to have been the work of anonymous Jews of Cyprus and Cyrene, whom the persecution that followed the death of Stephen had driven from Jerusalem. St. Luke relates how Barnabas, himself a native of Cyprus, was sent by the Apostles from Jerusalem to continue the work at Antioch which his countrymen had begun; he tells how Barnabas associated Paul with him in that labour, travelling to Tarsus to seek him out; he knows the names of the principal teachers of the Church at the time, names otherwise so obscure that they have left no mark in Church history; he gives Antioch the honour of the first organisation of missionary efforts among the Gentiles; and there, we may say, was held the first missionary meeting, when Paul and Barnabas returned from their circuit, and assembled the Church to hear the report of their successes. To that city Luke also ascribes the first Christian organisation of charitable collections for the relief of temporal distress, when, on learning the approach of famine afflicting the poorer Church of Jerusalem, the Christians of Antioch made a collection, and sent their leading members as the bearers of it. St. Luke also mentions Antioch as the place where originated those disputes which afterwards formed one of the earliest and, for the time it lasted, one of the hottest controversies of the Christian Church, that as to the obligation of Gentiles to observe the Mosaic Law. The instances I have cited are enough to make it highly probable that the author of the Acts resided for some time at Antioch, and was well acquainted with the early history of the Church in that city; and therefore it is, as I have intimated, the most natural way of accounting for the remark in the text, that St. Luke's memory went back to the time before the name Christian for the new sect had yet been invented.

The name speaks for itself as one which could only have originated when that new sect set itself to make converts among the Gentiles, and when heathen were thus forced to take notice of the distinction between this and the other sects into which Judaism was divided, and to designate it by a name of their own. It need not be said that Christian was a name which Jews never would have given to the disciples of Jesus of Nazareth. If the word implied no more than belief that a Christ, a Messiah, was to come, they were all Christians themselves; but an acknowledgment that Christ had come in the person of Jesus of Nazareth was the very last thing that could be expected from them. Actually the name Nazarene or Galilean was that which, in the times to which the Scripture records extend, they gave to the new heresy; and afterwards the name " Minim," which would seem to have been a general word for heretics, came to be appropriated to this form of dissent from the creed of the dominant class.[1] But as the name Christian did not originate with the Jews, so neither was it assumed by the disciples themselves. The words disciples, brethren, the faithful, the saints, were those which they used to designate the members of their own body. So habitual did the use of them become that the last word slips out from St. Paul when he is addressing Agrippa, a man who could not be supposed to ascribe sanctity or holiness to the members of the new community. St. Paul tells him : " Many of the *saints* did I shut up in prison." When St. Luke has occasion to speak of Christianity or the Christian body his ordinary name is " the way," an appellation the technical force of which is disguised in our translation, which generally renders it " this way." Thus, the object of Paul's journey to Damascus was, that if he found any of " the way," whether they were men or women, he might send them bound to Jerusalem (Acts ix. 2). And so, when making his defence on the Temple steps, he says : " I persecuted 'the way' unto the death." St. Paul's separating the disciples at

[1] See Buxtorf's *Lexicon*, *s.v.*

Ephesus from the synagogue of unbelieving Jews is said to have been done because "divers were hardened and believed not, and spake evil of *the way* before the multitude;" and later on, Paul tells Felix: "After *the way* which they call heresy I worship the God of my fathers." But it is very intelligible that though neither the Jews nor the Christians needed a name to describe the new community, and though unbelieving Gentiles did not need a name as long as they confounded the believers in Jesus with other Jews, yet when the new sect began to make converts among the Gentiles, admitting proselytes without any burdensome preliminary conditions, then those who did not join it were yet forced to take cognisance of it, and required a separate name to describe it by. As I have already said, Antioch was, according to St. Luke's account, the first city where a purely Gentile Church was founded, and so it is natural that there a name should first have been given. The Gentiles would hear the believers express their faith that Jesus was the Christ, and the name Christ would catch their ear as that of the founder of the new sect. The meaning of the word was not understood—indeed the word was almost universally pronounced *Chrestus*, and it was taken to be not an official title, but the proper name of Him whom the disciples honoured as their Lord.

We habitually use the name in this way ourselves, and the usage is as early as the Apostolic epistles which have come down to us, in which, though the combination Jesus Christ is very common, the use of the name Jesus by itself is somewhat rare, and the name Christ is very frequently used instead, as if it were a proper name. St. James probably refers to this use of the word Christian when he says, "Do not rich men blaspheme that worthy name by the which ye are called." Actually, as most of you know, the word Christian occurs only in two other New Testament passages besides the text, and both times in connection with its use by heathen. The one is King Agrippa's well-known "Almost thou persuadest me to be a Christian." The other is St. Peter's admonition to his flock, that none of them should suffer as a thief, or a murderer, or other malefactor, but not to be ashamed if any of them suffered as a Christian.

To suffer as a Christian was a phrase that had then a very definite meaning, for the name Christian became the ordinary title of accusation against the believers, and the unreasonableness of this was a topic much dwelt on by the early apologists.[1] They said, "If there be any truth in the charges commonly brought against us, that we are a society connected by the practice of infamous vices, indict

[1] For instance, Justin Martyr (*Apol.* 4, 7).

us for these. Accuse us of being murderers or incestuous, or guilty of whatever other wickedness we are said to practise, and if any such guilt can be established against any of us, we acknowledge it to be right that he should suffer; but it is unreasonable to punish a man to whose charge you can lay no other fault than that he is called by the name of Christian. What's in a name? If there be anything in a name, this name ought rather to count to the credit of those who bear it, since kind and good is what is meant by Chrestus." And they contended that the name Christian ought not to be disparaged, even if it might be true that it was sometimes disgraced by the unworthy conduct of some who bore it. In fact, the Christian apologists did not undertake the defence of heretical sects. What wickedness *they* might or might not be guilty of they could not undertake to say, and they, in fact, thought it very possible that the calumnies concerning the Christians, which the heathen believed, were not pure invention, but had a foundation in some real misconduct of heretics. But they said, "We ought not to be held accountable for the wrong-doing of people whom, though they call themselves Christians, we count unworthy of the name. The name philosopher, for instance, is a good name; yet it is assumed by many who are in no real sense lovers of wisdom. It embraces many who are quite at variance with each other, and it would be unfair, indeed, to make one answerable for another's doings, merely because they have this common name. Let the name Christian be treated like the name philosopher, as a name good in itself, but sometimes assumed by those who have no right to it. Let, therefore, the use of the name not be made a subject of praise or blame to any; but inquire into their deeds, and if the deeds of any are found worthy of punishment, punish them; but punish them because they are murderers, or robbers, or incestuous, not merely because they are called Christians."

This question as to the proper extension to be given to the name Christian, which we see was agitated as early as the second century, or perhaps earlier (for we read of it in some of the earliest Christian documents that have come down to us), may still be said to be an unsettled one. Still the complaint is heard that many claim the name who have no right to it. As in the time of Justin, so still scandal is often caused to unbelievers by the misconduct of some whose life is unworthy of the holy name by which they profess to be called. Have we not heard of deeds of Europeans, it may be in isles of the Southern Seas, it may be in India, it may be in Mahometan countries, which have revolted the consciences of men whose creed we count less pure than ours; and what have we been able to say in order to dispel the scandal cast on our religion, except "These men who call themselves Christians are so only in name, not in reality. Their religion, if they would obey it, is holy, just, and good: their vices are their own."

In the second century the stricter discipline of the Church made it easier for Christians to disclaim connection with discreditable professors. If their vices were great and open—if their dissent from the creed of the Church passed certain limits—they were excluded from the communion of the Church, so that its members might reasonably object to being held responsible for the conduct of men from whom they had formally and publicly separated themselves. Even then, however, we can easily conceive that scandal may have been occasionally given by men who had not been cast out from the Church, and whose public misconduct first revealed that they did not deserve the name of Christian. In the present day no attempt is made in our own Church publicly to separate any from its body, no matter what their vices, or how absolute their rejection of the Church's creed. Scarcely any of the bodies into which Christendom is divided aims at greater strictness; certainly none approaches the strictness of discipline with respect to moral conduct which was exercised in the primitive Church. And should a man be excommunicated by one body of professing Christians, he easily finds a home among others who claim an equal title to that holy name. For the days have passed when the name of Christian was one of reproach, and when acknowledgment of it could only be made at the risk of imprisonment, tortures, or death; now men cling to the name even after they have abandoned belief in every doctrine that was once regarded as distinctive of the religion; and there was felt to be a certain audacity in the act when a wide dissenter from the orthodox creed put the question the other day, Why should we call ourselves Christians?

It is natural in the case of a word which has long been so vaguely used, that no small difference of opinion would be likely to arise if we were now to attempt to define it more strictly. We should be equally likely to hear murmurs of dissent if we threw open the right to the name too freely, or if we guarded it too exclusively. Some, for instance, might ask, Have we a right to give the name to Quakers and others who refuse to make that public profession and stipulation, and to receive that formal rite of admission which from the earliest times was accounted that which gave a man a title to be called a member of the Christian Church?

Others might ask, Can we at least give the name to a man who cannot sincerely make that profession which we know was always demanded from candidates for baptism, I believe in the Father, and in the Son, and in the Holy Ghost? Can he be called a Christian who uses the name of Christ merely as the personal appellation of a man whom he does not believe to have held in the world's economy any office peculiar to himself; who looks on him as a man different from others neither in his birth nor in his death; as one who, partly perhaps, in consequence of injudicious language of his own, or, at any rate, through the strong affection and excited imaginations of his followers, was placed on a pinnacle to which he had no right, and came to be worshipped as a God?

There are others, again, who would not allow that a title to the name of Christian is conferred by the most orthodox creed, the most moral life, the strongest desire to be owned by Christ as one of His on the judgment day. They require, besides, a certain felt assurance that such shall hereafter certainly be their lot. Those who cannot tell of having experienced some such feeling they do not encourage to call or think themselves Christians, while they who can boast of these experiences are taught, in a land where nearly all call themselves Christians, to claim this title as their special right, and enrol themselves as Christian young men, members of Christian conventions, and so forth.

I saw the other day in the report of one of the meetings of the last-named body, that it was thought a proper question to ask a child, Is your father a Christian?[1] The alternative contemplated not being that the subject of the inquiry was an avowed infidel, much less that he professed any different religion, nor do I suppose it was intended that the child should constitute himself the parent's judge, but the question was whether the parent himself claimed to be, in a pre-eminent sense of the word, a Christian.

You would feel that I had set myself a hard problem, and one not easily to be disposed of in the short time at my disposal, if I undertook to answer all the questions suggested by the remarks I have made, or to state and prove any compendious rule for deciding to whom the name of Christian might properly be given. I shall not attempt to propose any accurate definition of the word Christian, nor shall I venture to do more than make a few comments on the two opposite

---

[1] "Is your father a Christian?" said a gentleman to a little boy on one occasion. "Yes, sir," said the little boy, "but I believe he has not worked much at it lately."—*Dublin Daily Express*, Oct. 13, 1880. The report states that the answer was received with laughter, but it does not appear that either speaker or audience saw anything strange in the question.

extremes, that of restricting very much the title to the use of the name, and that of throwing it open too widely. But as there seems more to be said than can be conveniently said now, I shall only speak now of the first extreme, that of undue restriction of the use of the name, leaving it to next Sunday to discuss whether all who wish to assume the name can fairly be conceded to have a title to it.

It must be admitted on all hands that a distinction between real and nominal Christians must be made. Our Lord Himself compared the Church which He was founding to a net cast into the sea, which gathered in of every kind, both bad and good. In another parable He compared it to a field of wheat with many tares growing in it, which could not safely be rooted up, and concerning which His direction was, let both grow together until the harvest. Another evangelist records another parable, in which He likens Himself to a vine, His disciples to the branches; but distinguishes these branches into two kinds, the fruitful and those which bear no fruit; the fate of the latter being to wither, be cut off, and cast into the fire. In conformity with this teaching, St. Paul exhorts his disciples not to rest content in any outward privileges, as if any of these were infallible and irreversible marks of God's favour.

The Jews had their privileges like the Christian Church. All were baptized unto Moses in the cloud and in the sea—all did eat the same spiritual food and drink the same spiritual drink—but with many of them God was not well pleased, for they were overthrown in the wilderness, wherefore let him that thinketh he standeth take heed lest he fall. In a second epistle to the same Church he will not permit his disciples to content themselves with the knowledge that they were recognised members of the Church, but says to them, " Examine yourselves whether ye be in the faith : prove your own selves : know ye not, how that Jesus Christ is in you except ye be reprobates." That all who call themselves Christians do not deserve the name is implied by our Church in the words of the prayer which she puts into our mouths, " that all who profess and call themselves Christians may be led into the way of truth and hold the faith in unity of spirit, in the bond of peace, and in righteousness of life ;" that is to say, it is plainly implied that there are those who profess and call themselves Christians who still need to be brought into the way of truth.

Admitting, then, the reality of this distinction between nominal and real Christians, if we desire to apply it, I suppose a very obvious rule is, severity in judging of ourselves, charity in judging others. Yet in practice this rule is very often reversed. It often happens that men with the smallest possible amount of self-examination, relying solely on the confidence with which, in some moment of fervidly-excited feelings, they have been able to appropriate to themselves the promises of forgiveness of sins, pass a favourable verdict on themselves; and it is a principle with them that that verdict must never afterwards be re-examined. On the other hand, the name of Christian is denied to others, sometimes because they see no harm in amusements which their censors denounce as unChristian, sometimes because, being by nature so constituted that in them the intellect predominates over the emotions, their religion, though satisfying their understanding and influencing their conduct, has laid no very strong hold on their feelings.

We can perceive that our Lord foresaw that in this matter His followers would be more severe than Himself, for His warning not to pull up the tares lest the wheat should be rooted up with them, shows that He foresaw that His followers would be likely to reject as tares what He Himself would acknowledge as wheat. Those who are thus more severe than Christ, adding to His commands requirements of their own devising, not only make the hearts sad of faithful servants of His whom He has not made sad, but often keep back others from enrolling themselves as His disciples. By making His service appear a hard one, His yoke a heavy one, they deter men from undertaking it: they teach them to regard the being His servants as a thing which may be put off to a distant time, and that meanwhile they may contentedly own themselves not Christians.

For the purposes of self-examination there cannot be a better or more searching question than —Am I a Christian? Do I really walk worthy of the name, by which I should count it a disgrace not to be called? Do I, in my heart, believe the things I profess to believe? That is to say, since acting is the real test of belief, Do I act as if I believed them? Do those truths which I acknowledge influence my conduct? Do I, who call myself Christ's, set Christ ever before me, striving to be like Christ, aiming to do the things which please Christ, hoping to be ever with Him?

Useful as it is to put these questions to yourself, it might be very misleading to judge of others by the answers which they might venture to make to them. It need not be said how widely men differ from each other with respect to their willingness to take a sanguine view of their condition. It sometimes happens, too, that persons dishearten themselves by thinking it necessary to examine into the state of their feelings. I suppose no sensible person would perplex a child by asking it how much it loved its parents. It would be easy to ascertain whether it obeyed its parents; whether it liked to be with them; whether it was glad to do what would give them pleasure. But if you judged it by the account it might be able to give of its own feelings, a Goneril would be likely to be preferred to a Cordelia. Not so does He judge who seeth the heart; for, as there may be inarticulate prayer, which is not the less real because it knows not how to shape itself in words, so there may be love which, though never made the subject of conscious reflection, and which probably would not gain in purity or intensity if it were so made, yet has proved its reality by its influence on the springs of action.

The worst consequence of harsh judgments of others is, as I already said, when we teach these others themselves to acquiesce in them. For what have we done then but teach them to disbelieve in the love of Christ? but made them think of Him, notwithstanding all the revelation of His love which the Gospels contain, as an austere master —one so exacting in His demands that, however real and great His claims on us, however great the advantages of entering His service, however awful the peril of refusing to join Him, still it is better to postpone doing so as long as possible, and trust that some time before death a convenient season will arrive for joining a master whose rewards are all in the next world, while His yoke is intolerable in this? But the Gospel has been written in vain for any who can thus think of Christ. The message to the world which He preached in His life, and which He taught more effectually by His death, is that God is love. From Him every good gift comes; and He who spared not His own Son, but freely gave Him up for us all, will not deny us any needful blessing. His commandments are not grievous. Obedience to them has the promise of blessing in this life as well as in that which is to come. If we feel in our heart any striving after good, from His Spirit that godly motion comes. If we desire that it should be cherished and increased, we may ask Him for a further outpouring of that Spirit with as much confidence as a hungry child asks his parent for food, knowing that he will not be refused. None that cometh to Him will be cast out. Among the blessings which His providence has already bestowed on you, not the least is that you have been already enrolled as disciples of Christ and as members of His Church. Draw back from your engagement if your maturer judgment condemns it; if you have discovered that the master in whose service you have been enlisted is unworthy of your reverence and your love. But if this cannot be said, halt not between two opinions; be in reality what you are in name; walk worthy of the vocation wherewith you were called.

III

THE NAME CHRISTIAN.—II

"Every one of you saith, I am of Paul; and I of Cephas; and I of Apollos; and I of Christ."—1 COR. i. 12.

IT is natural to us to think of the first generation of Christians, who had the privilege of being taught by inspired Apostles, and whose unworthy members were weeded out by persecution, as superior to the weaknesses which have disfigured the Church of later times. It is, perhaps, with a little of the self-complacency with which men see their supposed superiors brought down to their own level that we read that, even in the Apostolic Church, men extolled the merits of their respective teachers, set up one as a rival to another, and divided themselves into parties known each by its leader's name.

Though we hear it at first with some surprise, we have no difficulty in accepting the information that there were parties in the Corinthian Church known by the names of Paul, of Apollos, and of Peter; but commentators have puzzled themselves much to explain how there could be a party assuming the name of Christ's. How could that have been the distinctive title of any which surely must have been the common name of all? Some have hoped to cut the knot by a violent effort of exegesis, and imagine that in the last clause the Apostle speaks in his own person. Others may say, I am of Paul, and I am of Cephas, and I am of Apollos, but *I* am of Christ. However good the doctrine thus elicited, no candid interpreter will maintain that it really represents the true meaning of the words read as my text; and we have independent proof of the existence in the Church of Corinth of a party arrogating to themselves the exclusive name of Christ's in St. Paul's remonstrance (2 Cor. x. 7), "If any man trust to himself that he is Christ's let him of himself think this again, that as he is Christ's, even so are we Christ's." I spoke on last Sunday of the extreme of over-narrowness in conceding this title of Christian. If any think himself aggrieved in having it denied him, he has at least the consolation of knowing that it is an affront which St. Paul himself had to bear, for that he was obliged to plead with a Church of his own founding that he had as good a title as others to this name of Christian.

I. What exactly was the position taken up by

this party at Corinth which called itself Christ's it would be unprofitable to inquire. Some critics, who do not think it a hardship to be asked to make bricks without straw, have boldly undertaken to solve the problem, and though we have no source of information but the two verses that have been read to you, have disputed with each other as to the tenets of this Christ party, and its relations of friendship or hostility with the parties of Paul and Peter.[1] It is enough for us to note the line taken by St. Paul when he hears that a party had called itself by his name. He does not put himself at the head of his zealous adherents, and prove for their satisfaction how superior was his view of the Gospel to that of Peter or Apollos, who had been put forward as his rivals. He is shocked that Christians should call themselves by his name or by any name but one. "Was Paul crucified for you?" he cries, "or was it into Paul's name you were baptized?" Plainly, in his mind it was unfitting for Christians to call themselves by any other name than that of the Master who died for them, and to whose service at their baptism they had pledged themselves. The same line was often taken up afterwards by Church writers against

---

[1] It was in an essay on this Christ party that Baur, in 1831, first put forward his peculiar theory as to the true history of the Early Church.

heretics. These last were generally known each by the name of the first inventor of the peculiar tenets of the sect. They were Basilidians, Valentinians, Marcionites, Carpocratians, and so forth.[1] The Orthodox, on the other hand, boasted that they had no other name than those of

[1] See, for instance, Justin Martyr (*Trypho* 35). Similarly Adamantius, in his dialogue with a Marcionite (Origen, xvi. 264, Lommatzch), presses his opponent to become a Christian, and the dialogue proceeds :—

Mar. What : am I not a Christian ?
Ad. How are you a Christian who do not even claim to bear the name ; for you are not called a Christian, but a Marcionite.
Mar. But you are called Catholics ; so you are not Christians either.
Ad. If we called ourselves after any man you would be right. But if we are merely so called from our being spread over the whole world, what harm is there in that ?
Mar. Show me, then, that it is not lawful to be called after a man.
Ad. I will show you that it is not lawful to bear the name not only of a bishop, but even of an apostle. Which was the greater, Marcion or Paul ?
Mar. Paul.
Ad. Listen, then, to Paul, etc.

So likewise Athanasius (Orat. *adv. Ar.* i. 3) : "Never at any time did Christian people take their title from the bishops among them, but from the Lord on whom we rest our faith. Thus, though the blessed Apostles have become our teachers, and have ministered the Saviour's Gospel, yet not from them have we our title, but from Christ we are, and are called Christians. But for those who derive the faith which they profess from others, good reason is it they should bear their name whose property they have become. Thus Marcion broached a heresy some time since and was cast out ; those who continued with the bishop who ejected him remained Christians ; but those who followed Marcion were called Christians no more, but henceforth Marcionites. So likewise Valentinus, and Basilides, and Manichaeus, and Simon Magus," etc. Similar passages in Western writers are too numerous for quotation.

Christians and Catholics, the latter name surely as much abused as that of Christ was in the Church of Corinth, when it is narrowed down into the name of a sect.

And very prudently did the Church refuse to tie itself to the authority of any human teacher; for it is found by experience that such teachers can only retain their authority on condition of losing their personality. Their name may still ornament a standard or serve as a rallying point, but it must not be too closely connected with the life and opinions of him who bore it. What Wesleyan now feels himself much troubled by researches into the history of the opinions of John Wesley? Does he think himself in any way bound to alter his own system of doctrine when it is first brought to his knowledge that John Wesley started as a very high Churchman, that he retained to the last many of the notions with which he set out, and in particular a very deep sense of the unlawfulness and the evils of schism. His attachment now is to Wesleyanism, not to Wesley; and though it is gratifying to him to think as highly as possible of the founder of the system, and to believe that everything in the system, as it stands now, had, or would have had, his sanction, still he looks on these as questions, however interesting, only of speculative history; and it is to the system as it stands now, however it arose, that his practical allegiance is given.

And so it generally happens when a man of great energy and originality of mind succeeds in stamping new ideas on the minds of his contemporaries. Full of gratitude for the new light for which they are conscious of being indebted to him, they are not anxious to scrutinise very carefully blemishes in his character or errors in his system. Nay, it is well if they are satisfied with overlooking or condoning his faults, and do not make them subjects for imitation. Meanwhile, they press along the path into which their leader has introduced them, and perhaps draw his principles out to consequences which he did not foresee, and would not have accepted. The spell of his name, however, still retains its power, and no very willing ear is given when first a colder criticism attempts to subject to exact measurement the services he has rendered and the obligations that are due to him. If in process of time those who call themselves by his name are forced to recognise shortcomings or errors in the teaching of him whom they profess to follow, it makes no difference to them now. The principles which had at first derived their vitality from the authority of another have now taken independent root, and are not killed by severance from the parent stem.

In the history of human progress the greatest individuals count but for little. When children play along the shore, and build their fortifications and dig their trenches in face of the advancing tide, it is a triumph to the child who has most ably planned his engineering, and whose channels have let the water into his moats, while those of his competitors are still dry. But a few minutes more, and his superiority is effaced as the flowing wave, forcing admission alike to all, obliterates all distinctions. Our age has profited by the accumulated knowledge and experience of the ages which have preceded it. And looking back now on the men who did most service in teaching their own generation, we sometimes doubt whether, if they had not arisen, other men would not have made the discovery for which the time was ripe. At any rate, we feel that we have a right to sit in judgment on the results obtained by men vastly superior in ability to ourselves; to hold fast to some of their conclusions, the soundness of which time has tested and acknowledged, and dismiss others as antiquated prejudices of a less enlightened age. The young man ceases to tremble at the schoolmaster from whose ferule he once withdrew his hand; the grown man criticises as an equal the dicta of guides whom he once regarded as infallible, whom he still thinks of with gratitude, as the men who did most to stimulate his youthful thirst for knowledge, and of his former enthusiastic reverence for whom he knows that he has no cause to be ashamed.

So, as the world goes on, men like less and less to label themselves by the names of great teachers of bygone days. In the scientific world the thing is almost unknown. While theories have still to struggle for their existence, and wrangling goes on as to their truth or falsity, they are known by their authors' names. So, while no school could drive its rivals off the field, there were Pythagoreans, and Platonists, and Aristotelians in former days; and there are Comtists and perhaps Darwinians now. But when once a theory obtains complete recognition, with its victory comes catholicity, and it has confidence that it rests on a better foundation than the authority of any name, however illustrious. To tie itself to any such name might only retard its development, as we know that they who called themselves Newtonians allowed themselves to be outstripped in the race of discovery through too exclusive adherence to the methods by which their master had won his triumphs. Even in religious sects there is, I think, an increasing reluctance among men to fetter themselves by the authority of ancient teachers. I notice that several who hold the doctrines commonly called Calvinistic often prefer not to call themselves Calvinists, not desiring to make themselves responsible for all that Calvin may have said or done, and saying, with good reason, that they are prepared to follow Calvin only so far as they can see that he has followed a greater authority than he. If in these days the reputation is assailed of those ancient teachers of whom we think most highly, and whose memory we regard with most affection, it hurts our feelings more than it disturbs our intellectual convictions. It may pain us to hear our reformers spoken of as "unmitigated scoundrels;" but this we know, that if the worst could be proved that has ever been said of any, and if that which is true of some individuals could be shown to be true of any large numbers, still it touches not our faith. Our faith is not built on men. The foundations of our creed are not shaken, if history should prove that some Liberius or Honorius of ours has fallen into heresy, some Leo of ours sunk into practical heathenism, some Alexander outraged morality. Let Cranmer or any other of those to whom we owe the casting off of a foreign yoke, have been time-serving, or vacillating, or inconsistent, or worse, we are not hurt as Protestants, any more than we are hurt as Christians, if we have to acknowledge that St. Peter at times betrayed cowardice, or vacillation, or inconsistency. In any case, we are

Christians and Catholics, not Cranmerians. We follow men only as far as they follow truth; and in religious matters what our Church has said of the most venerable assemblies of men we say of the most venerable of individual men, that they may err and have erred, and that things ordained by them as necessary to salvation have neither strength nor authority, unless it may be declared that they be taken out of Holy Scripture.

II. Thus, I think, at the present day, we are likely more and more to come to an agreement that it is not meet to say, I am of Paul, or of Cephas, or of Apollos. And now comes the question—Are we to carry our principles no further? Is it meet to say, I am of Christ? It is impossible to answer this question until we have first answered another—What think you of Christ?

That we must think of Him whom we know as Christ as one of the world's greatest benefactors all are agreed. It is certain that His influence rapidly outleaped the bounds of His own land, and that it has been in all the most civilised nations of the earth an immense power for good. This is much to say; but if it be all it is not reason enough why we, at so great a distance of time, should label ourselves by His name. Theories, as I have said, bear their authors' names as long as they are struggling for existence; but if we exclude those utterances ascribed to Jesus which speak of His own dignity, His doctrines are all acknowledged to be true by every theist. That we should admire and gratefully reverence His memory is natural, but why pay Him this exclusive homage? Why should we say, I am of Christ, any more than I am of Socrates? In placing the two names together, of course I would not be understood to say that, considered even as teachers of morality, the one is comparable to the other, either in the purity of the morality taught, or in the extent of influence obtained. But still the instance illustrates what I mean, that you would not dream now of enrolling yourselves as disciples of a teacher who lived two thousand years ago, however great your admiration for his character. Those two thousand years of accumulated experience have raised us to such a level that, dwarfs though we are, we can look down on giants who lived below. It is with a certain patronising discrimination that we cull over the results of their labours, holding fast to that the excellence of which has been proved by trial, and rejecting what we believe they, if they had known as much as we, would also have been wise enough to reject. If a man of independent mind often refuses to make the sacrifice of individual judgment involved in enrolling himself under a living party leader, notwithstanding the immense gain of practical power that party organisation confers, why should we not retain our entire independence of any one who belongs completely to the past?

The conclusion to which these arguments point is, that any one who believes our Lord to be mere man, so far from having any cause to complain if he is not called a Christian, ought himself to have no wish to be designated by that name. I spoke, however, on last Sunday of the mischiefs which follow from judging too harshly of others, and too lightly denying them a right to the Christian name. I had occasion to mention how early complaints were made that the name Christian was assumed by persons not properly entitled to it. Even in those days of persecution, when it was a common thing for men to be sent to execution, with no other crime laid to their charge than that they bore this name Christian— even then there were unworthy pretenders to it. And genuine Christians accounted for the evil fame that hung upon their name by the wicked deeds of men who claimed that title only to dishonour it. It is not strange that unworthy pretenders to the name should be found in later times, when in place of the profession being forbidden by the laws, it was in many of the most civilised countries a punishable crime not to profess it; and when public opinion even outran the law, and to reject the title drew on the rebel heavier penalties than the law could inflict, in the contempt and hatred of his countrymen. In our own country at the present day things have greatly altered, and disbelief in the most fundamental article of the established creed, proclaimed in the most offensive and aggressive manner, so far from being visited with legal penalties, does not even prevent a man from sitting as a member of the Legislature. And as a seat there had to be gained by the suffrages of a large constituency, it is plain that neither does public opinion affix any very severe stigma to the rejection of the first postulate of the Christian religion. Yet it would be untrue to say that public opinion is as yet completely indifferent in this matter. Its penalties may not be very severe, yet it is not to be denied that there is a certain coldness which the ostentatious rejection of Christianity may entail, and, consequently, that there is a temptation to cover secret rejection of the religion by a nominal profession.

Have we, then, a right to think, when men are eager to call themselves Christians, who, as we suppose ourselves to have proved, ought not in logical consistency to wish to call themselves so, that they are not sincere in their professed desire, and are only anxious to escape social ostracism by at least a nominal conformity with the prevalent belief? I am persuaded that it would be unjust so to think, and that at the bottom of their reluctance to part with the name of Christ there is a principle which it is quite worth while to examine. We may say to them, You regard Christ only as a great moral and religious teacher, as one who, if He was not the first discoverer of certain great truths, at least succeeded in making them accepted in the world as they had never been accepted before. Why, then, cannot you hold these truths without speaking or thinking of Christ? Archimedes was a mathematical teacher of pre-eminent genius: we have incorporated his discoveries in our elementary teaching, and daily make use of them without speaking or thinking of Archimedes. Why should we deal different measure to a teacher of moral and religious truth? Why can we not believe and teach all the truths which Christ discovered without thinking or speaking of Christ?

III. When the question is proposed we have at once an instinctive feeling that the Christian religion without Christ would be a nonentity. It never was so preached. Open up the New Testament at random, and if you find the work done by the first preachers of the religion spoken of by themselves, or others, it will not be said that they preached Christianity, but that they preached Christ. It was not so much a conviction of the truth of His doctrines as love to Himself that animated their missionary labours. And it was love to Him and gratitude for what He had done, quite as much as belief in what He said, which they tried to instil into their converts. So when St. Luke tells that the Apostles had been discharged from prison, rejoicing that they had been counted worthy to suffer shame for His name, he adds, "Daily in the temple and in every house they ceased not to teach and preach 'Jesus Christ.'" St. Paul says in one place, "We preach not ourselves, but Christ Jesus our Lord;" and more fully in another place, "We preach Christ crucified, unto the Jews a stumbling-block, and unto the Greeks foolishness; but unto them which are called, both Jews and Greeks, Christ the power of God and the wisdom of God." Or perhaps an example from a later Epistle will better illustrate how completely "to preach Christ" had become the established phrase for propagating His religion: —" Some 'preach Christ' of envy and strife, and some also of goodwill. The one 'preach Christ' of contention, not sincerely, supposing to add affliction to my bonds: the other of love, knowing that I am set for the defence of the Gospel. What then, notwithstanding every way, whether in pretence or in truth, 'Christ is preached,' and I therein will rejoice." When we find that all the first Christian missionaries thus "preached Christ," it is, I think, unreasonable scepticism to deny that in His lifetime Christ preached Himself: that He uttered such words as "I am the way, the truth, and the life: no man cometh to the Father but by me;" giving thus His own sanction to what His Apostle afterwards taught, "Through Him we both have access by one Spirit to the Father."

And if we look for the secret of the power of the Gospel, whether as preached in ancient or in modern times, it is when Christ has been lifted up that He has drawn all men unto Him. Men have learned to know Jesus as the Gospel records reveal Him, as the lover of men, among whom He went about doing good; teaching, rebuking, comforting, dying for them; revealing to them what God is, not by words only, but in His spotless life; making atonement for their sins, and enabling them to look on the God whom they had offended as a reconciled Father; reigning now in heaven at His right hand, the present Saviour of His Church, one to whom His people may fly for help in every time of need, who dwells in their hearts by faith, with whom they can hold intimate communion, and be always assured of His sympathy and love. And taught thus to think of Jesus as one living in the present, Christians feel towards Him as no one can feel towards any dead hero of the past. If I asked you, Do you love Socrates? you would have to stop and think whether the word love could with any propriety be used to designate the feelings with which we regard him. If I asked, Do you love Christ? thousands would answer without hesitation, and answer truly, Love Him?—I would die for Him.

Some early defenders of our religion appealed to the fact that the language of their opponents completely gave the lie to their professed belief, seeing that while they professed their belief in many gods, yet, in a number of phrases in daily use, they spoke of God in the singular number, the soul thus bearing unconscious testimony to the truth implanted in it of the unity of God. Surely, with still better reason, we may appeal to the " testimony of the soul naturally Christian,"[1] in that there are so many now also whose language gives the lie to their professed belief, who profess to believe that Jesus was a man like others, who lived many ages ago, who is now dead and gone, and lives only in men's memories and in whatever

[1] Tertullian, *Apol.* 17, and *De Test. Animæ.*

abiding results have issued from His labours. But their anxiety to bear His name, their pain at hearing their right to it contested, shows that there are feelings in their hearts for which their theory will in no wise account.

It was a necessary condition of the success of Christ's work in the world that He should be able to inspire such love as He has done. Truths that require only intellectual assent may circulate and make their way with no need to be accompanied by any author's name; but any seeds of practical action which such truths contain lie dormant until they are quickened by the influence of human affection. To make any cause triumph and show itself a power in the world there is needed passionate attachment to a great leader. In particular, religion, if it deserves the name, if it is to be anything more than a fetish charm for gaining the favour or appeasing the anger of unseen powers, must be vivified by emotion; fear must be cast out by love. Far am I from saying that pure Theism is not capable of developing such emotions in the human breast. We need only take up the Book of Psalms to find evidence to the contrary. We find such utterances as—"Whom have I in heaven but Thee, and there is none upon earth that I desire in comparison of Thee. My flesh and my heart faileth, but Thou art the strength of my heart and my portion for ever ;" or, " O God, Thou art my God. Early will I seek Thee, in a barren and dry land, where no water is; for Thy loving-kindness is better than the life itself. My lips shall praise Thee." And yet the feeling which such words express must be described as exceptional; rather that of higher and more thoughtful souls than of ordinary men. The Jewish history declares it so to be. No other nation had had presented to them so lofty a conception of Deity. They worshipped one uncreated Spirit, dwelling in light, which no mortal could approach, and of whom it was unlawful to attempt to make an image. But this conception was too abstract for popular acceptance. The people were constantly falling into idolatry—that is to say, striving, by some sensible representation, to satisfy their want of a God manifestly present among them.

Shall we say that the difficulties felt by the Jews of old sprang only from their imperfect civilisation, and that with the progress of cultivation men find it easier to make the unseen the object of love. Our experience tells us the reverse. As with men's increased study of inanimate nature they know more of the order and regularity of the vast machine, they seem to become incapable of looking behind it, and recoil, as if from anthropomorphism, from the recognition of an author of nature to whom our love may be given. If there be a God, they say, He cannot be known. We can only smile at the alternative of Atheism which Agnostics offer us. We are permitted to believe that there may be a God, provided only we own that His omnipotence is limited in such a way that He is unable to reveal Himself to His creatures, and make them know and love Him. Others, recognising that men have unmistakably aspirations and emotions which need a religion to satisfy them, have invited us to exchange our worship of a God whom we do not know for a worship of man whom we do know; not, however, of any individual man, who must be acknowledged to have faults and imperfections which render him unworthy of our adoration, but of collective humanity. Such a religion may serve for the closest speculation of a so-called philosopher, but can never attract the hearts of mankind. Men have worshipped stocks and stones, but then it was because (however foolish their belief may have been) they supposed the object of their worship was a real being, with power to kill or injure them, and with consciousness of the adoration offered it. But who can worship a mere abstraction of his own mind, destitute of any real personality, unable to know whether any one gives or withholds his worship?

But the inventors of the new religion of which

I speak overlooked that the old religion which they forsook contained a much truer and more practical worship of humanity than theirs, in the worship of Jesus. Take the highest ideal of all that is most noble in humanity that any can form; tax your imagination to conceive all that is highest in purity and active goodness, and you will have formed no fancy portrait of impossible perfection, but only some sketch of what was actually realised in the life of Jesus. If you delight to let your thoughts dwell on such a model, you will not be indulging in unprofitable dreamings on a picture of your own imagination, not even in ideal reproduction of the historical past. It is permitted you to hold real communion with One whom, though He died, death could not hold; with One whom you may, if you will, find ever at hand to counsel and to help you; One who can turn your meditations on His goodness into a means of making you like Him; whom, if you really learn to know, you will not be able to help loving; nay, who will make you not merely like Him, but one with Him; so one with Him, that His riches shall supply your poverty, His strength support your weakness, His righteousness cover your sinfulness; so one with Him, that death shall no more be able to hold you than it held Him, and that where He reigns you shall dwell with Him for ever.

Men have obeyed a very natural impulse in enlisting themselves under human teachers, and saying, " I am of Paul, or of Cephas, or of Apollos." All that they mean the Christian means, but infinitely more, when he says, " I am of Christ."

IV[1]

A SCIENTIFIC TEST APPLIED TO ATHEISTIC THEORIES OF RELIGION

"Then said Jesus unto the twelve, Will ye also go away? Then Simon Peter answered Him, Lord, to whom shall we go? Thou hast the words of eternal life."—ST. JOHN vi. 67, 68.

WHEN St. Peter gave this answer it may seem that there was no lack of other teachers to whom he might have gone. There were at that time venerated Rabbis, recognised expounders of the law, who held in the estimation of the Jewish people a place far higher than that which was allowed to the Galilean carpenter's son. And many of those other teachers professed to have the words of eternal life. The doctrine of a future life and of a resurrection from the dead had been taught in the Jewish schools before Jesus began to preach. St. Paul, when brought before the Jewish Council, could hope to enlist the sympathies of a powerful party in his favour by declaring that it was concerning the hope and

[1] Preached in Belfast, December 1875.

resurrection of the dead he was called in question. His profession to Felix was, "I have hope towards God, which they themselves also allow, that there shall be a resurrection from the dead both of the just and of the unjust." With far more force can we reply—To whom shall we go? if it is proposed to us to abandon our Lord. If we turn to the teachers who are supposed able to supersede our antiquated Gospel, and ask them, "Have *you* the words of eternal life?" they reply, "Eternal life, we know not of such a thing. Nothing is eternal; least of all the life of man. In a few short years the matter of which his body is composed is resolved into its elements, and of anything in him apart from matter we know nothing. It is as vain to seek for man after his earthly life has fled as it is to look for the cloud which has melted away in the azure of the sky."

Such being their gospel, we need not be surprised if its preachers give no very warm invitation if we ask themselves, Shall we come to you? The teachers of infidelity of the present day are by no means of the race who compassed sea and land to make one proselyte. There was a time when unbelievers, generally, were men of coarse moral fibre, whose lives were such that they had good reason to wish that Christianity might not be true —who never troubled themselves to inquire whether it would be more for the happiness of the world that it should not be true—who, therefore, flung round freely their scoff or their objection against any doctrine which presented difficulty; rejoicing if they had gained a disciple, careless if by their jeers they had wounded the deepest feelings of their hearers, or if by the doubts they raised they had robbed some soul of its happiness, and deprived it of the spring of all its energies for good. The race of such infidels is not quite extinct; but not such are they who have any influence on educated thought at the present day. No unbeliever now is likely to find a hearing if he is one incapable of understanding what a power religion has been in the world, what empire it has exercised over the emotions and the conscience, what consolations it has administered in the hour of sorrow, what restraints it has imposed in the hour of temptation.

No wonder that any one who does understand this should have misgivings whether the knowledge he has to impart is any compensation for the faith he takes away. So that, as I have said, they give but a hesitating answer when we ask them, Shall we come to you? "Come," they say, "if you have culture such as to qualify you to become our disciple: but it is not every one that is capable of receiving our doctrines, nor is it every one that is able to bear them. The thin air of the heights on which we dwell is not such as the lungs of every one can breathe. We have, we think, the words of truth, but we do not pretend to have the words of comfort. If you come to us you must be prepared to welcome truth, and be content with it, no matter how unpleasant an aspect it may bear." And so they own, to begin with, that the great majority of one sex is not at present qualified to receive their doctrines, nor likely to be bettered by receiving them—in other words, that those doctrines are unsuited to about half the human race. There are few infidels who have any zeal to make a convert of their wife or of their daughter. They are not anxious to disturb the simple faith, the beauty of whose results they admire. Their rule is well expressed in the lines—

> "Leave thou thy sister when she prays,
> Her early heaven, her happy views;
> Nor thou with shadowed hint confuse
> A life that leads melodious days.
> Her faith through form is pure as thine;
> Her hands are quicker unto good."

If religion may be pronounced a necessity for the great bulk of one sex, there is certainly a considerable portion of the other who would find it equally difficult to dispense with it. There are men whose hands have been indeed quick unto good, men of the purest lives, of the most active benevolence, who will tell you that you would dry up the source of all their virtue, as well as rob their life of the fountain of its purest enjoyments, if you took from them their faith in their Father who is in heaven. There are others, no doubt, who could give up religion without a pang; nay, who would feel a certain relief to know that they might, without danger, shake off the restraints which it had imposed on them. Then, indeed, they might without misgiving take their fill of the grosser enjoyments which they delight in. Let us eat and drink, they would cry, for to-morrow we die. Yet were it well for the world that the restraints which had hitherto kept them in check should be removed? Where else should we find the controlling power which the hopes and fears of a hereafter have hitherto exercised? We may talk of the dignity of virtue and of the duty of self-sacrifice; but if he on whom we bestow our words reply that he does not choose to sacrifice himself, that his own happiness is more to him than that of all the rest of mankind, and that our pronouncing pleasures unworthy of him does not prevent his finding his happiness in them, and being determined to enjoy them if he can, what further arguments have we wherewith to influence him? So much has religion contributed to the welfare of society, that it has been said by no very religious man "that if there had not been a God it would have been necessary to invent one."

All that I have said is perfectly well known to the chief intellectual leaders of the irreligious philosophy of the present day; and so they have no anxiety to make disciples of the vulgar. They rather put forth their doctrines as the truths which are to be reached by mankind in some further stage of the development of the race, but for which at present only some of the most highly-cultured souls are ripe, and which must now not be forced on those who have not had the training necessary in order to receive them profitably. Well, then, may the bulk of you ask—To whom shall we go? Other teachers there are, but they confess that they have nothing to tell us that will make us wiser or better, and so they are not solicitous that we should flock to them for instruction.

II. But there may be some here such as they do invite to come to them, and for whom the terms of their invitation have no small attraction. For they profess to be able to teach the truth, and the truth is what those of whom I speak want to know, whether it be pleasant to hear or not. I can conceive such persons listening with some impatience to the topics which I have already brought before you. You are trying to prove to us, they would say to me, that Christianity makes men happy, or that it makes them good, when what we want proved is—that it is true. We don't want to be bribed, by any supposed good consequences, into believing anything without evidence. It may give a man great comfort to believe that in all the trials of life he has the power of holding communion with an ever-present and Almighty Friend, but we do not care for such comfort if it is based on a delusion. It may be very good for society that a belief should be propagated among the masses in a future state of rewards and punishments, but we care not to share that belief if it be only a cunning invention of politicians. It may not be very agreeable to be told that our father was an ape, and that we ourselves are but machines, and that our future is annihilation ; but if these things be true, better the ugliest truth than the most beautiful lie that ever was invented.

Most heartily do I sympathise with such a feeling. There can be no solid comfort for man's life if it be not founded on truth ; nor do I believe in the usefulness of any belief that has not a basis of truth. Ever, when it has been supposed that to shake some well-established prejudice might have some dangerous consequence, has it been found that the knowledge of the truth has done more for the world than the accepted falsehood could have done. We Christians, of course, believe that the God who made the world is a God of truth, that in seeking to know the truth we do Him acceptable service, and that He has so ordered the world He has made that the successful search for truth is richly rewarded. And this is the conclusion of which experience convinces philosophers, whether their creed be religious or atheistical. They are convinced by the history of philosophy that every truth they can discover will be a gain to the world; that with every accession to our knowledge of the truth will be gained some new power over nature, some benefit to enrich the life of man.

We may, then, confidently say that experience has proved to us that the belief in no lie can really benefit the world. Well, then, does it not follow conversely, that if a belief really benefits the world it cannot be a lie. Now, I need not go back on what I have said as to the practical confession made by so many of the anti-supernaturalists of the present day, that they know that the general reception of their teaching at present would not add to human happiness. For whatever dispute there may be as to the truth of Christianity, I can hardly conceive any as to the usefulness of a belief in it. If you were forming in your imagination a scheme for the happiness of the world, could you conceive anything better than that every individual in the world should, from his heart, accept the Gospel of Christ, and act on it as his universal rule of moral obligation? Only imagine what a world it would be if every one in it were, not in name only, but in heart, a Christian; if every one in it constantly set before his mind that perfect ideal, both in precept and example, which the life of Jesus has supplied; if each strove to live in constant communion with the model of the best and purest he was capable of conceiving, and ever acted as if all that he did was witnessed by Him; if each were armed against the vicissitudes of life by faith in the infinite love of Him who sways the power of heaven and earth, producing perfect acquiescence in all that was ordered by all-seeing wisdom and perfect goodness; if each, in imitation of Him who went about the earth doing good, strove by every means in his power to benefit his brethren in Christ, not seeking his own, but in lowliness of mind preferring other to himself, not rendering evil for evil, but ever following that which is good both among ourselves and to all men.

Oh, brethren, we have cause to be ashamed that

there should now be need to preach about the evidences of Christianity; for if the lives of Christians generally corresponded to their profession there would be no need of other evidences. We ought ourselves to be the living Gospel of Christ, preaching the most effective of all sermons by the practical exhibition of a life moulded by the doctrines of the Cross of Christ. And yet, however short the conduct of the professed followers of Christ has fallen of the standard it ought to reach, the world has seen in too many cases what an amount of self-sacrificing zeal for the good of mankind the belief in Christianity has generated, to leave any room for doubt that the greatest possible amount of human happiness would be secured by the universal and practical conviction of its truth. Can there be a stronger argument for the Divine origin of Christianity?[1] Who but God alone, the God of the spirits of all flesh, could have made an instrument of universal adaptation, in perfect harmony with the moral constitution of man, meeting the necessities of his nature at every turn, satisfying its highest and noblest aspirations, supplying it with the strongest possible motives when temptation presses, renewing the will, purifying the affections, re-creating in the soul the

---

[1] I have in this part of the Sermon borrowed largely from the Bishop of Llandaff's Charge for 1875.

image of God after which he was originally formed, and making him a partaker of the Divine nature for this very purpose that he might escape the pollution which is in the world, supporting the soul in the trials, and guiding it in the perplexities of life, and inspiring the full assurance of a blessed immortality in the life to come.

III. And now, I think you will see that other teachers take a line which it is impossible for them to maintain if they venture to say to us, We own your doctrines are the most consoling, that they are those which are most capable of inspiring a high-toned morality, that they are those a belief in which is most calculated to promote the happiness of the human race—but ours are the truest. Before they say this they are bound to produce some instance in the whole history of philosophy when the discovery of a new truth involved a loss of power to those who accepted it. Just the reverse has ever been the case. It is now an axiom that knowledge is power. Let us but know the laws that govern events and we gain power to control them. Science has ever been the handmaid of human life, and has enriched it with abundance of blessings. If the life that we live now so far exceeds in comfort that which was lived by our savage ancestors, that even the poorest among us would think an existence such as theirs hardly tolerable, it is to science we owe it. Science taught us to give rules to the wandering stars of heaven, and mark their appointed paths; science has taught the mariner by their means to guide himself across the trackless ocean, and to bear to our shores the produce of a thousand lands. Science has enlisted all the powers of nature in the service of man. It has found in steam a slave more powerful and more obedient than the genie of the eastern tales; it has forbidden the lightning to touch our buildings, and taught it to bear our messages; it has trained the sun to paint our pictures, and the poor can now have memorials of the features dear to them more faithful than the rich could once have obtained. Science has ever been the benefactor of man, so that if what comes in the name of science threatens to take from man his happiness, and deprive him of his power, we are safe in rejecting the pretender as an impostor.

But this is precisely the characteristic of the science, falsely so called, of the present day, which arrays itself as an adversary to religion. Just observe the course by which, in other instances, science proceeds to make its discoveries and to gain its powers. It takes intelligent notice of some of the changes that happen under our eyes, and it sets itself to inquire their cause. If it succeeds in finding the secret of the force which effects them, it knows then how to set that force again in operation, and thereby produce effects ten thousand times greater than any casual exercise of it would have elicited. The man of science takes notice how the lid of a kettle dances up and down on the fire, and he asks what makes it dance. When he has learned the true answer, he finds that he is the master of a force which will not only produce again the small effect which he at first observed, but which will accomplish any task he may be pleased to set it. And it is ever so. Practice proves theory. If you want to know whether you are in possession of the true theory of any of the processes of nature, you may judge your theory by its fruits. Will your theory teach you how to imitate these processes, how to regulate their results at your desire, to remove those which are injurious, to set those working on a larger scale which you find to be beneficial?

IV. In this way we may test the theories which profess to give an account of the power which religion has exercised in the world. Prayer, for instance, is confessedly a power. There are disputes as to the limits of its power, whether or not it affects the external world; but there is no dispute at all as to its power on the heart of him who practises it. Every one acknowledges that the worshipper employs perhaps the very best means to elevate his moral nature when he places himself thus in communion with the best and purest Being he is capable of conceiving, when he directs his aspirations after his highest moral good. As he prays, it is owned, temptation loses its power, sin becomes more hateful, the vexations of life become more bearable, ills have no weight, and tears no bitterness; in the heart springs up a fountain of strength against the seductions of vice, of comfort in sorrow as the will of the worshipper is more and more brought into conformity with that of the Being whom he worships. These effects are owned by everybody, and so an irreligious philosopher of the present day exhorts his disciples not to be ashamed if they are caught praying. Reason, he thinks, cannot justify the practice, but it is good, he says, to follow the instincts of our nature, even though we may not be able to give a satisfactory explanation of them.

Here, then, we have a force which exercises a real power in the world. Does any one profess to be able to give a scientific explanation of the operation of that force, we shall know at once whether his theory is the true one by seeing whether the knowledge of the theory enables us the better to employ and direct the force. A philosopher tells us, "I can explain the efficacy of prayer. The being with whom you conceive you hold communion is but the creation of your own imagination. When you ask him to give you grace and strength you are really invoking a non-entity. The grace and strength, it is true, come, but they do so in virtue of the laws of the action of your own mind, and not by any influence from without." We need think of no other answer than this: "If a man knows the true theory of anything he is the better able to do the thing. You say you know the true theory of prayer. Well, then, pray."—He can't. If the instincts of his nature surprise him into prayer, he is obliged for the time to put his theory out of his mind. If he thinks of it he smiles at his own inconsistency. He blushes if he is caught on his knees, and starts to his feet with lame apologies. To such a man I would say, "The thing is so contrary to experience that it may fairly be pronounced impossible, that to know the true theory of any process can unfit you for performing it. If prayer is a folly which ought to be suppressed, then perhaps your theory may be right; but if you own that it is good for man to practise it, then certainly that cannot be the true account of it which unfits a man for doing it."

V. I take another part of religion, its empire

over conscience, the sanction it gives to the rule of right and wrong, the prerogative it claims to direct the life. Looked at from this point of view, religion is, unquestionably, a force, and one of enormous power. What would the world be if it were not for all that a sense of duty makes men do and all that it keeps them back from doing? How many indulgences are declined, how many passions are ungratified, simply because it is felt to be wrong to gratify them; in a multitude of cases the feeling that it is wrong is so strong that we feel under scarcely any temptation to an act which we look on as practically impossible. What should we be if every one did that which was right in his own eyes, and if that was right in each man's eyes which it gave him pleasure to do? The fear of others, indeed, might be some restraint; yet human laws can reach but little way, and if there were not the check of principle and conscience, the dread of punishment from others would do but little in keeping a man from evil. Still more is this the case when the question is not of abstaining from action, but of doing. Would it ever be possible to have laws compelling men to make those sacrifices for the good of others, to undertake the unselfish labours which have been cheerfully performed at the call of religion and duty? No one can doubt that it would be a fearful calamity for the world if men generally were not controlled by conscience, and if they lost their sense of right and wrong.

Well, then, we want to know the true theory of this great and beneficial force. We ask of those who reject the account that conscience speaks with authority to us because it is the voice of God who formed us—in short, who deny that there is any God who formed us—what explanation they give of the origin of this sense of right and wrong? They tell us that these feelings of moral approbation, and the reverse, are nothing but the growth of prejudice and association. Acts which other men feel to be injurious to themselves individually, or to the community of which they are members, they regard with dislike. The expression of that dislike is exhibited to us in early years, and so what we call a disapproval of these acts has been associated with them in our minds from a time earlier than we can remember. Or, without being generated by anything that has taken place in our own experience, such feelings may have been inherited by us from our ancestors, in whom they took their origin in the manner I have described. A theist may give such an account as this of the origin of conscience, and conscience yet preserve for him its authority; for he can allow conscience to be but a growth, and still own it as the voice of Him who designed and planned that it should grow. But if we do not acknowledge anything divine in the origin of our feelings of moral approbation, why should we regard them? It will be as impossible to maintain the authority of conscience after we have accepted this theory of its origin as it is to scare any one with a dressed-up ghost after he has once gone up to it and pulled it to pieces, and learned how it was made. So here, again, we have the same story; a theory claiming to be true, but which, the moment we try to make a practical use of it, turns out to be not only useless but mischievous.

VI. I might, if time permitted, go on in like manner over the other chief points in religion, and examine what account is given of them in modern theories. I might speak, for instance, of the desperate attempts which have been made to retain for mankind the consoling hopes of a future life, notwithstanding the abandonment of Christianity. I might tell how some of those careful weighers of evidence who have found the proof of our Lord's resurrection insufficient, have asserted the possibility of getting more trustworthy assurance of a life after death on the testimony of spirit-rappers. But I cannot pursue details. I have said enough to show what answer is to be given to those who claim to have made the heroic choice of preferring the doctrines which are true to those the belief in which is only comfortable and useful. We do not believe in the possibility of such a divorce between truth and utility. If it were possible that the pursuit of truth could ever cease to be useful to the world we should have to revise all our morality, and inquire whether, on such a supposition, truth ought to be pursued. But the fact is, that the one point they are sure of is that their doctrines are neither consoling nor useful. What they are not sure of is that they are true. Nay, that they are not true is proved by their complete failure to resolve the problems of human life. They have never attempted to refute the answer that religion gives to those problems. They at best aspire to be able to give another satisfactory account of them without making the hypothesis that the world was created and is governed by a wise and intelligent Ruler. And when we examine this account we find that it breaks down completely in all that concerns man's emotions and his conscience, that is to say, in all that regards the practical part of human life. Shall we, then, who have a key that completely fits the lock, give it up for one that only makes a show of fitting, and breaks in the wards when we try to turn it?

Brethren, I would beg of you all to weigh the responsibility that is thrown upon you by the line of argument I have now taken. I have contended that an argument for the truth of Christianity may be drawn from the benefits which it has conferred on the world, and from the power which it exhibits to direct the conscience and rule the life of man. To give force to such an argument, the theory of Christianity must be worked out in the lives of its professors. I have said it already, and say it again, that if this were done we should want no other evidence of the truth of Christianity. Are you, then, living witnesses to the world of the Divinity of the faith which you profess? It is no common-place morality which will give this witness. If you only shun those actions which would draw on you man's punishment, or which are visited with discredit in the society in which you live, then, as our Lord said in the Sermon on the Mount—"What do you more than others?" Do not even the infidels the same? The same, nay, many of them better, for the lessons that Christ taught are of such excellence that they commend themselves, even apart from His authority, and are practised by many who, perhaps on their own principles, could scarcely show sufficient reason for conforming to them. What, then, if you be found worse than they; if you who have accepted the call of Him who pleased not Himself, to take up your cross and become His disciples, if you be found selfish and exacting, seeking your own, unmindful of the claims of others ; if you be found not trustworthy in the intercourse of daily life, not to be depended on as much when you are not watched as when you are ; if you turn out dishonest work ; if you, followers of the meek and lowly Jesus, be found in your family intercourse passionate, or ill-tempered, or vindictive ; if you, followers of Him who is all purity, be impure in your language, or in your thoughts—then you are as far as in you lies bearing witness against the truth of the doctrines you profess.

We have come to see how high a place the morality of the Bible occupies among the evidences for its truths. There have been men who have tried to find antinomian doctrines in the Bible, and who have sought to make out that it was the doctrine of that book that men could be as dear to God and as much the objects of His favour while living in sin as while practising holiness. We know, now, that if they could succeed in proving that the Bible taught such doctrine as this, they would only prove that the Bible did not come from God. But to live Antinomianism is as bad as to preach Antinomianism. It was of men, not whose doctrine, but whose practice, was bad, that the Apostle said—"I have told you often, and now tell you even weeping, that they are enemies of the Cross of Christ." Surely those are enemies of the Cross of Christ who would rob the Gospel of the Cross of one of its proudest boasts—namely, that by the new motives which it supplies, and the spiritual strength which it ministers, it has made a fulfilment of God's law possible which otherwise could not be obtained.

And though there be many whose profession of Christianity is but a name, there are, thank God, many more who experimentally prove that this boast is no vain one. The superiority of their obedience is that it is an obedience which springs from love. For this may be briefly described as the peculiar characteristic of Christianity, that it is the only system which makes it possible for us to love the Ruler of the universe. In some other systems we see in the universe the working of passionless laws, which work regardless of man's welfare or his wishes, which we may wonder at or admire, but cannot love. Others, again, fix their eyes only on the misery of a world ruled over by death and the fear of death, and hold out to us the God who presides over it as an object of pity, or of hatred, because He either cannot or will not banish evil from the world. What an utterly different note is struck by those two great sayings of the Gospel—" God so loved the world, that He gave His only begotten Son." "We love Him because He first loved us." Has any one lived in a house where there was no love, where commands were harshly given, and obedience sullenly rendered ; and has it not been coming out of shivering night into sunshine to come into a dwelling where affection rules ? This is the great question of the present day—In what kind of a house are we living? Are we in the dungeons of a tyrant ; are we in a city of strangers ; or are we in the house of a father and a friend ? Is it really true that God is love, and that God deserves to be loved ?

Oh, brethren, if to banish that belief from our hearts would be to banish sunshine from the world, we have cause for the joy with which we commemorate that great birth which we are this week to celebrate—the birth of Him who revealed the Father, who brought life and immortality to light, who gave Himself to die for us. Eighteen centuries have passed since His coming. The world has made many advances in knowledge and culture—yet, still, if asked, To whom shall we go ? we must answer with the Apostle, " Lord, Thou hast the words of eternal life. We believe and are sure that Thou art indeed the Christ, the Son of the living God."

V

THEISM AND MODERN SCIENCE.—I

"The invisible things of Him from the creation of the world are clearly seen, being understood by the things that are made, even His eternal power and Godhead."—Rom. i. 20

A VERY few years ago I suppose it would have been generally agreed that a clergyman could not employ a sermon more unprofitably than in trying to prove to his congregation the being of a God. If his pedantic attempt to demonstrate what nobody dreamed of denying produced on the minds of his hearers any effect at all, it would only be that of teaching them that there was room for doubt or controversy on a point which they had always regarded as indisputable. But at the present day the work of defending the most elementary doctrine of religion can hardly be pronounced quite unnecessary; nor is there any risk, at least in addressing such a congregation as this, that I shall make you acquainted with doubts or objections which you would never have to encounter were I not to bring them before you.

The current of modern unbelief has passed from assaults on the special doctrines of Revelation to the scrutiny of principles of natural religion which were unquestioned by sceptics of a former generation. When Bishop Butler wrote his Analogy, he could at least assume the existence of a God as an admitted principle needing no argument on his part to establish it. In fact, the unbelief of his day did not seriously question it; those against whom he wrote, on the contrary, maintaining that this and all other really essential doctrines of religion were sufficiently known by the light of nature, and that any additional revelation was superfluous. Arguing on the principles which were common to him with his antagonists, Butler successfully showed that the objections then current against Christianity could not consistently be urged by any theist; that he who has once conceded that the existing course of things was originally framed and is still governed by an intelligent Author, is not in a position to reject as incredible anything that the Bible teaches concerning God's dealings with the world which He has made. The very cogency, however, of Butler's argument has had on some minds an effect the opposite of what he intended. Instead of following him to his conclusion, they go back and retract the assent they had given to his premisses.

Such, Mr. Mill tells us in his autobiography, was the case with his father. He owned the force of the reasoning of the Analogy, but he preferred to give up his theism rather than accept Christianity. And the alternative chosen by James Mill is that now adopted by the principal adversaries of revealed religion, the more eminent of whom may be described as, in the strict sense of the word, atheists; that is to say, not "anti-theists," for they do not venture to pronounce a negative on the question of God's existence, but they set the whole question aside as one which is perhaps beyond man's powers to determine in speculation, and which need not affect his practice. If there be others of them who still retain the doctrines of a personal God and of a future life, they rather cling to these doctrines as a matter of sentiment than hold them with strong rational conviction; nor is their grasp of them sufficiently firm to give us confidence to deal with them by Butler's method, and force them to follow out to their consequences the principles which they admit. The result might be that, instead of restoring their faith to its completeness, we might carry away the little that is left.

Thus, the effect of the victories won by the champions of the Church in former days has been merely to simplify controversies, reducing all to a few great issues. The Socinian controversy may be said to have been long since extinct. A century ago a dispute was actively carried on whether it was possible to reconcile with the New Testament the doctrine that Jesus of Nazareth was mere man. The assertion of His Resurrection, indeed, could not be eliminated from the book, but perhaps it might be possible to cut out the story of His miraculous Conception. St. Paul's "God blessed for ever" and St. John's "My Lord and my God" might be explained away as ejaculations. Perhaps some dexterity of interpretation might get over the "thought it not robbery to be equal with God," or even "the Word was God." We hear little now of this trifling; the progress of historical science has cast discredit on an uncandid mode of dealing with the documents on which history rests, and those who, looking on the New Testament as a merely human book, have attempted to deduce from it what were the opinions concerning Jesus of Nazareth, which were entertained by His immediate followers, have arrived at conclusions more closely allied to the orthodox than were obtained by those who looked on it as in some sense an inspired book, and were anxious only to ascertain what was the very minimum that, on its authority, they could be compelled to acknowledge. It will be readily owned now that Paul and John were not Socinians, and the question has simply become :—Are they authority for us, and are we under any obligation to adopt their opinions? As little successful as was the attempt a century ago to maintain the contest on the ground of Socinianism seems to be now the attempt to fight the battle on the ground of mere Deism. If, nowadays, we hear of scandal caused to pious ears by the open denial of some accepted doctrines of religion, it is usually the case that the doctrines controverted would have been acknowledged as truth by Butler's antagonists as readily as by himself.

The defenders of the faith have no choice but to meet their opponents on the ground which they themselves select. It is irksome, no doubt, that all our past work should seem to go for nothing, and that we should now be called on for proof of first principles, which we had come to regard as axiomatic, so readily had they been accepted by all parties as the basis of all religious reasoning. Still, true science demands that we shall always be ready to give a reason for our belief, and that none of our results shall rest merely on the acceptance given them by others or by ourselves in former days. If the proof was good then, it will be able to bear examination and verification now. It is true we have not time to be perpetually going over the same ground, and we may reasonably refuse a hearing to men whom we have good reason to think likely to bring forward no arguments that we have not already considered and found worthless. We do not care to enter into a discussion with one who professes to be able to prove that the earth is a flat surface, and that the Newtonian theory of gravitation is false. But when received opinions are challenged by men whose knowledge and ability give them weight, it would be an arrogant assertion of our own infallibility if we vouchsafed them no other answer than that we had already considered and determined the question. In matters of science a new trial must always be granted whenever there is any reasonable ground to suppose that new evidence has turned up, or that any fault can be found with the processes by which, from ascertained facts, inferences have been drawn.[1] Looking, then, to the weight and scientific reputation of those who

---

[1] It will be seen that I reject the doctrine concerning certitude laid down by Dr. Newman in his Grammar of Assent. The main source of what I regard as Dr. Newman's errors is that he holds that any principle which he supposes himself to have once demonstrated must never afterwards be re-examined, no matter into what absurdities the admission of it may lead him. Similarly, the principle of Hume's celebrated argument against miracles is that we are to refuse to examine into the evidences of exception to any law of nature the absolute universality of which we suppose ourselves to have once ascertained.

have declared themselves able to make satisfactory theories of the universe, in which no account is taken of the Divine existence, it seems to me not wise to turn from these theories in silent scorn, but that there is a call on us fairly to examine whether any flaw has been pointed out in the arguments which once satisfied us. I ask you, then, to review with me the reasons which led us to believe that there were in the universe marks of design which proved it to be the work of an intelligent Author, in order that we may know whether, in coming to this conclusion, we only deluded ourselves with sophisms, or whether what we then supposed to be true remains still an unshaken foundation for our faith.

And, in the first place, it is important to observe that no question is raised as to the facts on which the argument is founded. On the contrary, everything that increases our knowledge of nature adds to the number of striking instances which might be used to illustrate the argument from design in a work on natural theology. When men first with an intelligent eye surveyed, even in the most superficial manner, the external world, they could not but be struck with the beauty and order which prevailed, and they early drew the conclusion, " The heavens declare the glory of God, and the firmament showeth His handywork."

And ever, as they looked more closely, they found that the characters which had arrested their attention, as inscribed on the most prominent features of nature, were also distinctly written on its smallest parts, the minutest portions offering the same testimony as to their original. It required no scientific knowledge to draw from the Psalmist the exclamation, "I will praise Thee, for I am fearfully and wonderfully made. Marvellous are Thy works, and that my soul knoweth right well." The same thoughts suggest themselves only the more forcibly the closer acquaintance is made with the wonders of the animal frame. It is the branch of the subject which has yielded most of the illustrations to Paley's work on Natural Theology; and many still more striking have been added since, some by a distinguished member of our own University.[1] It matters not what department of nature we select, adaptation of means to an end is the rule everywhere. If Mr. Darwin's researches have suggested to many inferences adverse to Theism, at least no one of the present day has done more to swell the host of examples which might serve to illustrate the argument from design, in particular by his study of the singularly varied contrivances by which provision is made for the fertilisation of certain families of plants;

---

[1] See Haughton's *Principles of Animal Mechanics*.

for whether we acknowledge a "contriver" or not, the word "contrivance" is not shunned by Mr. Darwin himself as being the only one that seems capable of expressing the wonderful adaptation of means to ends.

The facts, then, being thus admitted, the question is, Why are we not to draw the obvious inference from them?—"He that planted the ear, shall He not hear? He that made the eye, shall He not see?" That any chance collocation of particles should assume the form of an organised structure is now more than ever felt to be a scientific impossibility. In former times, when stones were seen to exhibit the tracery of a leaf or the form of the skeleton of a fish, it was thought satisfactory to say that the phenomenon was a *lusus naturæ*, a sportive accident, in which minerals had mocked the forms of the vegetable or animal world. Now, rather than believe that any chance could imitate the wonders of organisation, we are confident that what are now firm rocks were once a fluid paste—that mountains now frowning above us in awful grandeur were once buried under the sea; we undertake to give the history of changes in the earth's surface, the accomplishment of which demands a number of thousands of years, which it baffles our arithmetic to calculate. Very consistently did Comte, whose classification of the sciences was at one time supposed to have some scientific value, omit geology from his circle of the sciences, and reject with contumely, as outside the domain of science, speculations concerning the original of the human race, such as of late have made so much noise. For as he refused to admit the legitimacy of the great inference of Natural Theology, which, from the characteristics of the works of nature, deduces that they have been framed by an intelligent Author, so he could not consistently recognise a science which is altogether conversant with inferences of the same kind, namely, in which, from the characteristics of existing objects, we infer their origin, as having noticed what causes now produce effects of a similar kind. In particular, geology has no hesitation in inferring from very slight indications the working of intelligence and design. Markings are observed on flints which to the eye of the unskilled observer appear scarcely different from the other pebbles among which they are found; but the geologist confidently pronounces them to have received their form by human workmanship, and rather than believe them to have had their origin in chance he has no hesitation in drawing conclusions as to the antiquity of the human race, unsupported by history, opposed to traditional opinion, and even to what was supposed to have had the sanction of inspired authority. Shall we admit the inference of design to be good in the case of the rude markings of a flint, and deny that we are entitled to draw a similar inference in the case of the infinitely more artificial structure of the hand that shaped the flint?

We have been told, however, that modern science can refer all the wonders of teleology to natural causes. The key is supposed to be found in the doctrine of evolution, which Mr. Darwin has done so much to popularise. This is not the place to discuss the scientific merits of Mr. Darwin's theory, and therefore, for the purposes of argument here, I am content to treat that theory as if it were established as a scientific fact. I am willing to argue on this hypothesis, because I can imagine the possibility that hereafter some theory of evolution may be so established; but I am far from thinking that this stage has been at present even approached. In the progress of scientific discovery guesses ever precede proofs. The imagination of the inquirer hurries on to a generalisation long before it can be arrived at by any process of demonstration. The eye of genius, detecting some previously unobserved analogy, catches sight of a principle which will group several previously unconnected facts into order. It points out the establishment of this law as the work at which demonstration must labour, and long before that work has been accomplished the truth of the law will be held as a matter of faith. The history of science is full of the fulfilments of such predictions; and even when they have failed, the very proposing of such hypotheses has enabled us to interrogate nature more intelligently, and has led us into the most fruitful fields of research. We are therefore bound to treat with respect any scientific guess which promises to group many facts under one generalisation until that guess has been disproved. But there have been too many instances of the failure of such guesses to make it safe for us to treat an unverified generalisation as if it were a scientific fact. The speculations of Democritus, and Empedocles, and Darwin have, as I believe, been very fitly classed together;[1] they may be compared with the speculations concerning the mutual attraction of bodies which existed before Newton's time. But such speculations I count as but the protoplasm of science, not science itself.

The point at which the doctrine of evolution has at present arrived may be described as follows:—The belief of scientific men in the absolute fixity of species has been much undermined. We can at least in thought conceive a whole series of

[1] By Professor Tyndall in his Address to the British Association at Belfast, shortly after which this sermon was preached.

species filling up the interval between the very lowest form of life and the highest, and such that the transition from one species in the series to another may not impossibly have taken place by natural generation. Actually, however, such a series cannot be proved to have existed. When we attempt to trace it we find immense gaps, and we can only vaguely appeal to the possibility of lost records. Experience also fails to give us examples of the transition of any of the higher species into others. In the earliest pictured records we see not only existing species, but existing varieties of species. It is true we can assume for the purposes of speculation unlimited time, in comparison of which all over which human observation extends is evanescent. Yet observation, we should think, has lasted long enough to yield to the theory if it were true more support than it does; nor can we easily reconcile the great plasticity of species which the theory demands with their actual stability, and the narrow limits within which variations are confined. Again, the possibility of transition from inanimate matter to life has not yet been satisfactorily established. Just as the exposure of one false miracle after another has made men sceptical whether true miracles exist at all, so the exposure of the unreality of successive instances of supposed spontaneous generation creates a disposition to believe beforehand that newly produced examples will fail of establishment. The rule "omne vivum ex vivo" certainly holds in every case where the living thing is large enough to be easily the subject of examination; and there is, therefore, a certain presumption in favour of the notion that it is only the failure of our instruments of research which prevents us from securely establishing the prevalence of the rule in the case of the minutest organisms.

But though I regard it as very far from being scientifically established that all existing species were developed by successive evolution from the simplest primæval forms, I think it would be a great mistake if we made our theological systems dependent on the truth of the negative of this proposition. Neither our science nor our theology will be likely to be correct if we have on theological grounds prejudged any scientific question, and are not prepared with open minds to receive and candidly interpret any facts which future research may bring to light. And it is, therefore, that I go on to examine whether, in case a theory of evolution as complete as has ever been imagined should really be proved, any conclusions of Theism would be affected.

And first I would remark that the reason why we do not reject as incredible the supposition that facts may come to light establishing the universal reign of the principle of evolution, is because we know already so many facts exhibiting the general prevalence of that principle. Any new facts, then, that may come to light will be of the same kind as facts we know already, and if we have correctly interpreted the facts which we already know, the new facts when they come will not lead us to different conclusions. The child whom we catechise is taught to say, "I believe in God, the Father Almighty, who hath made me and all the world." We have not scrupled to teach him to say, "God made me," though it is no doubtful or recondite fact that he has not come at once fullgrown into being, but that he himself is a result of evolution, according to well-known laws. Supposing, then, it be ascertained that "all the world" has taken its origin under similar laws of growth and gradual change, the question of Theism remains precisely where it was; there is no new difficulty in my believing that God made all the world, but such as previously had not prevented me from acknowledging that God made me. And indeed it is obvious that to tell whether anything came into being instantaneously or gradually is an answer to the question *how* it was made, not by whom or by what agency.

In an indirect way, indeed, the doctrine of

evolution may be said to be unfavourable to Theism. It is only change which attracts our attention, and induces us to put to ourselves the question, What has been the cause of it? What goes on every day we accept as natural, as if it ever must be so; and it is only minds well trained to scientific investigation who ask about the "why" of thoroughly familiar phenomena. So an uninquiring mind might well at one time have acquiesced in the supposition that the world had always gone on as we see it at present, father begetting son like himself, all existing species being eternal; and might think that if this were so the problem of their origin needed no further explanation. In opposition to this idea, theologians dwelt on the signs of the comparative modernness of the existing state of things as proving that some small number of thousand years ago a creation must have taken place so unlike any change which now exhibits itself as to force us to account for it as an exercise of Divine power. The theory of evolution pushes back this necessity of a beginning to an immensely remote period. It allows us to conceive the laws at present in operation as reigning for unnumbered millions of years, the changes during all that time being like the changes we see now, not abrupt, but silent and gradual, and the existing constitution of things being but the integral of infinitesimally small variations from its state at its first beginning.

Yet the necessity for a first beginning has not been dispensed with by modern speculation, and there still remains whatever force there was in the old Theistic argument for the necessity of Divine power, at least to originate the universe. At the beginning of this century science taught us to look on the planetary system as a machine constructed to last for ever—the mutual perturbations of the heavenly bodies compensating one another in such a way as to be consistent with the perfect stability of the entire system. Modern investigation has thrown considerable doubt on this result, and the fashionable theory of evolution is altogether inconsistent with it. According to this theory, we are to account for the existing state of things as the necessary result of the gradual cooling down of masses of intensely heated vapour. The smaller bodies which had been thrown off have cooled most rapidly. The moon is burnt out, and is no longer fit to be the abode of life; the interior of the earth is still hot, but the surface has so far cooled as to adapt it for the development of living organisms; the sun is still a burning mass which bestows its heat on living things elsewhere, but is not yet in a condition to admit life upon itself. But this theory does not encourage us to look forward to an infinite progress, during which the human race shall by continual development be raised to something as much above their present level as Newton and Shakespeare were above their ape-like ancestors. In the great industrial activity of the present day we are rapidly drawing on stores of heat which were laid up long before mankind came into being. We are like a proprietor whose annual expenditure far exceeds his income, and who is only saved from ruin because he is still able to draw on the savings accumulated during a long minority. But when these are spent there is a diminished annual income to look forward to. For the process of cooling, however slow, is still going on. Century after century must witness a diminution in the heat radiated by the sun, until it becomes utterly unfit to fulfil the offices which it now discharges. For the process of dissipation of heat is one to which we can in thought put no limit, until that of the entire universe is equalised.

Thus the theory of evolution absolutely requires the assertion that the universe had a beginning. If its origin had been infinitely remote, we should ere now have reached the final term when, to use Mr. Mill's words, our system shall be reduced to a single and not very large mass of solid matter, frozen up with more than arctic cold. Mathematicians are even taking courage to calculate whether, on the assumption of the truth of this theory, it is not possible to assign a definite number of years within which the first appearance of life on our globe must have occurred. And so it becomes plain that it is not sufficient explanation to say that the laws of matter will account for the phenomena which the universe presents. As well might it be said that we have given the whole account of the motions of a clock when we have traced all to the action of the weight, failing to observe that the machine is running down under our eyes, and that there must have been a time when it was wound up. The modern theory, then, quite as much as the elder one, refers back our thoughts to an epoch of creation when the constituent atoms of the universe were endowed with attributes whence have flowed all the marvels which they have since exhibited. And it is to be noted, that modern speculation does not teach us to regard space as originally filled with homogeneous particles of matter that might be supposed to have eternally existed by the necessity of their own nature, but with molecules of different kinds, the proportion between which seems arbitrary, and yet from the due arrangement of which proportion all the subsequent order of the universe has flowed.[1] We can say that the universe as well as the indi-

[1] See J. Clerk Maxwell, *Discourse on Molecules.* Bradford, 1873.

I

vidual is the work of God, though both alike may have been developed from an elementary state which gave no apparent promise of its ultimate growth, because in that elementary state was involved the potentiality of all that has been since evolved from it.

The argument, however, that I have used, though conclusive as far as it goes, falls very short of what I desire to establish. It does no more than establish that at one time there *was* a God who framed the universe; but it says nothing as to His present existence, except so far as this, that if it be proved that He ever existed, we can conceive no reason for His having ceased to exist. This argument, then, is of less use in laying the foundation of natural religion than in overthrowing the chief obstacle to the reception of revealed religion. That obstacle consists in our disposition to make our own experience the measure of all possibilities in time or space. The rejection of miracle on the ground that it is difficult to conceive that things should ever have proceeded differently from the manner in which they offer themselves to our present experience, had been answered by an appeal to the necessity of belief in a creation, at the time of which the formation of plants and animals must have proceeded in a manner quite unlike anything we now have knowledge of. And though the force of this retort may at first sight seem disarmed by speculations which represent all existing species as coming into being by processes of completely the same kind as what we daily witness, yet we have now seen that this is not so, and that the argument remains in full force; for though we push back to a remoter period the beginning of the present order of nature, nothing has been done to dispense with the necessity of such a beginning. It becomes then impossible to maintain the principle which had been used as affording an insuperable presumption against the credibility of miracle, and as shutting out all the claims of revealed religion—namely, that nothing opposed to our present experience can be believed to have ever happened. I admit, then, the use of the argument we have been considering in the controversy concerning revealed religion; but as far as natural religion is concerned, we can dispense with it altogether. And should future speculation imagine, what science has as yet failed to discover, some method for winding up the machine again, and teach us to substitute the conception of successive cycles for that of a continued progress, yet the real question of Theism remains unaffected.

If, disdaining the humble paths of science, I could trust myself to soar on the wings of imagination, I could dream of a time when the doctrine of evolution shall have reached a point the way to which no one as yet has been able to get a glimpse of; a time when all the period during which our solar and planetary system has existed, or shall exist, shall be recognised as but a speck in the infinite of duration; when science shall tell how each sun and its attendant planets came into being, evolving, during the few millions of millions of years which constitute their petty span of existence, creatures in ever-growing perfection suited to their conditions of life, until the old age and decay of the world begins, and at last it arrives at that dissipation of heat which constitutes its death; and I can imagine that some future Darwin may give a theory of the transmutation, not of species, but of worlds: how out of the matter which had formed an extinct universe a new one might be evolved, capable of far higher perfection, owing to the new dispositions its molecules had received in their earlier state of existence. Such a speculation is now a mere dream; yet if it should become the science of the future, I should not feel that the evidence of a Creator had been lost, but rather that a higher conception had been obtained of the majesty of His works.

In fact, the speculations concerning the origin of species which have come before us may be looked on in a double aspect. They may be supposed to dispense with the conception of a creation altogether, or at least to push it back to an indefinitely remote period; but, in truth, what they really teach is, that creation is a process which goes on every day. Every time that an animal is born possessing any property which did not belong to its parents, or possessing any property in a higher degree, we have been taught to see that an act of creation really takes place. The change may be small, but it suffices that by accumulation it should become sensible, when it is plain to all that the result is what can be described as nothing less than a new creation.

As for these new creations, it is to be noticed that they are not referable to any law. The law of the survival of the fittest undertakes to explain the preservation of certain varieties, supposing them to have once come into being. But as to how these variations originate no account has been given. Every appearance of a new quality in the offspring of existing living creatures is a phenomenon at present as inexplicable, though not as startling, as if a new creature came full grown into being. By two words, however, the necessity for a God is supposed to be dispensed with—law and accident. Does a phenomenon occur of precisely the same kind as others which we have witnessed before, then we refer it to a "law," and deem no other explanation necessary. If we find it wholly impossible to refer a phenomenon to any general principle, we think we have said enough when we describe it as "an accident."[1] Yet, once again, it must be observed that these words, law and accident, only relate to the "how" of events, and give us no help in answering any question that may be proposed as to their causes. They tell us whether any rule can be traced regulating the occurrence of the events, so as to

[1] The weak point in the atomic theory of Epicurus, fastened on by Cicero (*De Nat. Deor.*, i. 25), was that it was necessary, in order to produce a concourse of atoms, to suppose each to deviate somewhat ("declinare paululum") from its direct path. To account for these deviations was not attempted, except by ascribing to the atoms some kind of irrational free will. It was hoped to escape the necessity of explanation by representing the deviations as exceedingly small—

"Quare etiam atque etiam paullum inclinare necesse est
Corpora, nec plus quam minimum."
"Exiguum clinamen principiorum,
Nec regione loci certa, nec tempore certo."
—LUCRET., *De Nat. Rer.*, ii. 243, 292

It was evident that no real explanation was given as long as there was left an unexplained residuum in which it was owned lay the seeds of all the phenomena it was proposed to account for. There is precisely the same weakness in the Darwinian theory, which accounts for the preservation of beneficial variations, but gives no explanation of the origin of variations. We are to be satisfied to know that species have a tendency "declinare paululum," and because the deviation in each case is represented as small, to inquire no further. It is clearly absurd to set up as a rival to the Theistic hypothesis a theory which gives no real explanation of the origin of things.

enable us to predict or secure their return; but they tell us nothing as to the agency which brings them about, and so they help us nothing in answering the great question of Theism. We do not assert the existence of two Beings;—one, strictly called God, presiding over the startling and unusual; the other Being an abstraction called Nature, ruling all those changes the laws of which we have ascertained;—but we believe in one God who rules the future and the past, the usual and unusual alike. Consequently, it gives our Theism no disquiet when the dominion of law is enlarged and that of accident restrained.

The question of Theism with which we are practically concerned is not what power exerted itself in ages past; but what we are to think of that power which rules the universe now. There is a force, call it by what name you please, pervading the entire universe, manifesting itself in an infinite variety of forms, ruling the reactions of inanimate nature, and inspiring the breath of every living creature; a force which may not be defied or resisted, everywhere consistent, uniform; a force which seems to strive to elevate each being in the scale of creation, and bring it on to higher perfection, casting aside the less worthy forms, cherishing and advancing the nobler. The question is, Does this force act blindly, or is it directed by an intelligence which knows what it is doing? It would keep us longer than I can venture to detain you if I were to attempt now to deal fully with this question ; but I hope soon to have another opportunity of discussing it.

VI

THEISM AND MODERN SCIENCE.—II

"The invisible things of Him from the creation of the world are clearly seen; being understood by the things that are made, even His eternal power and Godhead."—ROMANS i. 20.

I HAVE not thought it an inconvenience, though some little interval has passed before I have been able to resume the discussion of the arguments for Theism which I commenced a few Sundays ago. I might, indeed, deserve blame if I had brought perplexing difficulties before you, and had left you for a considerable time embarrassed by them without attempting a solution of them. But in this case there would have been danger in postponement only if the orthodox faith which I had been trying to defend had been that the eye was *not* made to see with. On such a supposition I own it would not have been wise to allow you too long a time to ponder unassisted on the difficulties of your creed. In fact, that result which we call seeing is brought about by the combination of a multitude of delicate adjustments, the failure of any one of which would defeat the entire effect. And the eye is but one of a number of organs combined in the human frame, with respect to every one of which the same thing is true—namely, that the performance of the function now discharged by it depends on the accurate adjustment of many component parts. That mere chance should bring together in the same organisation so many successful combinations is an improbability which our arithmetic cannot distinguish from an impossibility. The supposition that the account of the origin of these combinations is that the parts were brought together with the design of producing the effect which results from them is far the most obvious one, and, as I believe, is still the only one on which our mind can rest, and which it can accept as satisfactory. And so, if I had spent a discourse in throwing metaphysical difficulties in the way of your accepting this account, it is very likely that my highest success might have been to produce some sort of conviction as long as you were listening to me; but that when you were left to yourselves the reasons for your atheistic creed would slip away from you.

And, in truth, it is impossible that the supposition of design in the works of nature can ever be disproved. We can imagine that science may hereafter arrive at a complete account of the process by which organisms are evolved; that is to say, may make the steps of the process easier for our minds to embrace by classifying them with other familiar phenomena of a different kind. If so, we who believe in an intelligent Ruler of the universe will be enabled to form some clearer conception of the method by which He works, but nothing whatever will have been done to overthrow our belief that He really is working. If even there should be ever so satisfactory proof of the existence of a natural process by which organisms could be evolved without design or contrivance, this would not disprove the supposition · that they were the work of an intelligent author; it would only give at most an alternative account of the matter.

We have now to inquire whether any such alternative account has been given; or whether Theism still remains the only admissible account of the constitution of the universe. The principle, you are aware, which it is now supposed will enable us to dispense with the supposition of Theism is that of natural selection, or the survival of the fittest. According to this, it is held that things are so shaped by their environment that, whether God exist or no, they could not be different from what they are. In former times, when it was attempted to make out a possibility that the present constitution of things could have originated by chance, it was said that out of the infinite number of possible combinations those only have survived which were compatible with existence; and then it was a good reply that innumerable combinations were compatible with existence far less perfect than those which now exist. Men, for example, might exist deficient or deformed in a thousand ways, so that on any principles of chance it ought to be far rarer to find a man possessed of all his senses than it is to find a blind or a deaf man now. The principle of natural selection appears to get over this difficulty. It shows that in the struggle for existence even small imperfections place a species at a disadvantage; and so that we need not wonder at now rarely meeting with inferior combinations, which, though in the abstract not incapable of living, are yet crushed out of existence by the pressure of others.

In former days those who assigned chance as the origin of the world were asked, If the letters of the alphabet were cast at random on the floor, how many ages might one cast before an orderly work, such as the Annals of Ennius, would arise from their chance combination?[1] The modern

[1] "Hoc qui existumet fieri potuisse, non intellego cur non idem

theory substitutes for a mere chance combination of letters of the alphabet such a mode of poetical composition as was imagined by the philosopher of Laputa, in which indeed the combinations were in the first instance made by chance, but those only which made sense were preserved. Yet a moment's thought shows how utterly unlike such a comparison is to the aspect of nature. In any system of chance combinations those which made sense would be the rare exceptions. The great bulk would be unmeaning gibberish. But in nature every one of the combinations makes sense. Take one of those cases where, in the struggle for life, a species of plants or animals is perishing out of a locality; and examine this unsuccessful competitor for existence, and you will find that, as far as the argument for design is concerned, it yields as many illustrations as its more fortunate rival. Every part is as accurately formed, all the parts as harmoniously combined. It is needless, then, to mention other difficulties which have been urged as showing that this principle of natural selection, however worthy of notice and important in a certain sphere, does not

putet, si innumerabiles unius et viginti formæ literarum, vel aureæ vel qualeslibet, aliquo conjiciantur, posse ex his in terram excussis annalis Ennii, ut deinceps legi possint, effici; quod nescio an ne in uno quidem versu possit tantum valere fortuna."—Cic., *De Nat. Deor.*, ii. 37.

give us the whole account of the transmutation of species; as, for instance, that many variations of structure, though advantageous to a species when they have proceeded to a certain degree, are by no means so in their first beginnings, and therefore that the principle does not explain how when they first occur they should be preserved and increased; or again, that the theory that species are entirely moulded by their environment, is disproved by the fact that whole families of the human race give evidence of possessing intellectual powers which their circumstances have hitherto never called into action. I have no need, I say, to dwell on these and other difficulties of the theory; because, as I have just observed, the principle of natural selection does not touch the argument from design at all. If the parts of the body had been brought together without design, combinations having an injurious tendency, or that were simply unmeaning, would be quite as frequent as those tending to advantage. We ask, then, those who reject the hypothesis of design to explain how it is that it is so extremely rare that there is any part of an animal even unmeaning, that is to say, in which we are at a loss to see a distinctly beneficial tendency; and that, if there be any part which in exceptional circumstances causes pain or inconvenience to its possessor, there is absolutely none which suggests the idea that it was formed with the object of causing pain or inconvenience. Current theories of evolution really assume the great principle of teleology, and sweep away all apparent exceptions to the proof of design; for wherever an organ is found that at present seems useless or dangerous, it is held to be a survival from a state of things when it was beneficial; so that we arrive at the universal proposition, that there is no part of an animal which has not a distinctly beneficial tendency, if not in the present, at least in the future or the past. In reply, the principle of natural selection is appealed to as a method by which unmeaning or noxious structures have been eliminated. But we answer that experience bears witness to nothing of the kind. We never see examples of the elimination of the noxious. Those species which fail in the struggle for existence, though less adapted to their surroundings, are not in themselves chargeable with fault or imperfection. This answer makes it unnecessary to press the further difficulty, how within any length of time that we can conceive as admissible the elimination should have become as complete as it actually is. If the first struggle for existence had been between a multitude of structures, each barely capable of living, that which might accidentally gain an advantageous development in one part of its organism might be the most defective in another. And, considering the length of time necessary for any one improvement so far to establish itself as to cause the absolute disappearance of all inconsistent forms, it is quite inconceivable but that now the victors in the struggle would still present a thousand anomalies and defects. I have already said that the time which the theory of evolution places at the disposal of speculators is distinctly not infinite. If it were, there would be no need of this principle of the survival of the fittest. We might calmly present mere chance as a sufficient account of everything, and say that the *Iliad* itself might be the result of a chance combination of letters, provided any one had life and patience to combine them long enough.

Thus, then, we have seen that if we permit ourselves to ask any question as to the "why" of the order of the universe, we shall inevitably find ourselves reduced to give one account of the matter—namely, that it is the work of an intelligent Author. But we are told we ought not to ask any question about this "why"; that we ought to remain in the conclusion that the universe is a system which works together harmoniously, and inquire no more. It is certainly true that whole generations of men have wasted their strength in investigations which were quite fruitless, because the subject chosen was beyond the powers of the inquirers; and in some cases, perhaps, beyond the powers of any human being. And yet philosophy has not been fortunate when it has attempted to draw barriers across the path of the human mind, and fence off from investigation whole fields of study. I had occasion, for example, on the last day, to remark that it was not only investigations concerning God's existence which Comte rejected as incapable of leading to profitable result. Not only did he proscribe several other departments of study in which science has won its triumphs during the last forty years, but he went on to dream of a state of things in which, enthroned as high-priest of science, he should be able to enforce his prohibitions. If he had had the power he craved, Mr. Darwin's researches would have been summarily put a stop to; Bessel would have been restrained from measuring the parallax of a star, and so falsifying one of the seer's predictions within some four years of the time when it was delivered; and the students of spectrum analysis would have been checked in the profane attempt to make a science of stellar chemistry.[1] So dangerous is it for one

---

[1] " Disgusted with the insatiable curiosity which leads scientific thinkers to pry into the secrets of nature in all directions at once,

who is not himself omniscient to assign limits to the possibilities of knowledge.

But never has a greater extravagance been committed under the name of philosophy than when it has been attempted to shut out the question of God's existence from the field of legitimate inquiry. For such an exclusion amounts to this. Philosophers are too modest to pronounce a negative on the question of God's existence. There may be such a Being: they will not

---

often spending years upon subjects which to self-complacent ignorance or Philistinism seem entirely trivial, Comte enacted that 'some one problem should always be selected, the solution of which would be more important than any other to the interests of humanity, and upon this the entire intellectual resources of the theoretic mind should be concentrated, until it is either resolved or has to be given up as insoluble ; after which mankind should go on to another, to be pursued with similar exclusiveness.' It only remains to add that this all-important problem was to be prescribed by the High Priest of Humanity. When now, knowing as we do Comte's intense aversion to certain kinds of inquiry, we consider what would have been the result could such a system have gone into operation forty years ago ; when we reflect that Bessel would never have been allowed to measure the parallax of a star, that the cell-doctrine in biology would have been hopelessly doomed, that Mr. Darwin's researches would have been prohibited as useless, that the correlation of forces would have still remained undiscovered, that psychology would have been ruled out once for all, that the new chemistry would not have come into existence, and that spectrum analysis would never have been heard of; when we reflect upon all this, we may well thank God for the constitution of things which makes it impossible that the well-being of the human race should ever be irrevocably staked upon the wisdom or folly of a single speculative thinker."—FISKE, *Outlines of Cosmic Philosophy*, vol. ii. p. 495.

undertake to say. Only one thing they are sure of. If there be a God, it is beyond His omnipotence to reveal Himself to the creatures He has formed; impossible for Him to give them any certain knowledge of His existence. That God cannot be known indeed we readily grant, in the sense that He cannot be adequately known; that when, by enlarging the ideas derived from the study of our own minds, we have striven to form a conception of His majesty, we must be infinitely below the reality; that men have rashly presumed who have ventured to form theories of the Divine thoughts, and feelings, and decrees, as if He were altogether such an one as we. We also own that it is impossible to know Him as He is in Himself, or otherwise than in relation to the faculties of our own mind; but this is true also of every substance and every person in the world; and the only question is, whether through His manifestations we cannot form some idea of His attributes, at least so far as to be justified in ascribing to Him wisdom and goodness. Unless we can, we may look on the force which reigns through nature with awe and wonder, or rather with dismay, but can regard it with neither trust nor love.

Two reasons are mainly relied on to check us from the inference that that force which works order and harmony in the universe knows and intends what it is doing. One is, that experience only tells us of thought and intelligence in connection with the action of the brain, or other similar matter, and that therefore we take an unjustifiable step when we assert the existence of intelligence where there is no such organisation. You find a watch and you believe it to be the work of a man, because you have seen other men make other watches, but you have never seen a God make worlds.

The question evidently comes to this: Have we any right to say that thought cannot exist under conditions different from those under which human thought takes place? It is certainly natural to us to think that things which we always find to go together must be inseparably connected; yet there is no connection which we feel under less temptation to erect into a necessary law than that between thought and modifications in the structure of certain gray matter. It is a connection which, however little we may be disposed to dispute its reality, must still appear to us arbitrary and unaccountable. And, in fact, this connection is made known to us, not by experience, but by analogy. We have direct experience of our own thought, but our own brains we neither have seen nor can see. We have no direct experience of the thought of other men, but we infer from the marks of intelligence displayed in their actions that they have thought such as we are conscious of in ourselves; and finding that they have got brains, we make the second inference from analogy that we ourselves are similarly made. But our having made this second inference is no bar to our, on occasion, repeating the first which is in order of thought antecedent, and on the legitimacy of which the other depends.

Metaphysical difficulties as to the validity of the proof of God's existence are as powerless against conviction as similar difficulties concerning the validity of the proof of the existence of the external world. Any proof of the impossibility of our having certain knowledge in either case is like the famous proof of the impossibility of motion—*Solvitur ambulando.* I cannot undertake to explain the passage from the ego to the non-ego; but that problem which has baffled so many a theorist has been practically solved by the babe who lies smiling in his mother's arms, and who looks up into her loving eyes and reads in them sympathy responsive to his every feeling. He has already learned to be sure of the existence of a being not himself, who shields him from danger, who supplies his wants, who soothes him in his sorrows. And is it not equally true that theorists who perplex themselves with doubts whether they have adequately proved

God's existence, are puzzling over a problem which thousands, babes in knowledge, have practically solved? I need only mention the difficulty there is in preaching on my present subject in any pulpit but this, where the consideration of speculative difficulties is not out of place. Elsewhere I should be heard with exactly the same impatience if I tried to demonstrate God's existence as if I tried to prove my own, and strove to convince my hearers that they were under no delusion in imagining I was addressing them.

And in real truth we never should have heard of doubts as to the validity of the proof of the Divine existence if it were not for the difficulty which I have next to consider. If in all the phenomena of nature we could read purpose written as plainly as in the structure of the eye; if natural selection were as wise in every particular as it is in its general operation; if the higher were never sacrificed to the lower; if the petitions we made to God were as regularly answered in the way we desired as the requests a child makes to his parent, it would be practically as impossible for us to doubt of God's existence as it is for a child to doubt of the existence of his mother. But the difficulty is that the forces of nature are so often seen to work blindly and regardless of consequences. When pent-up volcanic fire struggles for an outlet, it matters not that the hills beneath which it is confined are crowned with the fairest works of human hands; the lava flood, indiscriminating, covers vineyard and hamlet with unsightly ruin, and ashes bury for centuries the busy cities of men. The earthquake does not respect the temples of the God who rules it, nor does it forbear its heavings through tenderness for the lives of innocent thousands who had vainly hoped to find security within the sacred walls. European literature bears permanent traces of the doubts concerning Divine providence which were stirred by the occurrence of such a calamity more than a century ago. The sacrifice of higher forms of life for the benefit of lower is a thing we witness every day. Scripture records the terror inspired by the locust and the palmerworm and the cankerworm; and though these be but names for us, yet we well know how in the struggle for life the food on which nations of men are depending is at times pre-appropriated by hosts of minute creatures for whose existence we in our pride of superiority can see neither necessity nor use. Descending still lower in the scale of creation, let the poison germ of fever or of cancer have fixed itself in the body of the best, the wisest, the most useful of our race, and it goes on evolving itself according to laws of its own, which inexorably claim their due while sorrowing thousands weep and pray in vain. These are the things which countenance the view that the force of nature is a blind *nisus*, which benefits us without love and injures us without hatred, and so has no more claims on our gratitude or affection than the great wheel of a factory has on the love of the workman whom it supplies with power for his daily task, but whom it will as readily tear in pieces if he be so careless as to allow himself to be tangled by it.

When we reflect, however, on the difficulty we have stated, we see that it reduces itself to this, that the working of nature proceeds according to general laws, uniform in their operation, and which are not relaxed on particular occasions when, to our view, it seems that great immediate benefit might be gained by swerving from them. It is not that we discern any fault in the laws by which the world is governed; nay, the more we study them, the more reason we find to admire their wisdom and to acknowledge their general tendency to advance the perfection of all created beings. But we are oppressed by the rigorous uniformity with which these laws are maintained. Yet ere this fact induces us to conclude that the universe is not ruled by a Being of surpassing wisdom and goodness, we must convince ourselves that it is more worthy of such a Being to be changeable than uniform, more befitting Him to alter His plans in compliance with each wish of His creatures than to teach them to rule themselves according to His will. In short, all turns on this, that we live in a world of which evolution is the law, in which things are not at once framed in the highest perfection of which they are capable, but grow to it. Man himself is thus in a constant state of education and progress. And the very condition of his advancement is that he can place undoubting trust in the truth and faithfulness of Him who displays Himself in nature. Whatever he has once learned as to the rules according to which He acts, may be relied on as sure not to be altered.

In fact, in this case that is true which was said many years ago of another controversy, and which we cannot fail to observe to be true of so many controversies, that both parties to the dispute say the same things; only that, it may be, what the one proclaims aloud the other utters in a whisper. On the one hand, many who are called Atheists repudiate the appellation, willingly giving the name God to the universal power which reigns in nature, not venturing to deny that that power is possessed of intelligence; rather preferring to think that there is some Being or Thing in nature which knows more about it than we do, and declaring themselves to be only anxious completely to purge of anthropomorphism their conception of God, and to protest against the popular representation of God as merely a magnified man. On the other hand, this degrading conception of God is distinctly rejected by our sacred writers, who have long since announced as attributes of the God they worshipped some of those properties of the force that rules in nature which Theists are supposed not easily to reconcile with their creed. Their God is the everlasting and immutable Jehovah, who changeth not ; whose words are faithfulness and truth ; not a man that He should lie, nor the son of man that He should change His mind. His judgments are declared to be unsearchable ; His counsels unfathomable by man. He may not be judged by human standards ; it is noted as the folly of the wicked to think that God is altogether such as themselves. There is, then, an anthropomorphism which Christians and their opponents will unite in condemning ; but to purge altogether from anthropomorphism our conception of God is really to make an induction leaving out the most important of the facts. It is admitted that we cannot know the absolute directly ; and therefore that God can only be known to us as He reveals Himself in His works, or, if you prefer to call them so, in His manifestations. The fuller our knowledge of these works the less inadequate our conception of

God must be. And so those notions of God which men drew solely from the analogy of their own minds, and which were tinged with human caprice and fickleness, if not with worse infirmities of man, were purified as men came to know God as He reveals Himself in inanimate nature, working by uniform laws, untiring, unhasting, unchanging. But far more unworthy of the truth even than purely anthropomorphic conceptions of God are those which are solely founded on the processes of inanimate nature, leaving out man himself. For among the products of the force which rules in nature—that is to say, among the works or manifestations of God—chief and foremost is man himself. To say, then, that our conception of God shall be in no degree anthropomorphic is to say that, in reasoning from God's works to His attributes, we are deliberately to leave out the greatest and noblest of His works, and that in which His character is most distinctly revealed. What, in short, is nature apart from man, but molecules of matter in more or less rapid motion, impinging and rebounding from one another; now uniting in close contact, now separating in order to form other combinations. In such a spectacle some would have us behold the best and highest that nature has got to show us. But it is no self-flattery to say that a spectator from without, who had witnessed in the world nothing but the attractions and repulsions of matter, would recognise the presence of a higher and nobler element the moment that a being made his appearance endowed with self-conscious thought. Man, to use Pascal's well-known words, is but a reed—one of the weakest things in nature. A vapour, a drop of water, will suffice to take his life. But inasmuch as he is a reed that thinks, even though all the forces of the universe should combine to slay him, he is more noble than they all. For he would know that he died, but the force that destroyed him would take his life unknowing what it did, unconscious of its superiority over him.

What kind of philosophers, then, are those who in their view of nature shut their eyes to its highest and noblest manifestations, and so dream of the force that reigns through all as blind and unconscious. A miserable result of philosophy, if it were a true one; for noble though we boast the mind of man to be, it would be miserable to think his shortlived and limited intelligence the highest thing in the universe. Perhaps I should not say in the universe; for we are graciously permitted to contemplate the possibility that there may be in some distant orb thinking animals with intelligence even superior to ours: but at least the history of that part of the universe of which we have certain knowledge, according to this theory is, that intelligence made its appearance late, and was long confined within the narrowest limits, tribes of simious men gradually groping their way, amid many mishaps and blunders, from savage ignorance to such limited knowledge as we enjoy; and that, after a certain moderate improvement, thought again must perish out of the world, as in the progress of ages it becomes unable to sustain human inhabitants. If there be intelligence in any other globe, there as here it must be a mere temporary efflorescence; and the days must come when the universe shall be left a desolate blank, uninhabited by any thinking mind. Such is the Gospel which modern philosophy offers us in exchange for ours—a Gospel which leaves man without a friend in the present, without a hope in the future.

It has been my object to show that the method of this philosophy is as faulty as its results are unsatisfying; that the source of its error is that, in forming its theory of the characteristics of the force which manifests itself in nature, it has left out of its induction that power which exhibits itself in the thought and intelligence of man. But all that I have as yet said is open to a similar criticism, for man is much more than thought and intelligence; nor is it this part of his nature which speaks most plainly of God; the home of religion is in his conscience and his affections. I have said how a spectator from without would recognise it as a phenomenon of an entirely new order when, in a previously lifeless world, there first appeared a being endowed with conscious thought. But let that thought expand to the dimensions of the noblest intellect earth has ever witnessed, and it would still be a phenomenon of an entirely new, and shall we not say, a higher order, when there appeared one whose breast could thrill with the sense of beauty, one capable of admiring, reverencing, trusting, loving. And of a new order and higher yet again when that capacity developed itself which not only recognises the beauty of truth, purity, justice, kindness, but which assumes the character of a sovereign and a judge, passing all our actions under review, dictating to us the course we ought to follow, and visiting us severely with its displeasure if we disobey. I cannot help feeling now as if I had wasted the time at my disposal for addressing you, in having spent almost all in speaking of those tokens of God's presence which our intellects can discern, leaving myself scarcely any to speak of the testimony borne to Him by our hearts and consciences. Yet it was safest to omit that part of the argument which can best speak for itself, and which is absolutely free from difficulty. No one can deny that there are in man emotions and affections which find in religion their highest expression and their fullest satisfaction. In the history of our race the religious sentiment is found to be the spring of all the principal events; it has inspired the most stupendous exertions, the most heroic sacrifices. Nor can we believe that this sentiment will ever be eradicated. Centuries ago a noble poet sang the pæan of victory of philosophy over religion, and triumphed in the boast that science exalted to heaven thence beheld her ancient tyrant trampled beneath her feet.[1] Premature was the vaunt; the poet found but scant audience for his luminous exposition of philosophy, and the great birth which the womb of time was preparing when he wrote was that of a religion surpassing every other in its power to enchain the mind of man. There is no danger now that the right of religion to empire over the affections will be disputed. Atheists themselves are well content that their wives and

[1] "Ergo vivida vis animi pervicit, et extra
Processit longe flammantia moenia mundi;
Atque omne immensum peragravit mente animoque;
Unde refert nobis victor quid possit oriri,
Quid nequeat; finita potestas denique cuique
Quanam sit ratione, atque alte terminus haerens.
Quare religio, pedibus subjecta, vicissim
Obteritur, nos exaequat victoria caelo."
—LUCRET., *De Rer. Nat.*, i. 73.

daughters shall be devout. I need not relate the history, so laughable if it were not so melancholy, how Comte found himself driven to invent a new God to replace Him whom he had banished. At the present day Mr. Herbert Spencer does not offer his agnosticism for the acceptance of the masses; he but holds it as a matter of faith that hereafter in the progress of the evolution of the human race a stage may be reached when his doctrines will suffice to satisfy men's hearts and rule their consciences. Professor Tyndall calls it the problem of problems of the present day, how to yield reasonable satisfaction to the religious sentiment immovably fixed in the nature of man.

There is one way in which it is certain that satisfaction cannot be afforded, the way which he himself seems to suggest, that religion shall be allowed free sway in its proper sphere, the emotions, on the terms of being banished from the region of knowledge. Our emotions absolutely refuse to arise if there be not a basis of knowledge to justify them. We cannot lavish the treasures of our reverence and trust and love on a God whom science has discovered to be a nonentity.

This, then, is why I have thought it right, abandoning that part of the subject on which it would be easiest to expatiate, but also which is now scarcely contested with us, to spend my time in examining the difficulties on the purely intellectual side. And if the result of that examination had been no more than to leave Theism a possibility, the remainder of the evidence would turn the possibility into a certainty. For no theory of the universe is deserving of consideration which refuses to take account of some of the most important of the facts. I have already said that, on the grounds on which I discussed the matter at the beginning, it is impossible that Theism can be disproved; so that if my discussion were a total failure, the result would be only that the two explanations would be equally admissible;—that the eye was made to see with by some Being who knew what he was doing, or that the forces of nature shaped it so, unconscious what they did. But now follow on the two explanations and see how they fit in with the rest of the facts. The outcome of the one is Pessimism; the universe turns out to be a gigantic bungle, the forces of which bring creatures into life only to make their existence miserable by pain and sorrow; in their highest manifestations giving birth to man who, poor and weak though his understanding is, has yet enough to be able to criticise the power that formed him, and detect its unskilfulness and clumsiness; man cursed with aspirations doomed never to be realised, who "builds him fanes of fruitless prayer," and stretches vain

L

hands of supplication to a heaven destitute of inhabitant; man who would fain dream of some dignity in his existence, but is instructed by philosophy to know that his frail and futile life is but one of the foambells tossed up by nature in its cycles of unmeaning and objectless evolution; man who has learned to know the sacredness of pity, the tenderness of compassion, who has learned to hate injustice, and if need be to give his life for truth and right, but who discovers that the attributes he thinks noble are not those of the power which rules his life, which is pitiless towards the weak, and when it deals its blows scorns to discriminate between the righteous and the wicked. What nobler does this philosophy leave to man than to lie a Prometheus chained on his rock of suffering, defying and denouncing the unmoral tyranny which has bound him there.

Take now the other explanation which insists that all the witnesses shall be called into court; that not only the facts of inorganic nature shall be interrogated, but that account shall be taken of the existence in the world of beings able not only to plan and contrive, but formed for love, and pity, and reverence, and prayer; above all, formed to recognise the claims of duty, and own conscience as supremely entitled to command. These facts are not set aside by any theory of the genesis of the moral sentiments; in other words, the things of which I speak cannot be annihilated by writing their history; however they came into being, there they are. Take then, I say, the explanation which takes all the facts into account, and the universe from a chaos becomes a kosmos. I do not say that every anomaly is explained, but so much is explained that we can easily believe that nothing but the finiteness of our understanding prevents us from seeing the explanation of the rest. Admit that we are the work of a Creator, and we have not to look abroad into the world to learn His attributes; we have the evidence in ourselves. We hear His voice in our consciences, ordering us to be good, and just, and merciful, and loving, and truthful; we despise and are ashamed of ourselves when we are wanting in these qualities; and we cannot gravely discuss the hypothesis that He who formed us lacks them, and that He made us so that when we come to know Him as He is we shall despise and be ashamed of Him.

The character of God being thus revealed to us from within, we look on the world without, and ask if what we see there is inconsistent with that character. Well, we do see general laws rigorously observed with seeming disregard of consequences in particular cases; but it is unquestionable that the general working of these laws is both benevolent and moral. Assuredly there is an eternal power that makes for righteousness. The longer I live the more I am filled with wonder at its operation, so that at times I shrink from using that argument for a future life which we commonly employ, founded on the inequality with which happiness is dispensed here, when I mark the accuracy with which retribution takes place even in this life,— the good that a man does rewarded to him even more fully than he could dare to claim as his right, and yet that reward not exempting him from tasting the bitter fruits of the evil he has committed. And when the general law seems in a particular case to work undeserved evil, other laws are seen to start into operation repairing that evil, or by a wondrous alchemy turning it to good. Thus, though the fear of God and the study to do His will does not shield a man from being overtaken by temporal calamity, yet God's servants when so overtaken have never complained that He has dealt ill with them. Their experience, after they have tasted the discipline of sorrow, has rather been, "It has been good for me that I was afflicted." "I know that it shall be well with them that fear the Lord." "Though He slay me, yet will I trust in Him." Does this last expression of faith seem extravagant? It is not so. The man of science puts faith in the universality of a general law; when having seen one apparent exception after another reconciled with it, he cannot help believing, even before full proof, that all remaining anomalies will be ultimately accounted for; so the Christian's faith in the goodness of God would be justified were that goodness only known to us by induction from without, still more when it is revealed to us from within.

And anomalies perplex us the less as we become conscious of our own incompetence to deal with the problems of the universe. If one word of ours could banish all pain and sorrow from the world, should we have courage to speak that word, when we reflected that at the same time we must banish all those lessons which man now learns in his school of trial. Should we venture to make this a world in which there would be no need of prudence, where the giddy and thoughtless might run without fear of slipping; a world ignorant of patience, or fortitude, or resignation; a Capua where holiday soldiers should be lapped in pleasure, not thought worthy to learn the stern joys of conflict or to win the crown of victory; a world ignorant of pity, or sympathy, or compassion, where each, sufficient for himself, might dispense with all help from others. Would such a world be a better and a nobler world than ours?

I had put aside as alien to my subject the institutions for which your help is asked to-day.[1] Yet these may teach us how defective are those accounts of the characteristics of nature which refuse to take note of man. We are told that nature is pitiless; that this is a world which has the survival of the fittest for the law of its evolution; a world, therefore, of which self-assertion is the rule, and where, in the universal struggle for existence, the weak are trampled on or hustled aside, and the strong alone remain. If you would know whether this representation gives the whole of the truth, go to the hospitals. There the rule is not self-assertion, but self-forgetfulness; the strong are the servants of the weak, the healthy of the diseased, the rich of the poor. Those most disadvantageously circumstanced for fighting the battle of life find themselves in their hour of suffering surrounded by skill and care, which their more fortunate rivals might well envy. No question is raised as to the value of the life which is at stake. Men who have gained power to benefit the world through their mastery of all the

---

[1] In connection with the Hospital Sunday movement, a collection in aid of the Dublin Hospitals was made on the day this sermon was preached.

resources of science devote themselves to the succour of the most insignificant ; and in order to prolong a life, perhaps worthless to all but the possessor, the valuable life of the helper is freely imperilled, sometimes nobly sacrificed. When we ask what it is to follow nature (a question lately treated by Mill in strange ignorance that a greater thinker had discussed it before him), are we to take nature in its rudest and lowest manifestations, or in its ultimate and highest ? If the God of nature be as pitiless as He is accused of being, whence that divine instinct of compassion, to be wanting in which we now regard as a mark of degradation in man ?

We count that we have other evidence as to the character of the God of nature. I have regretted that the necessity of continuing my subject on the only available day has obliged me to occupy the first day of our Christian year with a discourse in which our specially Christian belief has not been touched on. Yet, let me in conclusion remind you how, when He came among us, whom we own as Deity manifested in flesh, His rule too was not self-assertion, but self-sacrifice ; to seek and save the lost and perishing was His mission ; not the whole, but the sick, were those who had most claims on Him. He came not to be ministered unto, but to minister, and to give His life a ransom for many. Remembering how in His earthly life it was as a healer He was known, you will count it as a privilege that in this work of mercy to the poor and sick in which you are asked to join to-day, you have the opportunity of being like Him.

NOTE.

Since this sermon was preached, the doctrine of material atheism has been explicitly taught in an article called "Body and Mind," by Professor Clifford, in the *Fortnightly Review*, December 1874. He holds that in an act of sensation that without us which we perceive is matter in motion, and that within us which perceives is also matter in motion, the one matter being, though not of the same substance, of similar substance with the other. He holds that, even according to received principles, the fact that all the consciousness we know of is associated with brain, leads to the conclusion as highly probable that there is no mind without a brain; but that if his exposition of the connection between mind and matter be correct, this probability becomes the highest assurance that science can give, a practical certainty on which we are bound to act; nay, that mind without brain becomes a contradiction in terms. The question, then, whether there be any mind pervading the universe, in his view, becomes—Is there any evidence of the existence of a vast brain? and on this we need have no hesitation in pronouncing a negative, at least as far as regards that portion of the universe to which our knowledge extends; so that "we seem entitled to conclude that during such time as we can have evidence of no intelligence or volition has been concerned in events happening within the range of the solar system except that of animals living on the planets." In answer to the objection that his conclusions make the world a blank, as taking away the object of very important and widespread emotions, he consoles us with the reflection that "we have no right to call the world a blank while it is full of men and women, even though our one friend may be lost to us." Professor Clifford is courageously prepared to follow out the principle that there is no thought without motion of matter, to the converse that there is no motion of matter without thought—thought such as ours in the case of complex organisms like our brains, a simpler kind in lower organisms; and since organic matter must have arisen by physical processes out of inorganic, in order to save continuity in our belief, it must be held that, accompanying every motion of inorganic matter, there must also be some fact corresponding to the mental fact in ourselves.

In the text I have disputed the principle that experience only tells us of thought in connection with brain-motion, on the ground that it is only by analogy we conclude that there is thought in other beings than ourselves, and that the same argument equally reveals to us an intelligent principle pervading nature. If the analogy between its acts and ours is not as close as between the acts of other men and ours, it only follows that that intelligence differs more from ours than theirs. This argument of mine gains immensely in force if Professor Clifford's theory be true ; for when, in the passage cited above, he states that we have no evidence of volition concerned in events except that of animals living on the planets, the exception he makes is not consistent with his theory. For he excludes our volitions from any place among the causes of events, his theory of our actions being that impressions made on our sensory nerves are transmitted, according to mechanical laws, to the motor nerves, either directly or through the brain, without our volition once interfering in the chain of connection. It follows that the actions of other men would be precisely the same as at present if they were actually devoid of intelligence and volition ; so that we have no ground whatever for ascribing these attributes to them except such as analogy may furnish. In this theory, then, the proposition that we only know of intelligence in connection with the movements of a brain falls completely to the ground. We know nothing of intelligence except in ourselves, and though it may be a reasonable supposition that beings outwardly like ourselves possess it too, we are in no condition to deny that things unlike ourselves may possess it also. In short, Professor Clifford, in getting rid of the evidence for God's existence, has also swept away all evidence for the existence of mind in other men. If, notwithstanding, we find it impossible to doubt that they have intelligence and volition like our own, we need as little doubt that there is in the universe an intelligence and volition which bears the same relation to all the changes that take place there that our own volition bears to the acts of which we imagine ourselves to be the doers.

VII

EVOLUTION

"And He said, So is the kingdom of God, as if a man should cast seed into the ground; and should sleep and rise night and day; and the seed should spring and grow up, he knoweth not how. For the earth bringeth forth fruit of herself; first the blade, then the ear, after that the full corn in the ear. But when the fruit is brought forth, immediately he putteth in the sickle, because the harvest is come."—ST. MARK iv. 26-29.

IT would be an unheard of literary paradox if a critic were to lay down the rule, that the claims of a book to proceed from any particular author must be rejected, in case the work bears all the characteristic marks of that writer's style, but be admitted at once, provided only the work be utterly unlike all his acknowledged compositions. Yet this is literally the manner in which men judge of the works of God. By the study of the works of nature we can learn to recognise the style of its great Author. Then when any phenomenon presents itself, striking by its unlikeness to that style, the confession is ready to rise to the mouths even of irreligious men, This is the finger of God. But the advocates of religion are supposed to have difficulties to conquer, and certainly have prejudices to overcome, when they claim as God's work that which has about it nothing startling or unusual, but which conforms completely to the laws which sum up the results of our observation of the characteristics of the ordinary working of the Author of nature.

We must ask if men really believe what they say when they speak of God as the Author of nature. It would rather seem as if they looked on Nature and God as two distinct beings: Nature presiding over all ordinary phenomena, the laws of which are perfectly understood, and God interfering at rare intervals when some urgent necessity arises for a deviation from these ordinary laws. The very opposite spirit to this pervades the teaching of our Blessed Lord. In all the ordinary operations of nature He sees the hand of God; it is God that maketh His sun to rise on the evil and the good, and sendeth rain on the just and on the unjust. And He constantly impresses on His disciples the unity and continuity of God's working, and especially in His teaching by parables, illustrates by analogies from the kingdom of nature the laws of that higher kingdom of which He claimed to be the founder. In the parable which I have taken as my text to-day He states, as one of the laws of His kingdom, that principle which in men's habits of thoughts distinguishes what they ascribe to nature from what they are willing to ascribe to God; the principle that progress is ordinarily made by gradual, imperceptible growth. In opposition to the expectations of His followers He declares that that kingdom of God which He came to proclaim and to found shall constitute no exception to the rule universally prevalent in the natural world, that progress is ordinarily made by a process of slow, silent development. It would be a work of much time to trace this law of development in all its practical applications, to illustrate the diversified forms in which it exhibits itself, and to discuss the various questions which its working has suggested. On the present occasion I take as my thesis to establish the single principle that the fact that in any province this law of progress by development is found to prevail, offers no presumption that in that province God is not working.

From one point of view this principle appears so self-evident that it would seem as if words must be wasted in arguing in defence of it. It sounds like an ironical understatement of the truth to say that no presumption *against* God's working is caused by our being able to trace the prevalence of a law which universally dominates in God's natural world, and which, in His revealed word, Christ has signalised as characteristic of His supernatural dispensation. Yet, undoubtedly, it would be unwise to expect that a few words, showing its unreasonableness, would suffice to dissipate a presumption founded on habits of thought stronger than reason. As we may well believe that our first notions of causation are suggested by our own power to interrupt an expected habitual sequence of phenomena, so when there is no such interruption we are little tempted to look for causes. If things go on in their natural, accustomed order, we see nothing which requires explanation. The conversion of a seed into a spreading tree, of an infant to a full-grown, reasoning man, is in truth a change as complete as any that ever presents itself, and did it take place suddenly it would excite our utmost wonder. But the slow, gradual passage from one stage of being to the other appears to us only natural, and the thought of a necessity of a God, of a great first cause, has commonly been forced on men by the spectacle of what they regarded as new things coming into existence, rather than by any gradual alterations which took place in the old.

With the progress of philosophic investigation men's notions came to be seriously modified as to what can be properly pronounced new, what ordinary and natural. What had seemed to the uncultivated as the startling appearance of something new was shown to be only the recurrent reappearance of something which had been observed before, or the transformation of old matter according to laws now perfectly understood. And as men successfully classified phenomena and reduced their conceptions of them to order, they supposed they had accounted for them, forgetting that no success in explaining *how* and according to what rules anything is done in any degree answers the question *by whom* and *why* it is done. Even to religious men those processes of nature which were found to be regular and capable of being reduced to law ceased to convey any striking evidence of God's working; and writers on natural theology found it important to lay stress on the work of creation as affording less questionable proof of Divine interference. The line of argument was to show that things cannot always have continued in their present order, that in particular there is reason to believe that the human race has been of comparatively recent introduction into the world, and that consequently, at some time more or less remote, this earth must have been the scene of the inauguration of a totally new era, for the commencement of which a distinct Divine interference only can account. And then it was felt that the cause of Theism was suffering an injury when modern speculation undertook to reduce creation itself to law; when men professed to write the natural history of the genesis of worlds, and to show how a condensed fire-mist might be gradually peopled with living creatures; when they pushed back to a more distant time man's first appearance in the world, and tried to explain how he might have been developed from some of the inferior animals. This is not the place for discussing the scientific value of such theories, or for inquiring whether some things have not been too hastily admitted to rank as proved facts which were at best probable speculations. But I may take it as a first application of the principle which I have undertaken to illustrate to-day to point out that whatever may be the fate of these theories the question of Theism is not affected. It certainly gives no reason to doubt the existence of God if it should turn out that a certain unity pervades all His works, and if the history of worlds or of species resembles that of individuals, if in all cases the mature and perfect state is attained, not by a single act of power, but by a slow process of preparatory growth. Our knowledge that the world is ruled by an intelligent Agent is derived from the multiform proofs of design which exhibit themselves in every part of it, and these proofs are in no way affected by any increased knowledge we may gain of the processes by which the ends are worked out which it is the will of the Ruler of the world to accomplish. For example, a glance at patterns wrought in a web might suffice to inform us that we were looking at a work of human art, and that conclusion would not be shaken if it turned out that the work we were inspecting had not been produced by human fingers directly, but by one of those wonderful machines which simulate the action of man's intelligence. Nay, in the latter case, we should feel that human skill had been exerted in a higher degree than in the former. And so if it could be shown that all the wonderful regularity and beautiful order of the world had been evolved from the gradual cooling down of heated vapours, this would in no degree affect any argument founded on the adaptation of means to ends in the works of nature. We could still trace the ends aimed at, and the result produced, and the inference of design would be precisely the same, whether the result were produced by an immediate act of power or by a gradual process of preparation. And certainly in works of human art a stronger impression of intelligence and design is produced in proportion as the time necessary for perfecting the work is longer, as the materials must be sought out and prepared long beforehand, and as the application of them requires continuous patient care. Without going behind the present state of the universe we can convince ourselves that it must have had an intelligent Creator; and if we learn that its present state is the result and development of other preceding states, we have only the more cause to admire the foresight and wisdom of Him who planned that out of these preparatory stages should spring its present order.

II. Let me take in quite a different region a second illustration of the principle that our recognition of anything as God's work is not rightly affected by the fact that what claims to proceed from God can be shown to have had regular growth. If there be any part of our nature which can claim to be specially Divine, it is the voice of conscience which speaks within us as the voice of God, demanding supremacy over every other part of our constitution, directing us what to choose and what to avoid, and rebuking us when we disobey its indications. In fact, it is to this voice from within, far more than to their observation of external nature, that men owe their knowledge of God. Outward nature can make known to us that God exists, and it can reveal His power and wisdom, but all His moral attributes are taught us by the testimony of our own hearts. If it could justly be asked, "He that made the ear, shall He not hear? He that formed the eye, shall He not see?" with still more force was it asked, "He that chastised the heathen, shall not He correct? He that teacheth men knowledge, shall not He know?" He who has made us so that we cannot but approve goodness, truth, justice, must He not Himself look on these qualities with favour: must He not Himself possess these attributes in the highest degree? for we cannot conceive a Being calling creatures into existence, and so constituting them that they could not help hating and despising Him who formed them, and being persuaded they were right in so doing. And if we are so formed as to hate meanness, treachery, falsehood, and malevolence in others, to be ashamed if we are guilty of such faults ourselves, and to know that we are worthy of disapprobation, is there not ground for the fear which accompanies the sense of ill desert, justified as it is by the knowledge that He who is sovereign over the universe Himself hates and is able to punish those things which He has made to be hateful in the eyes of His creatures? Somewhat such as this was the Theistical argument founded on the revelations of conscience; but its foundation seemed to be destroyed when it was maintained that conscience itself was but an artificial growth, that there was no uniformity in its decisions, many things which we now count scandalous and disgraceful having been at other places or times judged to be quite consistent with virtue: that there was, therefore, no ground for believing in the existence of a moral sense, and that the genesis of the moral feelings could be satisfactorily accounted for by the natural associations of dislike to things which we have either ourselves experienced as the causes to us of suffering, or which having been found by other men to be injurious to the constitution of society, have come to be distasteful to them, from whom we catch the feeling, partly by unconscious sympathy, partly by direct education, partly, perhaps, by inheritance.

Whatever may be the fate of such speculations, they leave untouched the argument which infers the character of God from our moral judgments. For in judging of the designs of the Creator we must regard His works, not in the state in which they first came into being, but in that to which they grow in the circumstances in which He has placed them. It were absurd to regard Him as the Author of the seed, not of the plant—of the babe, but not of the full-grown man; or to maintain that the Creator did not plan, or intend that

His works should possess any properties which do not show themselves in their immature and undeveloped state. No argument can be founded on the imperfections of the moral judgments of minds in a state of imperfect growth or cultivation; nor again, is it material whether men are gifted with a special sense by which they discern the beauty of virtue, or whether the true account of the matter is that our Maker has placed us in such circumstances that wrong-doing is necessarily followed by unhappiness, so that we learn to hate it by the discipline of personal or inherited experience. In either case the argument has like force by which, from the testimony of our nature, is inferred the character of Him who has given us that nature.

III. In the third place, I notice the attempts which have been made to disprove the Divine origin of Christianity by tracing the rise of our religion to natural causes. It had been assumed by unbelievers, and too hastily granted by many religious men, that if Christianity came from God, its introduction into the world must have been an abrupt and arbitrary act—a miracle worked whenever it was the pleasure of the Almighty to work it. And then the question was asked, Why was this miracle worked just eighteen hundred years ago, and not some thousands of years sooner? Had not the evils which Christianity was to remove or to mitigate existed for centuries, and how is it intelligible that the Creator should have deferred applying a remedy to them until a comparatively late period in the world's history? And then, on the other hand, it was shown that there were natural causes which gained for the doctrines of Christianity, at the time they were published, a favourable reception they could not have met with had they been promulgated before. But we are not concerned to deny the existence of such causes. It is no part of our case to deny that God educated His world by a long preparatory process for the lessons our Lord was to teach it, so that it was only in the fulness of time that God sent His Blessed Son into the world. It is not quite impossible to see some reasons why He came when He actually did, and not sooner. To the Jews God had given their law as a schoolmaster unto Christ. But the lessons which it taught them were necessarily long confined to their own nation, shut up by barriers of rigid exclusiveness from intercourse with others. Not they alone, but every tribe of man was separated by contempt and hatred from others. Those of the heathen whom we know best, the Greeks, believed in the pre-eminence of their race far more strongly than did the Jews in the pre-eminence of circumcised over uncircumcised. For it was held by some of the wisest of the Greeks that the pre-eminence of Greek over Barbarian was not the accidental growth of circumstances or education, but the necessary result of the original nature of things. And the distinction of races was held to extend to the supernatural world. Each tribe of men worshipped its national divinities charged with the special defence of their own clients, who could not be overcome until their supernatural defenders had been either flattered into abandoning them, or were overcome by the superior might of the patrons of some other people.

The idea of the universal brotherhood of men as children of one God was little likely to find general acceptance, until the establishment of the Macedonian Empire welded together into one political society a multitude of diverse nations; and the throwing down of barriers between nation and nation, which was then commenced, was more completely effected by the Roman Empire. The union of so many nations under one empire not only made the work of the first preachers of the Gospel easier, by affording facilities of travel and intercourse between people of distant lands, by dispersing through every great city of the civilised world Jews who, though they went not as missionaries, but in search of gain, were able to leaven many of those among whom they lived with a knowledge of great religious truths preserved by their people ; not only thus did the union of many people under one empire aid the progress of Christianity, but it had already broken down the prejudices which would have impeded the reception of one great Christian truth, that God is no respecter of persons, that all are equal in His sight, that "there is neither Greek nor Jew, circumcision nor uncircumcision, barbarian, Scythian, bond nor free, but Christ is all and in all."

Time will not permit me to speak of other Christian doctrines—the doctrine of a personal God, the doctrine of man's immortality, the doctrine of sin, and of man's need of a Sanctifier and Redeemer—subjects concerning which men were more ready to accept Christian teaching after they had sought in vain, in different philosophies or superstitions, a solution of the great problems concerning humanity which had engaged their thoughts. It may be granted, then, that the seeds of our Lord's teaching, which sprung up and bore fruit because they were cast into a prepared soil, would, according to human calculation, have been choked, and have come to nothing, had they been sown at an earlier time. It may be granted, too, that the preparation of that soil was a gradual process effected by causes, many of which it is in our power to trace. And yet, according to what I have been insisting on all through this sermon, in acknowledging that much of the establishment of our Lord's kingdom upon earth is the result of a process of gradual development, we are not precluded from asserting also that it was the work of God.

IV. Lastly, let me apply what is taught in the parable as to the quiet, silent growth of the heavenly seed to the work of God upon the heart of individual men. And here, too, the tendency on which I have commented is widely prevalent —namely, only to recognise that as God's work which is sudden and violent. It is owned without difficulty that it is God's work when a persecutor like Saul of Tarsus is in a moment stopped in his career and is brought, trembling and astonished, to exclaim—"Lord, what wilt Thou have me to do?" It is owned to be God's work when, as at times happens, a sinner, who has run a wild course of vicious indulgence in defiance or forgetfulness of God, breaks off abruptly from his sins and turns to God. And it is owned to be His work when one who has groaned under the burden of unforgiven sin at length ventures to cast himself unreservedly on Christ's work, and proclaims that at the Cross he has found peace and forgiveness. But it is little thought that there can be a work of God in the soul of him with whom one day has passed like another, who has only to tell of some small temptations daily resisted, some small good habit strengthened, who has experienced no agony of doubt, no rapture of reconciliation. Yet the text may suggest that though God is not limited to any one mode of operation, still were we called on to pronounce what mode was most in accordance with the analogy of His works, and therefore to be regarded as most characteristic, and on that account likely to be most usual, we should rather say the mode in which the seed sown silently springs and grows up, man knoweth not how. Nor indeed is it easy to say how much that seems to us abrupt change is in truth the result of long-continued silent preparation. It is an abrupt change when water flashes into steam or congeals into ice, yet either is but the final result of a gradual process of addition or diminution of heat, during which little apparent change takes place in the condition of the fluid. And in the moral world the sudden clearing away of obstacles which have opposed the reception of great truths sometimes reminds us of the sudden falling of the walls of Jericho, where, in the unexpectedness of the triumph, we are tempted to forget the seven days during which the city was encompassed with no visible result. Take even such a miraculous conversion as that of Saul of Tarsus, who passed in a moment from the condition of a persecutor to that of a believer, and we may well believe that before the final blow was struck at those bulwarks of prejudice which in his mind opposed the reception of the Gospel, they had been undermined by the words he had heard from Stephen and the other martyrs whom he persecuted, and by the spectacle of their patient endurance for the testimony of the truth ; that the misgiving must sometimes have seized him—Is that altogether a lie which these men witness? and that though the thought may have been resolutely put away from him, yet the voice of Jesus from heaven only made him in a moment *know* that to be true which he had suspected might be true before.

And in like manner it will be found in nearly every instance of sudden conversion that it was not that truths then first proclaimed gained immediate acceptance, but that truths which had been often presented and repelled, returned in such overwhelming force as to bear down opposition. It is an abrupt and startling change when a mass of rock detaches itself from some lofty cliff and comes thundering down into the valley ; yet such a change is but the final result of disintegrating influences of frost and rain long and silently working. Thus you will see that while I most freely grant that both in the natural and in the spiritual world startling changes at times occur, yet, I contend that these are not to be regarded as opposed to the analogy of God's dealings, according to which change is preceded by a preparatory process. But at least to repeat once more what I have been urging all through, it were absurd to hold that what absolutely and strictly conforms to the analogy of the Divine processes is less God's work than what is apparently an exception to it. And it is especially needful that the young should be warned in this matter, lest while they are expecting some future time when God may descend on their souls in the earthquake, the tempest, or the fire, they shut their eyes to the still small voice of His Spirit pleading with their hearts. It is His gracious work that the truths of Christ's Gospel should have been already made known to you, that they should be from time to time pressed on your acceptance by the voice of His ministers, by the admonitions of religious parents, instructors, or friends, by the public services of the Church, by His word read in private, by providential dispensations inclining you to give heed to it. If you have already in any degree given heed to it, and, guided by it to know where strength is to be found, have striven in that strength to resist the temptations of the world, the devil, or the flesh, doubt not, but earnestly believe, that that Spirit has been at work in your heart who has power to bring to perfection the work which He has begun, and let it be your earnest desire *to grow* in grace, and in the knowledge of our Lord and Saviour Jesus Christ.

VIII

THE EVIDENTIAL VALUE OF THE EUCHARISTIC RITE[1]

> "And as they were eating, Jesus took bread, and blessed it, and brake it, and gave it to the disciples, and said, Take, eat; this is My body. And He took the cup, and gave thanks, and gave it to them, saying, Drink ye all of it: for this is My blood of the new testament, which is shed for many for the remission of sins."—ST. MATTHEW xxvi. 26-28.

I DO not know whether it is necessary to offer any explanation of the fact that of the Gospel history about one-third part is occupied with the account of the sayings and events of the last week of the Saviour's life on earth. To say nothing of the intrinsic importance of those deeds and words we feel how natural it is that the thoughts of any, from whom has been taken one whom they loved and valued, should dwell on the memory of all that he said or did immediately before he was parted from them. Parting words live long in the memory; a dying charge has a peculiar sacredness. There were, then, no words of Christ

[1] Reprinted here from series of Sermons published in 1873.

which it was so impossible for any who heard them ever to forget as those in which, when about to be separated from His disciples, He appealed to their love, and taught them how it was His wish that they should keep Him in memory after He was gone. And for all who love Him no words, it might be supposed, are more suggestive of matter for solemn and peaceful meditation. Yet it has come to pass now that with us these words are suggestive of strife; and I doubt not that many of you as soon as you heard my text prepared yourselves to expect a sermon occupied with controversy. The subject is certainly one on which it has now become impossible to escape controversy; and elsewhere it is my duty this term to enter into a full discussion of it; but at present I intend to speak only of those things, the truth of which we all agree in admitting; and though my treatment of the text will be controversial, the controversy will be directed against those who are without. I wish, in short, to dwell on the bearings on Christian evidences of the history recorded in the text.

On the revival of learning and the birth of modern critical science it was discovered that many documents, handed down from previous generations, and which had met from them with uninquiring acceptance, were unworthy of the reverence which they had received. At first this process of rejection went on but slowly. It seemed presumptuous to question what men in former days, entitled to honour for their learning, had with one consent admitted. Assaults were only made on those works which were least strongly guarded by prescriptive reverence; and even with respect to these the battle was, for a considerable time, stoutly contested. But one victory after another emboldened the assailants. At length nothing was too sacred for attack; the records of our faith have been subjected to the severest scrutiny, and, often on grounds which scarcely warranted a suspicion, sentence of absolute condemnation has been pronounced. There are symptoms now that the era of merely destructive criticism is passing away. The adversaries of Christianity do not content themselves now with scoffs and objections against the faith which we profess; they acknowledge the necessity of substituting something of their own; they own themselves bound to answer the question, what *they* think of Christ? what facts must they admit as certainly proved concerning that real human life on earth which undoubtedly has had such abiding influence on the history of our whole race? For writing the history of this life we have scarcely any materials but those Gospel narratives which some of the historians, to whom I refer, treat with such scant respect; and it is, therefore, well that we should fully use the few opportunities we have of testing the truth of these narratives by independent evidence. One of these opportunities is afforded in that history which I have taken for my subject to-day, that of the Institution of the Christian Sacred Feast—a history which could be established by satisfactory proof even if none of the four Gospels had reached us. As far as we can trace back the history of our religion this solemn feast was an essential part of Christian worship. In early times, indeed, there was some reserve as to stating publicly in the presence of the heathen what the Church believed as to the food which they there received. "That which the faithful know" was the common phrase when speaking in the presence of the uninitiated. Yet the veil thus used was so transparent, and those who employ it at one moment lay it aside so carelessly at another that their reserve appears to be rather that of reverence than of mystery. Certainly Christians of the very earliest times made no affectation of concealment. In the second century Justin Martyr, in his Apology addressed to heathen, gives a full description of the mode in which the rite was then administered; and goes on to declare that Christians had been taught that the food over which thanksgiving has been made is

N

the Flesh and Blood of the Incarnate Jesus. "For the Apostles in their memoirs, which are called Gospels, have delivered that Jesus so commanded them, that He having taken bread and given thanks, said, 'Do this in remembrance of Me. This is My body;" and likewise, having taken the cup and given thanks, He said, 'This is My blood.'"

The account just cited is professedly founded on the Gospel History. But we can go back a century earlier for decisive testimony as to the belief of the first generation of Christians; namely, to the account given by St. Paul in the first Epistle to the Corinthians—an epistle, the genuineness of which is not contested by the most sceptical of critics. St. Paul says, "I have received of the Lord that which I also delivered to you, that the Lord Jesus, the same night in which He was betrayed, took bread; and when He had given thanks, He brake it and said, Take, eat; this is My body which is broken for you: this do in remembrance of Me. After the same manner also He took the cup, when He had supped, saying, This cup is the new testament in My blood; this do ye as oft as ye drink it in remembrance of Me." This account is in verbal agreement with that given by St. Luke in his Gospel; but there is no reason to think that the one was copied from the other. On comparing the history of the appearances of our Lord after His resurrection, given in the fifteenth chapter of the first Epistle to the Corinthians, with that given in the Gospel, we have every reason for believing in the independence of the two accounts. In particular, if St. Luke, when writing the Gospel, had before him the Epistle to the Corinthians, it seems unlikely that he would not have told us something more about the appearance to St. James, or about that to the five hundred brethren at once. It is the more remarkable, then, that St. Luke's account of the institution of the Eucharist should be in close verbal agreement with that of St. Paul, though not so with those of Matthew and Mark. Yet the matter receives a very simple explanation if we only suppose a liturgical usage to be apostolic which we can otherwise trace back very close to apostolic times—namely, that of reciting the history of our Lord's institution of the rite at the time of consecration. For if this were so, St. Luke, who must have been so often present when St. Paul celebrated this memorial of his Lord, must have repeatedly heard these words recited by St. Paul, and therefore might be expected to record them in his Gospel in the form in which Paul had delivered them unto him. On the whole, then, there is absolute historical proof that at the time when the majority were alive of those who professed to have seen Jesus of Nazareth after He rose from the dead, it was the universal belief among Christians that their Master, on the night He was betrayed, had given to His disciples bread and wine, had assured them that in partaking of that food they should eat His body and drink His blood, and had commanded them to continue that celebration in remembrance of Him; and it is certain that they did so continue it in obedience to that alleged command.

The next question is—Is it possible that this belief and this practice could have arisen if the account which Christians themselves gave of its origin were not the true one? Reverence forbids me to describe this Christian institution in the language we should employ if we had never heard of it before, and if we came to know it now for the first time as a religious rite practised by some newly-discovered tribe. But the more there is shocking and seemingly absurd in the language used concerning this institution, the less likely is it that Christians would have spontaneously imagined this mode of doing honour to their Master, and showing their love and gratitude towards Him. We could quite understand the Christian society maintaining and ratifying their relations of mutual friendship by the institution of a common meal. The doctrine of the common brotherhood of all, and the duty of mutual love, would be aptly symbolised by all joining on equal terms to partake of a common meal, consisting of bread and wine, the simplest, and in those countries the most universal articles of food ; and while thus owning their mutual fellowship, acknowledging also their dependence on God, whose gifts they owned these blessings to be, to whom they returned thanks for them, and to whom they dedicated not only their offerings, but themselves. If the Eucharistic Feast were nothing more than a simple repast, forcibly expressing the common human wants of all, and their common dependence on the bounty of the same Father, it would commend itself to any one as a reasonable and wise institution, and we should have no difficulty in understanding how good men might have imagined it. But it is mysterious that the disciples should use concerning their rite language which would imply that theirs was a banquet on human flesh and blood—not ordinary human flesh, but the body of Him whom, when alive, they had most loved, and whom now they worshipped as God. It was no uncommon charge brought of old against different secret societies or bands of dark conspirators, that in order that the members might testify their readiness to sacrifice every prejudice and disregard every law, human or divine, which might interfere with the fulfilment of their duty to the society, they were compelled on their initiation to taste of human blood. Such charges were, no doubt, in many cases as mere calumnies as the accusation of Thyestean banquets commonly brought by heathens against the Christian community. In all cases the charges come to us on the testimony of enemies; but there is no instance of a society really innocent of such practices choosing to use language that implied it was guilty of them. Least of all should we expect to hear such language from the lips of Jews. Not merely was food at which all men revolt abhorrent to them, but it was the peculiar boast of a pious Jew that nothing common or unclean had ever polluted his mouth. To eat swine's flesh was in their eyes as heinous as an offence against the moral law; to taste the blood of any animal was as much forbidden as to drink human blood; the very touch of a dead body was pollution. Now we know for how long a period the obligation of the Mosaic law was insisted on; how many thousands of Judaising Christians there were who wished to include this law as an essential part of the Christian system, and that it was at least a century after the Apostles' times before these Judaisers were completely separated from the Christian

Church. But we can trace the Eucharistic rite as existing from the earliest times, and as common to all parties in these disputes, however strong their attachment to Mosaic ordinances. Again, if the rite were first heard of in a later generation among men to whom Christ was but a mere name, we might explain the language used as some mystical Eastern mode of expressing their desire to enter into most intimate union with Him whom they venerated as their Founder. But St. Paul's testimony makes it certain that Christians spoke of eating our Lord's flesh and drinking His blood, to whom Jesus was not a mere abstract name for typical perfect humanity; but at a time when the majority were still living of those who professed that they had seen Him after He had risen from the dead; while those were still alive who had known and loved Him as a human friend; who had thought no balms or spices too costly to do honour to His mortal remains, and to whom the thought of violating their sanctity would be as revolting as a similar thought in the case of one of our own dead friends would be to any of ourselves. Thus it appears that the origin of the Christian Eucharistic Feast is absolutely inexplicable if we reject the simple account of it given by the sacred writers—that the disciples use no language concerning it except what their Master Himself had taught them to use.

I daresay I shall seem to many of you to have strangely spent time in painfully elaborating a proof that we may accept as literally true what it never occurred to you to doubt—that our Lord on the night He was betrayed took bread and brake it, and gave it to His disciples with the words: "Take, eat, this is My body; do this in remembrance of Me." I have done so because of the important consequences which I regard as following when this fact is proved; as to our Lord's Divine foreknowledge, His intention to found a Church, and the relation which He declared that He Himself personally bore to the spiritual life of all men—a doctrine involving pretensions extravagant on the part of any merely human teacher, but strange, indeed, when coming from the mouth of One who is supposed at the time to have given up all hope of a successful issue to His enterprise, and to be looking forward to the prospect of an approaching shameful death. On account of the importance of these consequences, I have desired, before attempting to draw them, to show that our belief in the fact on which they are based does not depend on our belief concerning the inspiration of the Gospels, nor even on our belief concerning their antiquity and integrity. Just as we could prove by plain historical evidence, if the Gospels had never come down to us, that the original preachers of Christianity hazarded their lives in attestation of the assertion that their Master rose from the dead, so we can prove independently of the Gospels that it was their belief that He instituted the rite of which I speak to-day, and I have given reasons for holding that the very existence of such a belief among the first generation of Christians is a sufficient proof of its truth.

The importance which I attach to the proof of this fact is justified by the reluctance to admit it exhibited by sceptical writers, who are clear-sighted enough to perceive that the fact, if admitted, would compel them to reconstruct all their theories concerning the life and character of Jesus. In Renan's *Life of Jesus*, for example, the institution of the Lord's Supper finds no place. His excuse is, that this event is not recorded by St. John, whom Renan, differing herein from the majority of writers of his school, accepts as giving the most trustworthy account of the closing scenes of his Master's life. He assumes, without a shadow of proof, that the breaking of bread was a mysterious rite of unknown signification habitually practised by our Lord; and his theory is, that afterwards, when the disciples came to look on our Lord's death as a sacrifice superseding the offerings of the Old Law, then the tendency of legends to gather round the story of the last hours of the life of Jesus referred the breaking of bread to the Last Supper, and made the wine then poured out to symbolise the blood shed for the salvation of the world. But it is needless to say how completely this theory leaves unsolved the problem of the origin of the Christian Eucharistic rite. That the Christians early looked on their Master's death as a sacrifice we readily admit; but there is an immense gulf between such a belief and the doctrine that Christians were bound in some manner to eat of His body and blood. If we could suppose John's Gospel intended for a complete account of all that Jesus said and did, his omission to explain a thing so much requiring explanation would be a sufficient reason for rejecting his authority; and the story, as given by the other Evangelists, would be plainly in preference entitled to credit. But there are numberless proofs which I have not now time to state fully, that St. John wrote his Gospel for men to whom the main facts of the Gospel history were already known; indeed, there is every reason to believe for men who had the other Gospels in their hands.

For example, we learn from St. John's Gospel that there were then current objections to the acknowledgment of our Lord's claims, which ran thus: "Jesus is not of David's seed, as it was foretold the Messiah should be. Jesus was born at Nazareth, but the prophet foretold that the Messiah should be born at Bethlehem ; therefore, Jesus is not the Messiah of whom the prophets spoke." St. John states the objections, but he never states the answer to them, viz. that Jesus really was born at Bethlehem and of the seed of David. In the first chapter Philip tells Nathanael, "We have found him, of whom Moses in the law, and the prophets, did write, Jesus of Nazareth, the son of Joseph," to which Nathanael answers, "Can any good thing come out of Nazareth?" an objection to which Philip makes no direct reply. The current objection is more fully stated (vii. 41, 42), "Some said, Shall Christ come out of Galilee? Hath not the scripture said, That Christ cometh of the seed of David, and out of the town of Bethlehem, where David was?" No solution of the difficulty is given either here or at the end of the chapter, where Nicodemus is taunted, "Art thou also of Galilee? Search, and look: for out of Galilee ariseth no prophet." I do not believe that St. John could have stated so formidable an objection without giving some hint of the answer to it, if he had not known that his readers had in their hands at least one of the Gospels which contain the genealogy, tracing our Lord's descent from David, and in which the birth at Bethlehem is related. As a general rule, this Evangelist studiously avoids repeating what he might assume was already known to his readers: so that his silence concerning any part of the history cannot be regarded as testimony against it. And certainly his silence concerning the institution of the Eucharist cannot be regarded as testimony against it; for strangely enough, one of the arguments used by other sceptical critics against the genuineness of this Gospel is the coincidence of the language of the discourse in the sixth chapter with language used in the second century when Eucharistic doctrine was highly developed.

Strauss, unlike Renan, prefers the Synoptic Gospels to the fourth, and therefore he cannot lay stress on the silence of John with respect to a fact attested by the other three. He hesitates, then, and seems unable to make up his mind how much to admit. He believes that our Lord, on this last evening, was depressed in spirits, understanding His real position, unrelentingly pursued by the fanaticism of desperate enemies, and feebly supported by followers incapable of understanding Him. He thinks it possible, then, that when Jesus, as master of the household, broke the bread and poured out the wine for distribution among His disciples, the thought may have involuntarily presented itself to Him that even so would His body soon be broken—so would His blood soon be poured forth; and that He may have expressed some such gloomy foreboding to His disciples. Nay, Strauss will admit it to be possible that, looking on His death as a sacrifice, He may have regarded His blood as the consecration of a new covenant between God and mankind; and in order to give a living centre to the community which He desired to found, might have commanded the perpetual repetition of this distribution of bread and wine. All this he says is possible, but whether it really took place is another question. If Jesus had expressed any anticipation of the approaching violent death, and if the Church had adopted the custom of distributing bread and wine in memory of His death, no doubt the institution of such a custom would be ascribed to Christ whether He were really the Author of it or not; and if the Church had come to look on that bread and wine as the body and blood of Christ, and the blood as the blood of a new covenant, no doubt, again, the story would soon obtain belief that Christ had Himself used language to justify such a belief. But who can grant the assumption which this "if" requires? How was it possible that the Church should come to give bread and wine the names of Christ's body and blood if He Himself had *not* authorised their doing so?

Let us see, then, what follows from the reluctant admission of our adversaries. On the last night of his life Jesus, though not possessing, as we believe, Divine foreknowledge of the future, had at least human knowledge that the toils of His enemies were closing round Him. He saw that death could no longer be escaped, and that the career which He had planned had ended in failure. Yet even then He calmly looks forward to the formation of a new society which shall own Him as its Founder. He foresees that that flock of timorous followers, whose dispersion on the next day He ventures to predict, will recover the shock of their disappointment and unite again. And as for this shameful death, the thoughts of which oppress Him, instead of anticipating that His followers will put it from their thoughts and blush to remember their credulity when they accepted as their Saviour one unable to save Himself, He commands His disciples to keep that death in perpetual memory. Notwithstanding the apparent failure of His course He conceives Himself to be a unique person in the world's history, and in Strauss's words, He regards His death as the seal of a new covenant between God and mankind. What other man has ever dared to set such a value on his own life? If such a belief were not true, it would surely be the very frenzy of insanity.

More than this—He makes it an ordinance of perpetual obligation to His followers that they shall seek the most intimate union with His body and blood, and holds out to them this closeness of perpetual union with Himself as the source of all spiritual life. One of the principal grounds on which some have urged us to reject St. John's Gospel is the lofty language which in that Gospel our Lord uses concerning His own person and claims; pressing these claims, it is said, in an exaggerated way, inconsistent with the meekness and humility which characterise his discourses recorded in the other Gospels. But in this narrative recorded by the Synoptic Evangelists, and not by St. John, we find Him making higher pretensions than on any other occasion, and making these claims under the very shadow of the Cross. It was no afterthought of His disciples to smooth away the offence of the Cross by ascribing to His death some mysterious efficacy; He Himself had taught them to look on His blood as shed for them and for many for the remission of sins. He intimates that the event then taking place was comparable with the first setting apart of the Jewish nation to be God's peculiar people; and as Moses had then sprinkled the people with blood, saying, Behold the blood of the covenant which God hath made with you, so now He calls His own the blood of the new covenant. This legislation for a future Church was made at a moment when His most attached disciples could not be trusted to remain with Him for an hour, and when He had Himself predicted their desertion and denial. Our adversaries make no difficulty about admitting that our Lord predicted His death; for this, they think, did not exceed the powers of human forecast, so plain were the symptoms of the storm gathering round Him. But no ordinary human foresight could then discern that the infant Church would survive the shock of its Master's death, and instead of being ashamed of the Cross would glory in it, and look upon His death as the source of all life. Thus, then, we have not only in the Last Supper a spectacle of faith, calm and unshaken in circumstances the most desperate, but we have a prophecy of success improbable in the highest degree, and yet which received the most complete fulfilment.

We all believe that that prophecy was no random guess: that faith, no blind enthusiasm; we know that Jesus was all that He claimed to be; that His death was the great sin-offering to restore the broken communion between God and man—union with Him the condition of our spiritual life. And we cannot doubt that it was no empty words which He spoke when instituting that sacred rite. If His words have been perverted so as to give rise to error and superstition there is the more reason for thinking that He who foreknew these consequences, and yet did not refrain from speaking, wished to make known truths more powerful for good than any of their perversions are for harm. We may believe that He then revealed a covenanted means which will enable those who use it in faith spiritually to eat His flesh and drink His blood, and to receive therein a pledge of all those blessings which His sacrificed body can yield. Not alone in this rite is He present to those who in faith seek for Him. Where two or three are gathered together in His name He is in the midst of them. Even the private lifting up to Him of a single heart is not unmarked by Him. But we may well believe that an especial blessing attends those who in faith obey His commands and seek Him in the ordinance He has appointed; not bewildering themselves in vain speculations *how* this man shall give us His flesh to eat; not, on the one hand, denying all supernatural grace, and reducing all beneficial effect to the results of the natural operation of laws of our own minds; nor, on the other hand, insisting that men shall believe in the reality of miracles, of which there is no evidence, save that it seems to us that, in order to make our explanation of His words true, it is necessary that God should work them. Such philosophising shows want of faith in Christ's true presence as much as the direct denial of it. Just as God's presence in this world was implicitly denied, not only by those who refused to lift their thoughts above His material works, but by those who strove to localise His presence and could not recognise Him except where there was some figure to represent Him made by hands of men. But, as I have said, my purpose to-day is not to discuss any of those points on which Christians disagree, but to show the place among the evidences of our religion occupied by the fact that Christians have from the first observed this institution; a fact of which no other explanation can be given but that contained in the Gospel account of the origin of the rite; and a fact which proves that our Lord, in the immediate prospect of approaching death, looked on that death not as the end of His religion but the beginning of it; a sacrifice for the sins of the world, the source of all good to mankind. He who spoke of Himself thus was confessedly a wise man, a meek and humble man. Could He have been only man?

IX

THE PARABLE OF THE SOWER

> "Behold, a sower went forth to sow; and when he sowed, some seeds fell by the wayside, and the fowls came and devoured them up: some fell upon stony places, where they had not much earth; and forthwith they sprung up, because they had no deepness of earth, and when the sun was up, they were scorched; and because they had no root, they withered away. And some fell among thorns; and the thorns sprung up, and choked them: but other fell into good ground, and brought forth fruit, some an hundredfold, some sixtyfold, some thirtyfold. Who hath ears to hear, let him hear."—ST. MATTHEW xiii. 3-9.

IT will not be unnatural if the thought has occurred to many of you on hearing these words read, that you know already all that can be said on so threadbare a subject. The verses I have read have served as the text for innumerable sermons; they have been expounded in various commentaries on the New Testament, and more fully discussed in special treatises on the parables; so that it seems as if all the lessons that could be learned from them must have been already fully drawn out. Yet every one who has studied the

Gospels must, from time to time, have felt how difficult it is to exhaust the meaning of any of our Lord's utterances. Trite and familiar as all His recorded words have become to us, yet some of them will at times come to our minds with new freshness, teaching us some lesson of which we have need, or presenting to us the key to some difficulty which had perplexed us; and we then seem to find in them a depth of wisdom which we had not suspected.

But how small a proportion do the recorded words of our Lord bear to those which He actually spoke. The fourth Evangelist has reminded us that any account of our Lord's earthly life must of necessity be imperfect, and that a complete record of every one of His deeds and sayings would require a work so voluminous as to be practically impossible. The discourses that have been, in fact, preserved were delivered on a comparatively small number of occasions, so that we must conclude that far the greater part of the teaching of our Lord during His sojourn in this world has been lost to the Church. Its effect, then, was only what it produced on the minds of the immediate hearers. And in many cases how small that effect must have been. We ourselves, as I have said, only learn in some degree to take in the full meaning of His words by dwelling on them, and meditating on them, and by learning from others who, under His Spirit's guidance, have succeeded in understanding what they were intended to teach. How little of them should we have known if we had only heard them once. But those who surrounded Him were dull of hearing beyond the least intelligent member of one of our ordinary congregations. We have been familiar from our childhood with our Lord's general manner of teaching, and with the leading principles of His doctrine, and, forgetful what help this has given us in apprehending His meaning, we are sometimes, perhaps unreasonably, amazed at what seems the strange stupidity of those who afterwards became the great teachers of His Church;—how they perplexed themselves by taking literally words which were plainly figurative, or by looking for some subtle signification in words which they knew not how to receive in their plain literal sense, as, for instance, when they were at a loss to understand what He could mean by speaking of His rising from the dead. Those who thus failed to understand Him were the best disposed, the most eager to learn, the most intelligent of His hearers. But how often must those about Him have been either unfriendly or careless,— men, perhaps, who whiled away an idle moment by listening to the popular teacher, but who were not likely to ponder over, or even retain in their memory, anything beyond some few of His most striking sayings, and those most probably distorted and misunderstood.

Thus we find that there once came into the world a Divine teacher, of whom hearers who came with no friendly intent were forced to confess that never man spake as He spake (and we know how infinitely below the truth were their conceptions of His heavenly wisdom), and that of immensely the larger part of His utterances no permanent record has been preserved. We have no reason to suppose that the sayings which have been lost to us were inferior in wisdom and suggestiveness to those that have been preserved. Again, there is every reason to believe that of all this great mass of teaching which was lost to the generations after the speaker, far the greater part was also without effect on the generation which heard Him, His words having been spoken to ears too prejudiced, or too careless, or too unprepared, to take in their meaning or appreciate their wisdom. The reflection, then, suggests itself, To what purpose was this waste?

Is it too bold to conjecture that such a thought may have troubled the human soul of our blessed Lord Himself as He saw how much of His labour was spent, as it would seem, in vain? At least we cannot but take notice of a certain difference of character between our Lord's discourses contained in the section from which the text is taken, and in other parts of the Gospels. Comparing the Gospels generally with the Epistles we cannot but perceive how much more in the former than in the latter the practical predominates over the speculative. A parable of our Lord usually presents to us a practical lesson taught, and taught in such a way that the hearer could never forget it. The parables, too, seem usually to have been suggested by thoughts which He saw passing in the minds of the hearers. He saw them trusting in themselves that they were righteous, and despising others, and He spoke the parable of the Pharisee and the Publican. He saw them expecting the immediate appearance of His kingdom, and He spoke the parable of the king who went into a far country. He saw them putting limitations to the extent of the commandment to love their neighbours as themselves, and He spoke the parable of the good Samaritan; or grudgingly measuring the limits within which they would accord their forgiveness of injuries, and in the parable of the unmerciful servant He so impressed His followers with a sense of the unbecomingness of an unforgiving spirit in men who had themselves need of forgiveness, that we find this lesson repeated by an Apostle who was not one of His personal hearers—" Be ye tender-hearted, forgiving one another, even as God, for Christ's sake, hath forgiven you." But the parables of which the text is one do not seem to have been suggested by any immediate wants of Christ's hearers; the difficulties with which they deal are such as were not likely to be felt by converts in the first enthusiasm of hope that He whom they were now prepared to acknowledge as the Messiah would win a speedy and complete triumph over His enemies. It was not just then that they would be perplexed with the difficulty how much of the work done for God in this world appears to be done in vain; how imperfect the success of that labour which seems not to have been altogether wasted. These difficulties are formidable to us who, after eighteen centuries of the preaching of Christ's Gospel, see so much still remaining to be done before the kingdoms of this world can become His; and it is a support to our faith under the trial of them that our Master from the first announced to us that such should be the character of His kingdom; but they are not the difficulties likely to have troubled the first disciples. So that, as I have said, these parables do not appear to have been suggested by any doubts which the Saviour saw to be troubling the minds of His hearers, nor by the immediate need to teach them any practical lesson, but they were meant to remove the stumbling-block which the imperfection of His success might place in the path of future disciples.

Our great English divine has made us familiar with the principle that the observation of analogies between God's mode of action in different provinces of His kingdom will often, if not completely remove all difficulties, at least immensely diminish their number, by showing us that what had seemed to be distinct difficulties are really but different examples of the working of the same general principle, the general principle being often easier to understand and account for than any of its particular applications. It may seem strange that in the many centuries of Christian speculative thought which preceded Bishop Butler, so little use should have been made of this line of argument; for the favourite method by which our great Master threw light on the problems of the spiritual world was to illustrate them by analogies from the world of nature. In the present case His preaching of the Word, with its widely diversified success, is illustrated by the analogy of the seeds which nature scatters in such bountiful and seemingly wasteful profusion; some lighting on beaten ground, where they perish without ever having made an attempt to germinate ; or it may be falling into shallow soil, where, though they begin to shoot, they can find nothing to support their growth ; or if they drop upon better earth, crushed out in the struggle for existence by other plants more congenial to the soil ; yet these local failures more than compensated by the success obtained when the seed finds its fitting home. Let it reach the good ground, and it multiplies thirty, sixty, a hundredfold ; that which is least among seeds growing into a tree, in whose branches the fowls of the air come and lodge.

To our Lord's hearers the one great practical lesson taught by the parable was, Take heed how ye hear. The same divine word sounded in the ears of every one in the crowds that thronged round Him. The same seed was cast upon every heart. Nothing was wanting to its excellence. If, in some cases, it bore abundant fruit, in others was without result, the difference was in the soil on which it fell :—whether it was received upon an honest and good heart, or in one hardened to spiritual impressions, or choked with cares for the riches or pleasures of this world. That same lesson remains for us that it is not enough that God's Word should be faithfully spoken to us ; our own hearts must be prepared to receive it, else the Word preached will not profit us.

But there is another lesson now that the Word of life is spoken, not by the lips of the Son of God, but by frail and erring men. Must we not say, Take heed how ye speak? For to each one of us has been the privilege bestowed, the duty entrusted to sow the good seed. Not merely words spoken in public, but words uttered in private, casually dropped, it may be, and without any intention to do good by them; not merely the set discourse of a clergyman, or a parent, or a teacher, but the chance remark of a young man to his companion, or perhaps of a child to his parent, or a learner to his teacher, may be the seed whence good fruit springs which shall endure to eternity.

But, alas, it is not only good seed which is thus sown. We read of an enemy who came, and while men slept, sowed tares among the wheat; and this enemy finds among men too many hands ready to do his work. And oh, how easily that work is done. One little sneer may shame away a vast amount of youthful enthusiasm for good. One cynical, uncharitable speech may wither up faith in the reality of unselfish goodness in others, without some belief in which there is not likely to be much of it in ourselves. One polluting tale may let loose in the mind of the hearer a riot of impure imaginations. There are those whose track in the world, as it would exhibit itself to an eye gifted to discern its spiritual aspect, would be marked by a thicket of noxious plants, the seeds of which he had abundantly strewn as he passed along. Nay, brethren, what of the seeds we sow ourselves? Are those seeds whereof fruit shall one day be gathered into life eternal; or shall it be that when the owner of the field shall take note of our life-work in the world, He shall say, "An enemy hath done this"?

It will repay us to dwell a little on the comparison of the text. The seed is the Word of God; or rather, since the chapter speaks not only of the good seed, but of the noxious seed sown by the enemy, we may say more generally, the seed is the word, whether spoken for God or for His enemy; and we may note how the germ of all our most important thoughts and resolves is the thought of other men which their words reveal to us.

II. The investigations of recent years have so forced us to take notice of the physical antecedents of thought, that there has resulted a tendency to look upon thought as a kind of material product. The brain secretes thought, some of the coarser materialists have said, as the liver secretes bile. But if we wish to see how completely *sui generis* thought is, we have only to take notice of the process by which thought is generated and sustained. No secreting organ in our system creates that which it secretes. Every particle of bile given out by the liver must have been contained in that which entered into the liver. The organ has done nothing but separate and form into new combinations the substance on which it acts. The chemist can find in the food the constituents of all the products of the animal frame. Is it so with our thoughts? Can we find them in the blood which courses along our veins and arteries, and which, entering into the blood-vessels of the brain, sustains the activity of that organ? Will a delicate analysis ever detect them in the food whence that blood was derived, and thus show that the brain does nothing but disentangle these thoughts from the envelope which had concealed them. Chemistry has taught how to vary the manure of a plant or the food of an animal according to the kind of product which he who rears them desires to obtain. Can we imagine that, in the progress of science, it will be discovered how the diet is to be varied, according as the product we desire to obtain is the poet's fine imagination, or the philosopher's deep speculation, or the mother's fond affection, or the martyr's stern resolve? If thought were matter, however cunningly transformed, matter would supply it. But thought can only be fed by thoughts. If we wish to write on any proposed subject, all that regimen can do is to keep our brain in a healthful state, fit for action, but the materials on which it works must be the thoughts of other men. Those of you who come here for education cannot be fitted for the work you have to do by any mere attention to your bodily well-being. By those wonderful means by which God has ordained that the thoughts of one mind can be communicated to another, you must be brought into contact with the thoughts of the wise and great men who have lived before you.

How little can the effect which words produce be estimated by any mechanical calculation of the force concerned in their production. When an orator holds a multitude entranced by the magic of his eloquence and sends them forth stirred up to some deed of mighty import, as, for instance, when Europe, roused by the voice of the preacher of the Crusades, precipitated itself on the East with the cry, "It is the will of God," it will be a wonderful theory of the transmutation of force which will explain, on mechanical principles, how the power which set the speaker's lips in motion, causing thereby certain undulations of the air, thence put in vibration certain membranes of the ear of those who heard, and thereby so changed the conditions of their bodies (for on materialist principles there is nothing else to change) that these machines were each constrained to move as the speaker had desired.

When matter is variously transformed, it is a principle of modern science that there always remains a conservation of energy. The force destroyed in one form reappears in another. Nor is it only a vague relation of succession which is ascertained to exist when we find, for instance, that arrested motion will develop heat, and that from heat we can derive motion. We can tell the exact amount of heat which will be generated by every pound weight of matter falling through every foot of space, and the same heat can be used to reproduce the same amount of motion. But where are our measures when we compare mental results with their physical antecedents? When death removes one to whom a Church or a nation has looked up as a guide and a counsellor, what consolation has science found for mourners gazing on the pale cold lips whence they shall hear wise words of counsel no more? Can she apply now her doctrine of the conservation of energy? Can she tell those who know their loss too well that nothing really is gone, that they have still in other forms an equivalent for what seems to have departed? Nay, he who is dead may yet speak, but it is only as his words and deeds live in the memory of the survivors. And if some comfort stronger than this is needed, Christianity, not science, must supply it.

Again, we cannot trace to any transformation of matter the resolutions of the human will. If we wish to sustain in another a fixed resolve, chemistry has discovered no volition-generating substances, by introducing which into his bodily frame we can make his will as strong as we desire. The suggestion of a thought can make the weakest able to baffle the tyrant's utmost force. Often has a confessor dragged before the tribunal of his judge a frame worn out with imprisonment, wasted by fasting and hardships: if the will be but a form of bodily action, all that cruelty can do to enfeeble the body has been freely used; yet it has been used in vain, and that though exerted on those whose age or sex made them least able to resist. The tender virgin has been stronger than the persecutor who could take her life, but not make her deny her Lord. The weight of eighty-six years did not bow down the resolution of a Polycarp never to change the Master whose goodness he had so long experienced. And if in that hour of trial external support has helped to keep the resolution from wavering, the support has not been given to the body, but it has been supplied through the medium of words to the mind. As in the Jewish story of old, the mother has exhorted her sons to give to the torture the bodies which her womb had borne rather than forsake the God who had given those bodies life, and who of His mercy could give them breath and life again.[1] In one of the earliest authentic records of Christian martyrdom we read of the sufferings of a young lad who expired in torture, and we are told how the heathen spectators could mark that what had kept his resolution unshaken was the words of a fellow-sufferer, a tender woman, subjected to still greater variety and intensity of torture.[2] And in other equally well-known stories of martyrdom in the ancient Church and in our own, the son has bid the father not to change his resolution through anxiety for the children whom he was leaving behind, and the wife has cried to the husband, whose life was dearer to her than her own, to yield that life rather than deny his faith. What physical agent could communicate the force which the breath of these few words administered?

III. Thought then, and nothing else, is the food of thought. The word is the medium by which that food is supplied. But, as suggested by the parable we have been studying, the word

[1] 2 Macc., vii. 21-29.   [2] Euseb., *Ecc. Hist.*, v. 2, vi. 2.

is but the seed. If the world is wiser now than it was four thousand years ago; if we have now more knowledge, more power over nature, it all results from this, that the thought of one man passing into the mind of another does not remain untransformed. Of little worth is the instruction which makes the pupil the mere echo of his teacher. True it is that, as in the world of nature, seeds without number fall, and are not incorporated with the soil into which they drop, and so they lie ineffective, and after a little time no trace of them appears. But let them fall upon the good ground, and the produce will often be as much greater than itself, as the tree in whose branches the fowls of the air rest is greater than the little germ from which it sprung. I suppose we may assume that the great work of Butler, to which I have already referred, was suggested by the remark of Origen which he quotes at the beginning, yet under how many eyes before Butler's time had the remark passed without suggesting anything. And how little probably was Origen himself aware of all that was contained in the principle which he employed.

This is but one example out of a thousand how a thought expands and fructifies. But need we any other example than that which is suggested by the result of our Lord's own teaching? For what has been the history of the religious thought of the civilised world for the last eighteen hundred years but that of the attempt to draw out all the lessons that are involved in the words which He spake during the years of His earthly sojourn, or rather in that fraction of these words which in God's providence has been preserved?

I have said how our word is the seed of thought in others, but I ought not to omit to notice how it is also the seed of thought in ourselves. Our thought, while unexpressed, is vague and unfruitful; but the process of giving it shape in words suggests a multitude of new thoughts. As we formulate our ideas their mutual relations disclose themselves in a way we had not perceived before; and often it happens that a difficulty which had perplexed us, when drawn out and distinctly put into words, suggests its own solution. Our beliefs, too, do not attain the strength of convictions until they are put into words. It sometimes happens that our reason leads us to a conclusion at variance with our prejudices, and we are afraid of it, and suspect it to be mere paradox; but no sooner have we committed ourselves by making known our opinion to others than the difficulties which had deterred us are seen to be unsubstantial, and quite melt away. Our purposes again are easily altered, until, by the expression of our resolution, we pledge ourselves to them. Thus it has been that since the commencement of our religion no one was accounted really a Christian until he had publicly expressed his belief in our faith, and his resolution to shape his life in conformity with it; and so, while with the heart man believeth unto righteousness, with the mouth confession is made unto salvation.

The considerations on which I have dwelt lead to some important lessons for those who own it to be their duty to help in sowing the Divine seed in the world. Their work is but to sow seed. In any mechanical labour the result obtained is the exact equivalent of the work expended, and the workman may fairly count himself the author of the product. It is not so with him who sows a seed. He may go his way, and sleep and rise, and the seed will spring up he knows not how. For other forces then have taken up the work— the expansive power of the seed itself, the nourishing elements of the soil, the rain and the sun from heaven. These give the increase; these bring the seed to maturity; and the result may be out of all proportion to the labour originally expended. And it is only in a subordinate sense that he who sowed the seed can be called the author of the harvest. He is so in the sense that without him the result would not have taken place; but he has done no more than call other forces into operation, and the work is theirs, not his.

I have already spoken of the lesson of responsibility that follows from what has been said, the duty of taking heed what seeds we sow. For as the seed we sow may multiply sixty or a hundredfold, that which might be considered trifling as far as it merely affects ourselves may show itself in a very exaggerated form in our work upon others. Nor shall I delay to dwell on the lesson of humility taught to those whose privilege it has been to do any successful work for God in the world—a lesson which St. Paul has drawn from the same image, reminding his converts that it was God's husbandry they were. Paul had planted, Apollos had watered; but it was God who had given the increase. But a few words may be said as to the lesson of encouragement to those who, while desirous to work for God, are conscious of feeble powers, and despondent because such work as they have done shows little signs of success. With respect to feebleness of powers it is sufficient to say that it does not require great power to cast a seed. In other words, the reflection how very small a part of the work is really ours is one that not only suggests humility to the successful but encouragement to the despondent; for if they honestly fulfil, to the best of their ability, the task committed to them, they call into action forces far more powerful than they. The good seed which they sow has a Divine power of its own, and when it falls into an honest and good heart, and is watered with blessing from above, its growth is not affected by any weakness in the first planter.

But no sign of success appears. Well, it is not to be expected that every seed cast should spring up. When our Lord in His own person sowed the seed, it was but a small minority of His hearers in whose hearts the word spoken took root and bore fruit. And in those cases where the seed takes root neither does the fruit appear at once, nor does he who sowed it always know of it. I suppose every one can tell of decisions on some important occasions influenced by words which were not spoken with any intention of influencing them, and of the effect of which the speakers were never aware. Most persons, too, can tell of new views of things or of the character of persons to which their eyes were first opened by things said to them or said in their hearing; and it is not wonderful that the speakers should often be ignorant of this effect of their words, since the hearers might frequently find it difficult themselves to recall the origin of their changed opinions. Again, I daresay it has occurred to many who hear me to be surprised, and not always agreeably surprised, at finding that words of their own which had almost vanished from their memory had lived in the memory of others. It is indeed remarkable how long these buried seeds of thought retain their vitality. When Irenæus in advanced life records his youthful recollections of Polycarp, and tells how well he remembered the personal appearance of the great teacher, his manner of going out and coming in, and the general character of his discourses, he relates no uncommon experience when he says that these memories of his boyhood were more distinct than of events of quite recent occurrence. Any one who reflects on such facts will see how utterly impossible it is for any one to measure the influence his words may exert; and, observing how some seeds perish and others of less apparent promise live, must allow that despondence about our work is just as irrational as pride in it. The true lesson to be drawn from the uncertainty of the results of human work, the failure of some labours that seem to deserve success, and the blessing granted to others which seem less worthy of it, is that which the wise man drew long since, that we must have faith, regardless of results, to persevere in every good work our hand findeth to do. "In the morning sow thy seed, and in the evening withhold not thy hand, for thou knowest not whether shall prosper either this or that, or whether they both shall be alike good." "Cast thy bread upon the waters, for thou shalt find it after many days."

In conclusion, let me remind you once more that every one of us stands in the double position of sowing and receiving seed, and accordingly that we have the double practical duty of taking heed not only how we speak, but how we hear. In order that the seed may produce its effect, it must be received into an honest and good heart. No practical lesson would follow from this if it were true, as was taught by some heretics of old, that there are born into the world essentially different classes of men. On such a supposition nothing would be in our power. If an honest and good heart were not originally ours, we might mourn over the fact, but we could not change it. But far otherwise is the fact. Gracious influences from above are present with every one of you which, if you quench them not, will prepare your heart to receive the word which is able to save your souls. The condition of the soil, far from being fixed once for all, is in course of perpetual change. If warnings be neglected, if sin be yielded to, that soil which once seemed to yield a ready reception to the good seed may be so hardened that what is sown can find no entrance there. Or if the weeds, as they spring, be carefully cleared away, the place where once the good seed would have been so choked that it could yield no fruit to perfection, may be so improved that what is sown there will increase a hundredfold. Our Lord, in connection with this parable, taught the wonderful power which the seed, when received, has to prepare the ground for the reception of more seed. " Take heed how ye hear, *for* unto you that hear shall more be given ; for he that hath, to him shall be given ; 'from him that hath not, shall be taken even that which he hath." Beware, then, how you stifle any remonstrance of conscience, how you turn a deaf ear to any presented call of duty ; for it is thus that with your own consent the good seed is carried away from you, and then if through your own fault you be found to have not, there will be no injustice if the sentence be inflicted on you that from you shall be taken even that you have.

X

LEANING ON MAN'S OWN UNDERSTANDING.

"Trust in the Lord with all thine heart, and lean not unto thine own understanding. In all thy ways acknowledge Him, and He shall direct thy paths."—PROVERBS iii. 5.

"Boast not thyself of to-morrow; for thou knowest not what a day may bring forth."—PROVERBS xxvii. 1.

THE precept, "Lean not unto thine own understanding," is one in which, with advancing years, we are well disposed to acquiesce. In the days when we first awake to the real independent exercise of our intellectual powers, the light they give seems so bright and clear that we feel we may justly put confidence in it. We are weaned from the docility of childhood by being led, first timidly to suspect, afterwards distinctly to see, that those whom we had venerated as guides have fallen into error. And in our inexperience, ignorant that liability to error is not so uncommon that a proved lapse into it entitles us to deem a man inferior to his fellows, we despise our former masters, and, regardless of their authority, form our own conclusions. The more able and clear-headed a young man is, the more dogmatic and intolerant he is likely to be, the more impatient of the stupidity and prejudice which prevent others from seeing things as plainly as they appear to himself.

But one who has grown older, and who has really profited by the experience of life, must often have found cause to revise his own judgments. The problems to be solved turn out to be far from being so simple as they had once appeared to him. Many things that had once seemed clear to him he now finds were so because he had only seen half the case, and had not confused his judgment by fairly looking at both sides of the question. Demonstrations that he had regarded as irrefragable, and which might have been sound enough as far as regards the logical process of drawing conclusions from premises, he now finds to have been vitiated by his having taken for granted, without sufficient proof, the truth of the premises on which his argument was based. Thus he comes to lean less confidently on his own understanding, and at the same time to think with little respect of dogmatism in others. The shallowest waters are those which it is easiest to see to the bottom of. And the man who is always very clear in his views, who is quite sure that he has sounded the depths of every question, and is confident that there is nothing in it which he has not taken account of, is most likely to have simplified the problems for himself by leaving out all that constitutes their real difficulty.

What I have said relates mainly to the abatement of confidence in our decision of questions merely speculative. But it is much easier to be modest as to the wisdom of our practical decisions. On our right choice of a course of action much of our future happiness may depend, and yet we cannot feel certain that we are choosing correctly. We know that our discernment of character is far from infallible, and that those in whom we put confidence may prove unworthy of our trust. But even if we make no such mistake, things beyond our control play so important a part in the affairs of life that the best laid schemes are liable to disappointment, and the most far-seeing of men must feel uncertainty as to the success of his calculations for the future. In this world of change and sorrow experience soon teaches us the lesson, "Boast not thyself of to-morrow, for thou knowest not what a day may bring forth." The child finds its day of expected pleasure, long looked forward to, marred by some unexpected impediment; later on he may have to tell of a life's happiness wrecked because the person on whom his hopes of the future were built, and without whom he can have either no success or no enjoyment of his success, has been taken away. Sudden reverses overtake the most prosperous; the most sagacious make blunders through which their inferiors discover, with pleased surprise, that these wise men were, after all, not so much wiser than themselves.

The result of such experience might seem to be general distrust of the powers of the human intellect, but happily the exigencies of life save us from the danger of any unreasonable scepticism. We must act, and it is continually necessary for us to decide between different courses of action. In order to guide our practical decisions we cannot help having a mass of speculative beliefs, the truth of which we cannot allow ourselves to question without paralysing our energy. But as experience convinces us of the weakness of our understanding and our liability to go wrong notwithstanding all the light it gives us, we should all be glad if there could be supplied us any way of arriving at our beliefs which we might safely trust without the necessity of leaning on our own understanding. It is thus that the claim of the Roman Catholic Church to infallibility has been willingly admitted by multitudes who, persuaded of the immense importance of being able to give right answers to all questions of theology that may be proposed, but distrusting their own competence to answer them, gladly accept the assurance of an authority which undertakes to guarantee them against all responsibility.

So likewise in practical matters, men trembling with anxiety for the result of decisions as to which they could not see their way distinctly, have eagerly caught at what they imagined to be Divine indications of the right way. In times past it was regarded the part of wisdom to register omens and auguries; and it is whimsical to read, that in the greatest military nation of antiquity it was thought that the question whether a general ought to accept or refuse battle might properly be decided by observing whether or not a chicken had an appetite for its dinner. To disregard such indications was considered a presumptuous leaning on one's own understanding, after which no disaster need be wondered at.[1]

It is not in the Church of Rome only, nor in the superstitions of heathenism only, that the precept, Lean not on thine own understanding, has

[1] Nihil nos P. Claudii bello Punico primo temeritas movebit, qui etiam per jocum deos irridens, quum cavea liberati pulli non pascerentur, mergi eos in aquam jussit; ut biberent, quoniam esse nollent. Qui risus, classe devicta, multas ipsi lacrymas, magnum populo Romano cladem adtulit. Quid? Collega ejus Junius eodem bello nonne tempestate classem amisit, quum auspiciis non paruisset?—Cic., *De Nat. Deor.*, ii. 3.

been interpreted to mean, Lean on some one else's understanding, and that it has been stigmatised as insane pride of the human intellect if men presume to prove all things, and are unable to accept what others propound to them as correct interpretations of the Divine will. I may as well state here at once that I believe that the words of the first text I have read, when considered together with their context, will be found to have no connection with the use that is sometimes made of them. When we want to know what is meant by wisdom and understanding in the Book of Proverbs, we can find no better commentary than the saying in the Book of Job—"The fear of the Lord that is wisdom, and to depart from evil that is understanding;" or in the words of the Book of Proverbs itself—"The fear of the Lord is the beginning of wisdom, and the knowledge of the holy is understanding." The wise man of the Book of Proverbs is he who walks in the ways of holiness, who "understands the fear of the Lord, and finds the knowledge of God." If a man fancies that he can make a better calculation for his own happiness than by obedience to God's law, he miserably deceives himself; his wisdom is foolishness. Appearances may be in his favour. "But though a sinner do evil an hundred times and his days be prolonged, yet surely I know that it shall be well with them that fear God which fear before Him. But it shall not be well with the wicked, neither shall he prolong his days, which are as a shadow, because he feareth not before God." This, then, is what the writer of this part of the Book of Proverbs means to say in the words of the text. Be not deceived by any suggestions of the human heart which would lead you to fancy that God's precepts are not wise, and that you can find happiness in any ways which are not the ways of holiness. "Be not wise in thine own eyes, fear the Lord, and depart from evil." The paths of sin may seem to you smooth and easy; His way may appear rough and thorny; but walk in the path that He has marked out for you, and have faith to be assured that that will be the way which leadeth to life. "Trust in the Lord with all thine heart, and lean not unto thine own understanding. In all thy ways acknowledge Him, and He shall direct thy paths." The words of the text, then, contain no injunction to us to put out the candle of the Lord within us, that reason which supplies the light whereby we must walk, but only an injunction to us to hold fast the best conclusion which true wisdom furnishes, namely the conviction that it must be a vain search to look for happiness in any ways but His.

To come back, then, to the questions which

I commenced by discussing:—in matters of speculative belief, and still more in practical matters, we have no option but in some form or another to be guided by our own understanding. If we are acting as rational beings and not as mere straws blown by the wind, whatever line we embrace, we must be led by some reasons for embracing it which commend themselves to us as good. We may not have balanced for ourselves arguments for and against, but may have acquiesced in the decision of some authority; but then our understanding must approve the wisdom of submitting to that authority. At some stage or other a decision of our judgment must be the foundation of our action. Those who consider themselves safe in following the guidance of a Church which they deem infallible must still, if they are rational beings, have had some reason for adopting the opinion that their Church is infallible, and if that belief cannot be justified, then there is no certainty of anything they have received on her authority. It is quite true that the great bulk of our beliefs has not been attained by any process of independent reasoning. We catch our beliefs from others; a great part in childhood from our parents and instructors; more from our equals when we grow up. But however obtained, our beliefs are bound when challenged to justify themselves to our reason. If they fail to do this, their perishing is but a question of time.

I have seen an attempt made to show that the Roman Catholic is the only form of the Christian faith which is likely to survive the struggle with modern unbelief. Sentence of failure was passed on all Protestant attempts to defend their faith by argument. As it is now the favourite method of making converts to Romanism to scare them into the bosom of the true Church by the fear of scepticism, so Roman Catholic controversialists seem to look with a kind of satisfaction on the efforts of sceptical writers whom they believe to be doing their work, and are apt to rate at the very highest the success which such writers are able to achieve. Their own Church they can boast does not commit the fundamental error of endeavouring to justify herself by argument. She contents herself with demanding submission, and calling on men blindly to follow her guidance. They are to wait for proofs until they are in her bosom, or rather they are to continue their allegiance until they can prove that she is leading them wrong. And as, when once they have yielded themselves, they are taught that it is a sin to doubt or question anything she propounds to them, I am not prepared to deny that if the arguments on the side of unbelief are really the strongest, this may be the best way for keeping men as long as possible from yielding assent to them. But, after all, it is little to gain for any denomination of Christians only the boon of the Cyclops, to be devoured last. It is difficult, indeed, to believe even in the good faith of an advocate who builds his hopes for the success of his cause on the pertinacity with which it can evade a trial. I can understand a man refusing to listen to imputations on the character of a friend in whom he has perfect confidence. But if he gave as a reason for refusing to listen, that he was assured that the result of any examination would certainly be unfavourable, and that all who ventured to bring his friend's character to the test would be sure to think ill of him, how could men believe that he himself seriously thought well of him?

In sum, then, however little right we have so presumptuously to trust to our understanding as to dogmatise, as if there were no chance of our committing a mistake, the understanding God has given us is a trust, the responsibility of which we cannot shake off, and for refusing to use which we should certainly be guilty. I have joined together in what I have said our liability to go wrong in speculative and in practical matters, because of the light one throws on the other. If we think it hard to have to use our own judgment in forming beliefs which, if erroneous, may have consequences beyond the grave, let us consider how God deals with us in respect to the affairs of this life; how He disciplines us by throwing on us the responsibility of making decisions which may have the most serious results on our earthly happiness; how He does not save us from this responsibility even when the knowledge necessary to a correct decision is wanting to us; yet how, out of all our errors, He works out the ultimate good of those who put their trust in Him.

The truth that we know not what a day may bring forth seems to give a most disheartening view of human life. We have the burden cast on us of directing our own way, while yet the light by which to guide it is denied us. We have, as it were, to steer our ship, enveloped in a dense fog. Sometimes the fog lifts a little immediately in front of us. We use such skill as we may in avoiding the dangers which we discern; yet it may be that the events of the morrow prove that that course which seemed to us most prudent was in reality exceedingly unwise, and that in turning aside from one danger we have run in the way of a far more formidable one. And then when such evil comes upon us, it is a painful reflection that it was brought on us by our own act; that we should never have met with it if we had not missed the right turn at one of the turning points of our life, and when we might have chosen a path of safety, struck into one that led us to calamity. Arising out of this is a very natural and a very common feeling to shrink from the responsibility of making for ourselves one of the great decisions of our lives. We hesitate, and exclaim, Oh, if we could only tell what would come of it. We are glad if we can find any one to tell us with authority what is wisest for us to do. If no such person can be found, we are often willing to be guided by chance, and if circumstances should present some impediment to our taking one of the two courses between which we are hesitating, even though it is an impediment which we could easily overcome, we are yet willing to accept the existence of that hindrance as an indication that we may choose the other path, and think that if we meet misfortune there, we have not chosen it for ourselves. The wisest of us are scarcely free from superstition in this matter. We do not now own to having regard to omens; we do not break off a journey because a hare has crossed our path, or because a raven has croaked. But if a proposal to enter on a new line of action comes to us in some unexpected way, not sought after by ourselves, but suggested to us by some seemingly chance concurrence of events, we are apt to fancy that here we can discern a special indication of the Divine will; and that in accepting it we are trusting to the Lord, not leaning on our own understanding. And it is not uncommon to hear clergymen, when they have resolved on separating from a beloved people, justify themselves by considerations of this kind rather than by the more obvious inducements that the post to which they move is better paid, more honourable, and opens up greater prospects of usefulness.

Yet our reason might tell us that the responsibility of making a decision is one that we cannot escape. Whenever we are called on to act, we may act according to our own judgment of what is best to be done, or we may trust ourselves to the judgment of another; but then it is an act of our own to choose to whose guidance we shall commit ourselves, and if we choose an incompetent guide, we shall be the sufferers. If the blind choose the blind to lead them, both fall into the ditch. Or if we even abandon our course to be guided by chance, still the decision to do so is made on our own responsibility. It is we who interpret the chances; it is we who often unconsciously guide them, like skilful generals, seizing on the chances which lead in the direction to which our wishes incline, and disregarding those which point in the opposite direction. At all events the decision, however determined, is ours, and should evil befall us on the path we take, we have cause to blame ourselves, if by using more forethought we could have avoided it.

In this connection I would venture to criticise lines we often hear sung in church, though that was scarcely the use for which their author intended them—

"I do not ask to see
The distant scene; one step enough for me."

The beautiful verses, of which they are part, have gone to the hearts of many who have keenly felt that human wisdom is all too feeble to guide them through the darkness in which they have to grope their way. And if no more is meant than that we must thankfully use the light God has given us, without murmuring because He has not given us more, I have nothing to object. But if, when sufficient light has been given us, we take one step without looking where we shall next have to put our foot, this is mental indolence, not Christian faith. I make the remark because I cannot help suspecting that the author's own history illustrates the error I condemn, and that sometimes, when considering whether or not he would accept a principle, he rejected as a presumptuous looking too far forward the examination what consequences that acceptance would involve. Certain it is that since he joined the Church of Rome he has had to acknowledge doctrines as true which at the time he joined, and for some time after, he believed to be false. But he considers that by his acknowledgment of the Church's infallibility he accepted not only all the doctrines she had propounded at the time, but also all that she might subsequently propound, and that he is now precluded from reopening the question. Had he then taken into account the possibility of those subsequent definitions at the time he made his acknowledgment, or had he set that question aside as a looking at the distant scene instead of to the one step he was about to take? If a chess-player made it a rule that he would never look more than one move forward, it is very likely that he would soon find all his subsequent moves forced consequences of that one, but not so likely that he would bring his game to a prosperous termination.

It is natural to fall into the same sin as that for which the wicked and slothful servant was punished, who, because only one talent was entrusted to him, thought it not worth while to improve so small a fund, but laid his talent up in a napkin. When circumstances force us to see how small a way our prudence can reach, and how unforeseen events will disappoint the best concerted plans, it is a natural impulse to pronounce it to be useless that we should attempt at all to plan or to look forward. Yet we are bound to use God's gifts as conscientiously, whether they be large or small. If evil befall us, we have cause to blame ourselves if we have encountered it solely through our own recklessness, or through neglect to use the means which God has put within our reach for avoiding it. But we have no cause to blame ourselves should temporal suffering meet us in a path which we have chosen in prayer for God's guidance, and in accordance with the best judgment we could form at the time. The course of events may prove our judgment to have been erroneous, and we may then be tempted to complain that if we had acted otherwise we might have escaped all misfortune. But it is dealing unjust measure to ourselves to blame ourselves for our past decisions because at the time of making them we had not a knowledge of then future events. There is no more unprofitable waste of time—there is nothing more irritating to the spirit—than to go back over the past and bring against ourselves the accusation that if we had not acted thus, such a thing would not have happened, though at the time there was no good reason why we should not have acted as we did. Temporal sufferings which we meet in this way must be regarded as discipline sent us by God as really as if He Himself, by a voice from heaven, had directed us into the path where we met it.

For this is the truth which removes all sadness from the reflection that we know not what shall be on the morrow, that while a man's heart deviseth his way, it is the Lord who directeth his steps. That fog bank through which we wade, and which prevents us from rightly shaping our course, really extends but a little way. Above it and beyond it the sun shines bright, and in that full blaze of light is He whose guidance will never be refused us when we seek it, and whose protection has power to secure us from all danger. A child may be frightened in the dark, but his fears abate when he feels the grasp of his parent's hand. So, though the path which we tread may be dark and gloomy, we can walk it with courage if we feel that we have our Father and our Saviour with us. The Psalmist found it so long since when he said, "Though I walk through the Valley of the Shadow of Death, I will fear no evil, for Thou art with me."

I am far from saying or thinking that when we are in doubt how to choose, and beseech God to guide us, we may rely on it that He will protect us from choosing the path that leads to suffering, and will turn our feet into a prosperous way. His will respecting us may be different. But we may be sure that if we do encounter suffering on a path which we have chosen in prayer for His guidance, we may regard it as sent by Him, and may accept it as His loving chastisement. And this is what consoles us if we sometimes seem condemned to draw with blinded eyes a lot from the urn of our fate; to know that in truth it is a lottery in which there are all prizes and no blanks. Does this seem to any too strong a saying? It is not stronger than what the Apostle has told us —"We know that *all* things work together for good to them that love God." Just as in the world of nature the bounty of God sends from heaven the irrigating rain, and makes the ripening sun to shine, while He permits man to choose in what form this bounty shall shape itself; whether it shall clothe his fields with green pastures, or his hills with forest trees, or make his valleys smile with waving corn, or adorn his gardens with gay flowers to delight his sight with their colours and his scent with their fragrant perfume; so it is that if they who love God had faith to know it, when they are hesitating what course they shall take in reference to things of this earth, they are only hesitating in what form they will receive a blessing. One path may lead to temporal prosperity; and if that be accepted as a Father's gift, not enjoyed apart from Him or in forgetfulness of Him; if the good things which He sends be regarded as a stewardship to be administered for Him, then, instead of separating us from Him, they may bring us nearer Him, and may gain from Him the commendation, "Well done, thou good and faithful servant, thou hast been faithful in a few things; I will make thee ruler over many things." The other path may lead to trials and sorrows, yet will it be no proof of want of love that He has permitted us to enter on this way; for whom the Lord loveth He chasteneth. Just as under our cloud-mantled skies many a sweet-smelling and useful plant comes to maturity, which would have withered under the undimmed blaze of a tropical sun, so does many a grace ripen under the clouds of adversity, for whose exercise unmixed prosperity could afford no room. Were our own will always accomplished, we should not learn resignation to our Father's will, patience under His dispensations, confidence that He doeth all things well even though to our eyes it seem not so. We should not learn a lowly estimate of ourselves, since it is so very natural to accept the good things we enjoy as our due, fancying that it is in consequence of some peculiar desert of ours that we have more than others; nor should we learn that power of sympathising with the sorrow of others, which can scarcely be acquired by one who has himself never known anything of affliction or sorrow.

It is not only the prosperous man, who has goods laid up for many years, that makes the mistake of acting and thinking as if this world were to be his home for ever; often does the mourner murmur at his lot, forgetting that the brief time of his earthly sojourn is the time when the character is to be moulded in him which is to be his throughout eternity; the time when the Son of God is to be formed in him here if he is to be His for ever. Has he any cause of complaint if God subordinates the happiness of his short stay here to the training him for eternal happiness, if, by His blessed retribution, He compensates brief sorrow, short-lived care, with eternal rest, and uses light affliction which endureth but a moment, to work for him a far more exceeding and eternal weight of glory?

And hereafter, when we look back upon these earthly sorrows, how light and short will they appear. How short is sorrow to look back upon which has been the necessary condition of joy. Our Lord says—"A woman, when she is in travail, hath sorrow because her hour is come; but as soon as she is delivered of the child, she remembereth no more the anguish for joy that a man is born into the world." How interminable, as they are passing, seem the hours of a stormy voyage, yet when we have been a little time on land, in the midst of the friends whom we came to meet, our troubles are forgotten. How small now appear to us the troubles of our childhood, real though they were at the time, when perhaps we murmured at restraints or denials of our requests which then seemed harsh, but which now we know were dictated by the truest love.

Nor need we always wait for another life to know the need be of our present sorrows. In the text we read, " Boast not thyself of to-morrow, for thou knowest not what a day may bring forth." Sometimes there are those who need to be comforted with the exhortation—Despair not of to-morrow, for thou knowest not what a day may bring forth. Does the future seem to you all dark, is your day all overcast with clouds, and can you see nowhere any prospect of brightening? Perhaps the moment when your heart is most chilled with doubts may be that which the Lord will choose to lift up the light of His countenance upon you. Hear, in that beautiful 126th Psalm, the experience of men to whom deliverance came in so unexpected a form that they could scarcely believe themselves awake when they heard of it, and could not restrain the laughter which naturally arises when we meet with anything utterly strange and improbable. "When the Lord turned again the captivity of Zion, then were we like unto them that dream; then was our mouth filled with laughter and our tongue with joy. Then said they among the heathen, The Lord hath done great things for them. Yea, the Lord hath done great things for us already, whereof we rejoice. They that sow in tears shall reap in joy. He that now goeth on his way weeping, and beareth forth good seed, shall doubtless come again with joy, and bring his sheaves with him."

In sum, then, we have no right to say that God has dealt ill with us, though He has ordained that we should guide our course by a light so feeble and uncertain as that of our understanding. If because that light is not as full as we should wish it to be, we disdain to use it, and think that though we may not lean on our own understanding, we may lean implicitly on that of other men; if we take up our speculative opinions without reason, and let our practical decisions be guided by chance, then whatever evils befall us we shall have justly encountered as the deserved penalty of our perverse rejection of the means of avoiding them. But it is otherwise if we have in the truest sense followed God's guidance, by cultivating with conscientious care those faculties which He has given to lead us, and made the best decisions we are able with such wisdom as He has bestowed on us. Our calculations may be wrong; the events of the morrow may prove that we have entered on a stormy sea when we deemed we were embarking on smooth waters. But in any storm we shall have Him with us.

And if Scripture sometimes teaches us to say, "We know not," still oftener it teaches us to say, "We know." We know not what shall be on the morrow, but "*we know* that all things work together for good to them that love God." "*We know* that He hears us whatsoever we ask," and "*we know* that we have the petitions that we desired of Him." "*We know* that the Son of God is come, and hath given us an understanding that we may know Him that is true; and we are in Him that is true, even in His Son, Jesus Christ." "*We know* that Christ was manifested to take away our sins." "*We know* that when He shall appear, we shall be like Him, for we shall see Him as He is." "*We know* that if our earthly house of this tabernacle were dissolved, we have a building of God, an house not made with hands, eternal in the heavens."

XI

WISDOM

"Unto man He said, Behold, the fear of the Lord that is wisdom, and to depart from evil is understanding."—JOB xxviii. 28.

THE maxim of the text appears in slightly different forms in more than one of the Old Testament books. In one of the Easter Day Psalms we have—"The fear of the Lord is the beginning of wisdom; a good understanding have all they that do thereafter; the praise of it endureth for ever." And so again in the Book of Proverbs—"The fear of the Lord is the beginning of wisdom, and the knowledge of the Holy is understanding." And in several other of Solomon's Proverbs the same idea is expressed in slightly different words.

The name of Solomon has become proverbial among ourselves for wisdom. He deeply impressed his contemporaries both by his acquired knowledge and by his natural sagacity. He was held to be wiser than all men. His wisdom excelled the wisdom of all the children of the East Country and all the wisdom of Egypt. He was wiser than all whom the Hebrews of his day reverenced as sages, wiser than Ethan the Ezrahite, wiser than Heman, and Chalcol, and Darda. His fame was in all nations round about, and travellers came from distant lands to see his riches and to hear his wisdom. Yet in great part of the Book of Proverbs the word wisdom is used only as the name of a quality in which Solomon was confessedly not pre-eminent; only as another name for goodness and the fear of God. The more, however, we think of the matter, the more reason we shall see to be convinced that other qualities which have been honoured by the name of wisdom are but vain pretenders to that title, and that this alone in truth deserves it.

First—wisdom is not learning. A great part of what his contemporaries admired in Solomon consisted of the accumulated mass of facts with which his memory was stored. He could speak of trees from the cedar that is in Lebanon even unto the hyssop that springeth out of the wall; he could speak also of beasts and of fowl, of creeping things and of fishes. Yet it is an observation we are constantly forced to make, how much a man may know, and yet what a fool he may be. Even in his own subject, his industry in acquiring knowledge may easily outrun his power to make profitable use of it; and from weakness of judgment the opinions he forms on the subjects on which he has bestowed most labour may be absolutely entitled to no respect.[1] But even if he is completely successful in his own department, whether or not it be as common as men of the world are apt to think, it is assuredly common enough that a man may be a very great scholar and yet a simpleton in all that concerns the practical affairs of daily life. That Solomon, for instance, with all his wisdom was a wise ruler, we have not the slightest reason to suppose. He did successfully accomplish the ends which he made it his ambition to attain; but, as usually is the case with Eastern rulers, those ends concerned rather the magnificence of the sovereign than the real welfare of the people. He struck out new commercial enterprises, but these probably carried on as monopolies for his personal benefit, and adding nothing to the wealth of the nation. They enabled him to astonish his subjects with the sight of foreign luxuries not brought to Jerusalem before; horses and fine linen from Egypt, gold, and ivory, and apes, and peacocks imported from the distant East. Thus the Hebrew monarchy was, in his time, maintained in unprecedented grandeur, and the splendour of his Court surpassed all that his

[1] Mr. Casaubon, in *Middlemarch*, belongs to a type of which specimens constantly present themselves.

people had ever heard of, nor probably did either he or they for some time consider whether all this costly splendour did not overpass the resources of the small state which he governed. He had an enormous harem of 700 wives and 300 concubines; he had magnificent palaces at Jerusalem, summer palaces at Lebanon, stately gardens, golden plate in such abundance that silver was nothing accounted of in his reign. The hasty reader is so impressed with all that is told of this magnificence that he often fails to take notice of what is also told of the cost at which it was kept up, the *corvées* of forced labour, the grinding taxation of the subjects. We find that on the king's death the oppressed people insisted on an absolute change of system, and, failing to obtain it, hurled his dynasty from the throne; while all the wealth that had been brought together only served as a lure to attract the foreign invader, and in five years from Solomon's death Jerusalem had been taken, and all the accumulated riches carried off to Egypt.

Again, wisdom is not cleverness:—though it is often mistaken for it, especially by the young who are apt to give to a certain kind of intellectual ability a great deal more of admiration than it deserves. I refer to that kind of ability which finds it easy to invent arguments in favour of any line of action it wishes to commend, which is not easily taken by surprise, is ready with plausible answers to objections, and can throw into the most attractive form the reasons for coming to the desired conclusion. All this, however, is but the cleverness of the advocate; what we really want for our practical guidance is the wisdom of the judge. Suppose that a man urges us to go the way that it is contrary to our real interests to go, the more persuasive is his eloquence, the greater his skill in producing reasons for the wrong course, the greater the mischief he does to those that give ear to him, and to himself if he believes in his own arguments. So, again, in mere literary or scientific investigations, where we are not concerned with action, the cleverness which can maintain an ingenious paradox, or which can so marshal arguments as to make a false explanation of facts appear satisfactory, may receive admiration from the unthinking, but only disgusts him whose sole wish is to know what is the truth. It is natural that in our free country an exaggerated value should be attached to that oratorical or argumentative power which characterises the successful advocate; for skill to form the wisest schemes of statesmanship would be a barren gift if not accompanied by the ability to commend to others the conclusions which have been arrived at. In order that any useful measure may be carried, he who advocates it must be able to persuade a large number of persons of its expedience. Skill in such persuasion is, therefore, with us an absolute necessity of political success, and there are always among the rulers of the country some who owe their position to their eminence in it. And though no doubt there is a presumption that they who succeed in making others think that they are giving wise counsel really deserve the character they bear, yet it is a very different thing to be a brilliant orator and a wise statesman. Many instances might be given of persons who have exercised great influence in the House of Commons, though with powers of speech less than the average, solely on account of the trust that was put in their honesty and good sense.

But we may meet with illustrations enough in our daily life what very different things are cleverness and wisdom. It may happen you to be opposed by persons on whose friendship you thought you might have counted; unkind words may have been said to you, a slighting and disparaging estimate of you expressed. And you may have it in your power, by a stinging retort, to cover your assailant with confusion; and by exposing some inconsistency, or fastening on some weakness of his, to take ample vengeance. If you do this readily and wittily, you may produce a great impression of your intellectual ability. No intellectual ability at all is required for holding your tongue, and yet to submit in silence may be far the wisest course. In such a case the line of conduct dictated by Christian meekness may be also that approved by worldly prudence. A man who opposes you when your interests come into collision with his may not be really your enemy if you do not permanently make him so, or if you do not, by damaging his reputation, destroy his power as well as his willingness to serve you another time. And if you are angry because a more slighting estimate has been expressed of you than you think you deserve, why, in the first place, it is possible that it may be you who overrate yourself; but, if not, it may still be the wisest to wait patiently till misconceptions clear themselves away; for, as a general rule, people in the long run get quite as much honour as they deserve; and any anger or impatience about such a matter only delays the recognition of their merit.

But I find that in thus giving as an illustration the fact that Christian meekness is true wisdom, I am only anticipating in a particular case the general principle asserted in the text that the fear of the Lord is wisdom. From one point of view, it will occur to many that this principle must be undoubtedly true. If we look on practical wisdom as that which guides us to the line of conduct best calculated to secure our happiness, it must undoubtedly be wise to secure the favour of Him who is infinite in power, and whose rewards are eternal. It is quite a commonplace to point out the folly of the man who professes to believe in a future life, yet lives as if this world were to be his home for ever. It is just the same, it has been said, as if an officer under Government temporarily employed here, but who knows that he must soon expect orders to proceed to a distant station, and there take up his permanent home, were to invest all his property here in a form incapable of being removed with him. But we are not obliged to make our assent to the principle of the text depend on our faith in the sanctions of a future life. God's commandments are not grievous; and even as far as this life is concerned, it is our happiness and our wisdom to obey them. If we glance through the commandments of the decalogue, we cannot doubt the folly of disregarding them. We shall own that it is the fool who hath said in his heart, There is no God; that those are fools who put their trust in graven images, and bow down to the work of their own hands; and so on with regard to the other commandments which enjoin the duty of worshipping God, which maintain the sanctity of family life, proclaiming the duties of children to parents, of husbands and wives, which enjoin personal purity, which forbid injury to our neighbour in person or property, or in his family relations, and which guard the outward conduct by waging war on the sinful desires from which sinful actions spring; all these commandments are such that any thoughtful man must own that it is his interest as well as his duty to comply with them.

But when we turn to the New Testament, we find a basis for Christian ethics very different from that of the most enlightened selfishness. If we receive the teaching of that book, the spring of our actions must be love to Christ, and likeness to Christ the model of the perfection at which we must aim. And what was the character of Christ? The Apostle sums it up in the words, "Christ pleased not Himself." It does, indeed, sound like a truism to say that our Blessed Lord's life on earth was not one of self-indulgence. You are all so familiar with the details of His life that you need not to be reminded what He endured for man's sake. His victory over the temptations of Satan in the wilderness indicated the character of His entire life. The temptations which he rejected there, He rejected absolutely and for ever. The allurements of appetite, the charms of earthly power, the desire of popularity found no place among the motives of His conduct. Destitute of all the world counts necessary for happiness, He went about in ceaseless labours for the good of others, diffusing bodily health and spiritual instruction, regardless of selfish ease, regardless of the opposition He too often met with from those He came to benefit; mindful only of the great object for which He had come, to seek and to save them that were lost. You know that all that He previously submitted to for our sakes was but preliminary to that closing proof of love (the greatest, as He Himself said, that any can give), to lay down His life for His friends; nay, not even then His friends, since, as the Apostle tells us, while we were yet enemies Christ died for us. The Gospels, moreover, inform us that the Lord's humiliation was a voluntary descent from glory which He possessed with the Father before the world was; that His continuance in this humiliation was equally voluntary; that in the darkest hour of His agony legions of angels stood ready at His call; but the word of summons was not given, because then the Scriptures of the prophets would not have been fulfilled; those Scriptures which had inseparably connected the redemption of man with the travail of the soul of the Redeemer. And it was not merely that our Saviour's humiliation must have been felt more keenly as contrasted with the height of glory from which He had descended; what the Scriptures reveal as to the higher nature He possessed suggests other reflections as to the way in which that very nature must have increased the weight of what His human nature had to bear. His divine foreknowledge must have kept present to Him during the whole time of His humiliation, the bitterness of that agony by which, on the night of Gethsemane, His humanity was almost overwhelmed; while His knowledge of the hearts of men enabled Him to discern that even of those whom He had chosen out of the race for which He came to suffer, one was a traitor, and the rest would, in the hour of danger, desert Him. Privations present and anguish constantly foreseen, submitted to, thanklessly submitted to, for the sake of others, from all of which a word would, at any moment, have relieved Him; such is the account of the Saviour's life on earth. This was the life which His first converts set before them as the model for their imitation. As He loved us, so ought we also to love one another, was their maxim. It was ever vividly present to their minds what He, their Master and Lord, had suffered for them, and the thought what He had endured for their sakes was ready to rise to rebuke any selfish shrinking from danger, or toil, or privation, which their brethren's good required them to encounter. "Let this mind be in you which was also in Christ Jesus" was the Apostle's exhortation. "Christ pleased not Himself, so let every one of you please his neighbour for his good to edification."

Here, then, is the paradox of Christianity. "The fear of the Lord is wisdom," is the declaration of the Old Testament. Wisdom teaches us to provide for our happiness in the most enlightened way, rejecting those pleasures which are of a lower order, or which are but temporary, and will be followed by greater pain, and choosing those which are higher and lasting. But here we have what seems quite a different rule; seek not your own happiness at all; live and work for the happiness of others; give up all thought of self; all calculation how you may make yourself greater, or more honoured, or more prosperous. That may be more noble conduct, but can it be said to be wisdom?

The key to the paradox is found in that golden saying of our Lord, which St. Luke has preserved for us in an after-gleaning made after his history of our Lord's life had been finished—"It is more blessed to give than to receive." This strikes a higher key than is touched in some of those Gospel lessons in which our Lord had inculcated the duty of giving. Give, He had said, not to those from whom you hope to receive a return; not even with a view to men's praises. Let the praise of Him who seeth in secret be enough for you. Give to those who cannot recompense you, and ye shall be recompensed at the resurrection of the just. But here we have the doctrine, not of future recompense for self-sacrifice, but of its present blessedness. That it truly is more blessed to give than to receive, however paradoxical the utterance when first made may have sounded, we cannot for a moment doubt. Our Lord, in the Sermon on the Mount, had told His disciples that in not allowing their love to be repelled by the unworthiness of its object, they should be like their Heavenly Father, who maketh His sun to shine on the evil and on the good, and sendeth rain on the just and on the unjust. And if it must be happiness to be like Him who is all-blessed as He is all-bountiful, His blessedness cannot consist in receiving anything from the creatures who can add nothing to His majesty. To give where no return *can* be made must be His blessedness, and that must be happiness for those who are like Him. And there is no difficulty in understanding that this really is the case. Those to whom God has given powers find happiness in their exercise quite independently of the fruits these powers may gain. It is not true, or it is a mere fraction of the truth, that " love of fame is the spur which the clear spirit doth raise to scorn delights and live laborious days." An unsubstantial recompense, if this were all; nor would prudence find it easy to justify the giving up of solid comfort for the sake of having our vanity incensed by praise—praise that may, perhaps, never reach our ear, and may not come till after we are dead. But I believe the truth to be that though many, when trying to give an account to themselves why they lived laborious days, may have thought to vindicate their prudence by the prospect of future praise, this was not their real motive. Their happiness was in the work itself, and the laborious days brought them higher delight than selfish ease could have offered. And in the case of work done for others, it is not only that there is pleasure in the exercise of our powers; it is not only that it is more flattering to our pride to give than to receive; but the heart must be cold which does not find delight when through our gift happiness springs up for others, and their sorrow is turned into joy. Cases are of constant occurrence where no other reward is sought for efforts to give pleasure to others than some evidence that these efforts have been successful. Take, for instance, maternal love, that most striking example of the happiness love finds in giving without thought of receiving. If a baby laughs and crows, it is thought to make an ample return for all the attentions that are lavished on it.

If there can be any doubt as to the comparative wisdom of him who places his happiness in receiving or in giving when both are successful in their aims, we can have no doubt in the case when they fail. Indeed, when can he be said to succeed who places his happiness in self-aggrandisement? For ever as he reaches those whom in the race for greatness he had made it his ambition to overtake, it seems to him but a poor victory to have conquered these, when he sees, as he must, others still in advance of him who now appear the only competitors worthy of his rivalry. And when failure comes, as come it will, how ignoble are the sorrows of him who has sought great things for himself and found them not. How little sympathy we can give to the smartings of wounded vanity, to the disappointed graspings of ambition, to the confusion of him who, having claimed the highest place, is compelled to descend with shame to a lower room.

Contrast with these the worst sorrow that can be suffered by one whose happiness is giving—the pain of love repulsed. It will often happen that attempts to do kindness to others are not received in the spirit in which they are offered. If we needed proof that giving has a happiness of its own as much as receiving, we should easily find conviction from our experience that there may be as much selfishness in refusing to receive as in refusing to give. Sometimes the refusal may spring from unamiable perversity of disposition, which loves to disappoint expectation, and grudges a pleasure which it is perceived is counted on; sometimes it may proceed from scorn of the poor gift offered, which is disdainfully brushed aside, without appreciation of the kindly feelings, perhaps the labour and sacrifice made by the giver; sometimes it may proceed from a sturdy spirit of independence, too proud to bear the burden of an obligation, and willing to forego a coveted good, rather than be beholden to another for the enjoyment of it. That even in this last case, with feelings highly worthy of respect, there may be mixed up a great deal of selfish disregard of the feelings of others, we need not delay to point out. But we plainly are forced to own that it is not the selfish man alone who must count on meeting occasional disappointment; the most generous, the most loving, is liable to have his motives misinterpreted, or his love cast back.

How are we, then, to strike a balance? Can we say that the grief of wounded affection is less keen than the pain caused by the failure of schemes for self-aggrandisement? If we cannot say this, perhaps we might say that the sorrows of love are more noble than the delights of selfishness, and that it is a more blessed thing to have even felt disappointment in giving than to have had success in receiving. But it is more to the purpose to observe that such disappointment only brings pain with it in proportion as selfishness has animated the motives of the giver. There were some early Christians who imagined a flame through which all at the end of the world must pass, through which those would pass unscathed who were pure from earthly defilement, but which would fasten on all in the soul that was mean and base, and so give much or little pain in proportion as there was much or little that must be burned away. Of this kind is the pain which the bountiful receive when their gifts are rejected. If their generosity has been but refined selfishness, if they have given only because they wished to have their pride gratified by the acknowledgment of others' dependence, because they delight in receiving thanks and praise, or because in some other way they hope to be paid back again by those whom they have benefited, the disappointment of such expectations as these must not count among the sorrows of love; but goes rather to swell the list of the vexations to which selfishness, in all its forms, is liable. But if the giver's kindly act is really prompted by the single motive, the desire to promote the happiness of its object ; if it spring from that truly unselfish love which can rejoice in the happiness of those we love, even when they prefer that that happiness shall come to them in a way to which we cannot contribute, then the sting is taken out of disappointment, and what might have been at first pain to us is turned into matter of rejoicing. St. Paul may teach us the spirit proper to those who have their heart more in the cause for which they labour than in the credit to be won for themselves from promoting it. He heard of the exertions made in preaching Christ by men who were his rivals and his enemies, and he exclaimed— Whatever their motives, Christ is preached, and I therein do rejoice.

If, then, the New Testament has taught us to understand by "the fear of the Lord" somewhat more than had been distinctly revealed in the Old Testament; if it teaches us that it means to be children of Him who is kind to the unthankful and the evil ; to be followers of Him who gave His life for sinners, ungrateful and rebellious ; still we can truly say the fear of the Lord is wisdom. Butler has illustrated the profitable effects of virtue by imagining the prosperity of a community of perfectly virtuous persons. If you want to know what are the fruits of that which is a higher and a warmer thing than mere virtue, real love for others, such as that of which our Redeemer's earthly life is the highest pattern, we need only imagine His example followed by a single individual. Imagine that any one systematically wove into an entire life the practice of these lessons of our Lord, and you would have to own that such a one, whatever his or her intellectual gifts might be, was one of the wisest of human beings—wisest in providing for his own happiness, and wisest also if counsel were sought by others.

It is eminently true of love—give and it shall be given to you. If one were found by experience to be perfectly free from selfish aim, one by whom no unkind word was ever spoken, one who was always planning some act of kindness to others, who grudged no trouble to make them happier; it is impossible but that such a one would inspire such perfect trust, and would be surrounded by such love aud gratitude, as would brighten his own life as he strove to brighten those of others. To such a one we could come, in any difficulty, for advice, in full confidence that the counsel given would be prompted by no thought of the interests or wishes of the adviser, and that we should be told, not what was pleasantest for us, but what was really wise and right for us to do.

And in matters of conduct, perplexity as to the right course so often arises, not from any real difficulty in seeing what path duty points out, as from shrinking from trouble that following it might impose, or from a hankering after enjoyment of some kind to be found on another road, that mere singleness of mind and purpose confers an insight denied to those whose vision is clouded by selfish desire. Such insight will often prevent charity towards others from degenerating into weak blindness to their faults. For when the right course is discerned, it is impossible not to take notice when others turn aside from following it. And the disguises by which they justify their conduct to themselves become transparent to one of greater simplicity of character. It is no small part of practical wisdom in the course of this world's conduct, to have the gift of insight into character, and to be able to judge correctly who may be trusted, and how far. But you will not need to be told that it is wisdom in a higher sense than this to which the text refers, even though it may not have been amiss to point out how godliness has the promise of the life that now is, as well as of that which is to come. May we, brethren, ever daily strive to be more and more like Him who is the Eternal Wisdom of the Father, that hereafter we may be with Him where He is, where they that be wise shall shine forth as the sun in the kingdom of their Father.

XII

SELF-RIGHTEOUSNESS

"I tell you this man went down to his house justified rather than the other."—St. Luke xviii. 14.

How often does it happen that the paradoxes of one generation are the truisms of the next. The discovery which has been rejected as not only absurd, but dangerous to religion, after some resistance gains acceptance, passes then into elementary instruction, and the time comes when it seems as if men must always have known it. The striking remark which has startled its first hearers by its strangeness, as soon as its truth is recognised, is repeated by so many that it becomes a commonplace, from which we turn our ears, weary of its triteness. Something of this kind has happened in the case of our Lord's rebukes of Pharisaism and self-righteousness. The associations connected in our minds with the words are so entirely different that it is scarcely possible for us to feel how strange, almost how revolting to His hearers, was our Lord's preference of a Publican to a Pharisee. The word Pharisee now conveys to us the idea of hypocrisy, formality, attachment to external observances, combined with neglect of the weightier matters of the law, undue self-confidence, and unjustifiable contempt of others. But at the time our Lord spoke, the Pharisees put no higher estimate on themselves than the people willingly conceded to them. The name then expressed religious zeal as opposed to latitudinarian indifference. While the wealthy and powerful of the time preferred a quiet, reasonable religion, kept within proper bounds, making no demands upon faith or practice, except such as they knew not how to evade, allying itself readily with the State, and useful for keeping the lower ranks in order by adding a supernatural sanction to the commands of the law of the land, such a conception of religion did not satisfy the more earnest and more thoughtful minds. They wanted a religion which should be plainly no State contrivance, but should come to them as a law from above. To such a law they would measure out no stinted or grudging obedience, but willingly added fences to the letter of the command, so as, by habitually doing something more than was enjoined, to make sure that the law should not be transgressed. While others confined their view to the world of sense, they loved to recognise the supernatural. They thought it no impossibility that angel or spirit might bring them blessing from above, and they hoped for a life beyond the grave. Ruling their conduct by a religion which was to them a felt reality, if they compared themselves with others who lived for this world alone, they might not unreasonably feel confidence in themselves that they were righteous, and their confidence was amply supported by public opinion. To declare that such men might have less favour in God's sight than one of the Publicans, men whose profession was so condemned by strong national feeling that, having irretrievably lost the good opinion of their neighbours, they were unrestrained in their conduct by fear of loss of character, and so in the Gospels are commonly classed with the harlots—this was a paradox as revolting to Jewish ears as it would be to ours to be told that the outcast of the streets might be more acceptable to God than the devoted Sister of Charity who has spent her life in the service of others. But it is needless to show that there was something in Pharisaism worthy of admiration, for this is implied in the charge brought against the Pharisees of our Lord's times. They were accused of being hypocrites, of not being what they pretended to be; in which it is implied that if they had really been what they seemed, they would have deserved the praise they claimed. And doubtless there were some whose goodness was more than outside show, both in the first original of the sect and in those later times when Pharisaic culture prepared the soil in which the seeds of the Gospel most readily flourished ; for to this sect belonged the majority of the first converts, and the many thousands of Jews who believed are described as all zealous for the law.

But it has constantly happened that after the admiration of men has been justly won, that admiration continues to be claimed and given after it has ceased to be deserved. Children of Abraham claim Abraham's privileges who do not the works of Abraham. Men who have done real service to mankind are followed by others who claim to be their representatives and successors, but whose likeness to them is only outward, and who are destitute of their spirit. Ever since the time that the false prophets of the Jews " wore a rough garment to deceive," it has been found easier to imitate the true prophet in his outward accessaries than in his spirit. A peculiar garb or outward bearing, gestures, tone of voice, ceremonies which true reverence may have originally suggested, are caught and traditionally kept up, and are long accepted as unerring marks of the devotion which they did once really indicate. Formulæ, precious in their day for the service they did in asserting and preserving disputed truth, continue to be shouted out as watchwords by men who have no sense of their real spirit, and when the perils of the faith are very different. So it is that the earth is haunted by the ghosts of departed virtues, and men give their reverence to forms from which life has fled. The work of the Old Testament prophets was comparatively easy when they assailed open vice, which they who practised did in defiance of their own consciences. Our Lord's task was far harder,—to convince of sin men who were on perfectly good terms with their consciences, who believed themselves, and were believed by others, to be God's most zealous and devoted servants. But the work once done by our Lord has been done for ever. Since He showed that pretended religion was a more deadly enemy even than open sin, because it subjugates the whole man, and makes even the conscience its slave and its ally, others have found no difficulty in testing the pretensions of professing piety. His lessons, no doubt, constantly need to be revived, because the foe whom He assailed ever disguises himself in new shapes; for as the hollowness of one form of outward piety is discovered, and so that form ceases to gain men's admiration, they who have exposed it may, in turn, be made the model for imitation, by successors falsely claiming to be like-minded with them; and thus it happens that the respectable Christian of the present day is in outward appearance very unlike the Pharisee of our Lord's time. But still the lesson having been once taught, that we must not admit unquestioned that which passes itself with ourselves or others as zeal for God, it has not been difficult to detect the spirit of Pharisaism in the new forms in which it has showed itself, and to smite it with our Lord's condemnation.

In proposing, then, to speak to you to-day of self-righteousness, I have felt as if I were assailing that which has no friends. The self-righteous are condemned with one voice by the religious and the irreligious. It is only natural that they who despise others should not be popular with those on whom they look down. Nay, the charge of Pharisaism is brought against many who do not deserve it. For they who strive to live by a higher standard, however little they may pride themselves on their own performances, do silently condemn those who are content with lower aims, and these last will be ready to stigmatise as overrighteous, and possibly as self-righteous, any who exceed the measure of what they count sufficient.

On the other hand, our Lord has taught very plainly that a man is more accepted with God if he comes confessing his sins than if he comes boasting of his righteousness, that the best of us cannot make God his debtor, that if we have done all that is commanded we are but unprofitable servants, that the obedience of the best falls very far short of His commands, and that it is therefore a delusion to entertain the idea of being justified by our works. So it follows that Pharisaism cannot be more loudly condemned in the most godless circles than it is by all who profess to be our Lord's disciples ; and our pulpits resound with warnings against self-righteousness. Yet I cannot but think that many of these warnings miss their mark, that there is often much of unreality about them, and that while the preacher is loud in condemning a sin into which his hearers feel no temptation to fall, they may be left unwarned as to a self-righteousness of which they are in real danger. I think, then, that it will not be unprofitable if we try to examine what that self-righteousness is which we are bound to avoid, and wherein the danger of it consists.

And in the first place, I say that we are not saved from the danger of self-righteousness by our full knowledge and hearty recognition of the doctrines of grace. We may have been taught rightly, and be ready cheerfully to acknowledge, that of ourselves we can do no good thing. We may own the natural corruptness of our hearts, and may be persuaded that every good thing that is produced in us is the work of the Holy Spirit, from whom every good and perfect thing doth proceed. And yet this acknowledgment will not save us from the danger of trusting in ourselves that we are righteous. For this was precisely the case of the Pharisee in the parable. He did not dream of taking to himself the credit of the excellence which he supposed himself to have attained to. He acknowledged it to be all God's work in him. "God, I thank *Thee* that I am not as other men are, unjust, extortioners, or even as this publican." He carries with him the spirit of trusting to himself that he is righteous and despising others, at the very moment that he is thanking God who has made him to differ from them. Thus you see that we who own that our salvation is not of works, but all the free gift of a crucified Lord, who take not to ourselves the praise either of our justification or our sanctification, who confess that whatever fruits of holiness there may be in us are not the fruits of our own fallen nature, but the work of the Spirit of Holiness, are still not free from the danger of falling into the error of the Pharisee in the parable. When we come to God full of thankfulness, blessing Him for the wonders of His grace, and rejoicing that we are not as others who have not found the acceptance with God which we enjoy, it may be that some of those with whom we compare ourselves go down to their house justified rather than we.

Yet, on the other hand, it is not self-righteousness to be conscious of the attainments we have made in holiness: nor do those escape it who are ready to acknowledge freely the small extent of their spiritual progress. It is not required of a Christian that he should be blind to the work of God's grace in his soul. He is not required to live in a kind of inverted hypocrisy, confessing himself to be worse than he has reasonable cause to think himself, and pronouncing on himself a judgment which every one else must feel to be unjust. I have read the lives of some Roman Catholic Saints who, while they attracted the admiration of their brethren by their supereminent sanctity, yet professed themselves to be the vilest of wretches, a disgrace to the community, only fit to be trampled by them under foot, and whom they were amazed their brethren were willing to tolerate among them.[1] Yet when I find them

---

[1] "St. Rose of Lima was humble to a pre-eminent degree. She would frequently cast herself at the feet of a poor country girl who

not making confession of particular sins, which would really cost them their brethren's good opinion, but only such general acknowledgments as swelled their fame still higher by adding the praise of humility to their other virtues, I find it hard to recognise such language as prompted by true humility. St. Paul, indeed, has startled us by calling himself the chief of sinners, for when most honoured by God for the successful exertions he had been permitted to make for His cause, he could never forgive himself for having persecuted and wasted the Church of God. Yet he was not unconscious of what God had done in him and by him. "The grace of God," he says, "which was bestowed on me, was not in vain, but I laboured more abundantly than they all: yet," he adds, "not I, but the grace of God which was in me." Surely, when the Apostle owns what God by His grace had wrought in him, this is not self-righteousness; it would, on the other hand, have been hypocrisy if he had pretended to be ignorant of it. No; the humility of the saints of God is preserved in a different way. Not through refusing

worked in the house, and entreat her earnestly to beat her, to spit upon her, to trample her under her feet, and treat her as the most contemptible creature in the world. She thought herself a burden, useless to the world, and odious to nature; and if any misfortune befell the family, she said it was her own sins which had drawn it down as a chastisement from heaven."—*Life of St. Rose of Lima.* Dublin: Duffy & Co.

to see, or to acknowledge the triumphs of Divine grace, or the work of God's Spirit in their souls, but by the deeper sense of sinfulness, which the closer approach to God, and the more intense love of Him is sure to generate. Those sins which we once thought trifling, pardonable frailties, the way of the world, the infirmities of human nature, assume in our judgment a deeper dye as we are more penetrated with the love of Christ. Then it seems to us no small matter that His boundless love to us should be rejected with base ingratitude. Thus it was with St. Paul, that the insulting and persecuting the name of Christ which once had seemed to him his duty, appeared to him, when his spiritual eyes had been enlightened, such amazing wickedness as to fill him with neverceasing wonder that even he, the chief of sinners, had obtained mercy. And not only this, but the conscience of him who walks with God is strengthened; his spiritual discernment is increased; multitudes of secret sins start to view which had never been noticed by his conscience while formerly torpid and hardened by the deceitfulness of sin. And as he strives to walk closely with God, he becomes conscious of innumerable shortcomings; the more he strives to follow Him who is infinitely perfect, the greater the distance appears. He, in short, who is manfully fighting in his Master's cause will have some defeats and reverses to tell of, of which the man knows nothing who has never struck a blow in his Saviour's service. These are ways in which a Christian's humility is preserved, and not by his being ignorant of what God has done in him, nor by his being unable to say, through the grace of God I am what I am. In fact, the greater a man's real righteousness, the less danger he is in of self-righteousness.

And this brings me to the next point, and one by no means needless to be mentioned: Righteousness is not self-righteousness. The irreligious man, as I have already said, is apt to set down as self-righteous every one who can claim to be better than he pretends to be. Men of a different character, who have caught up the one doctrine, that we are not to put confidence in our own works or deservings, which is part of the Gospel, though not the whole of the Gospel, are seriously alarmed when they hear of any aiming at being righteous, as if it would necessarily follow that they must become self-righteous; or, if a preacher dwell upon works, as if he must teach salvation by works. That was a risk which St. Paul was not afraid of incurring, for great part of his epistles is taken up, not merely with general exhortations to holiness, but with very detailed instructions as to particular duties. The truth is, that as far as my experience goes, the danger is an imaginary one of a man's doing too much good works, and so being led to trust that he will get salvation by them. Many men do works that would generally be called good works without any thought of the next world at all; but among Christians who really concern themselves about salvation, the knowledge of Christ's atoning work is too generally spread to allow it to be a very common mistake to refuse to place trust in that to the exclusion of every other ground of confidence. In truth, there is nothing wrong in being righteous, or in doing good works. The only thing to be frightened about is, if the righteousness be not real, or the works not truly good. And, as I have just said, the less the real righteousness, the greater the danger of self-righteousness.

This is the easier seen if we use that analogy between the understanding and the will which throws light on so many questions. In intellectual matters, what answers to self-righteousness is conceit of fancied knowledge, the most deadly foe to real knowledge. And it is notorious that perfect content with one's attainments can only be had on the terms of knowing very little. Did any one ever hear of a philosopher whose mastery of his science was so profound that he had solved all its problems, and so had no further question to put to himself, no need of enlargement of his knowledge. On the contrary, every advance made by the successful inquirer enlarges his horizon. The discovery of the answer to one question suggests to him other questions which, but for his newly-acquired knowledge, it would not have occurred to him to put. The more he knows, the stronger his sense of the extent of the unknown; so that the saying is not unworthy of the great philosopher to whom it is attributed, that at the end of his life, looking back on his discoveries, he compared himself to a child who had spent his time gathering pebbles on the shore, while the great ocean of truth lay undiscovered before him. If you want to find a man completely contented with his knowledge, you must look for one who has spent no trouble in the search for it. You must listen to the undoubting decisions on theological questions pronounced by one who has never unsettled his mind by study of them, or on questions of political economy, or metaphysics, by one who scoffs at the very name of these sciences. Strange, indeed, it is that we value our opinions by a different rule from that by which we value everything else. Other things we value in proportion to the trouble it has cost us to obtain them. But our opinions are the more dear to us the less pains we have taken to come by them.

A philosopher may have taken years to arrive at conclusions, and yet be ready to modify them if new facts are made known to him; but the opinions men have learned from their fathers, or picked up in any other way without mental exertion of their own, are so precious in their eyes that they have burned men alive who have tried to deprive them of them. The very first step, then, towards the attainment of real knowledge is the disabusing the mind of this false persuasion of knowledge; and he whom the oracle pronounced the wisest of men is rightly held to have justified the praise by his making it his special mission to convince men that they knew nothing. Exactly the same thing holds with respect to righteousness. The very first step towards the attainment of true righteousness is the abandonment of false confidence that righteousness has been already attained; and the greatest progress in holiness has been made by men who have started with the deepest convictions of sin.

The analogy I have brought forward will help us in answering the question, What is the harm of self-righteousness? why is it to be regarded as a sin? why is God displeased with it? A very prevalent view is that self-righteousness is wrong, because it is an affront to God; a giving to ourselves some of the credit that rightly belongs to Him; a thing, therefore, to be avoided, lest it should excite God's jealousy. And so they think it a proper thing, when they come before God, to confess that they are miserable sinners, though they would deeply resent it, if any of their fellow-creatures were, out of church, to accept as literal truth their acknowledgments of sinfulness. It was natural that the heathen, whose gods were but slightly magnified men, should think of them as uneasy if men were put in competition with them, and as highly incensed if their praise was derogated from; so that the general was giving a challenge to misfortune who boasted that in this victory fortune had no share. But different thoughts suggest themselves when we form truer conceptions of the infinite majesty of God. Then, we understand the frantic absurdity of any creature's setting himself up as a rival to Him from whom he derives every power he possesses; and the equal absurdity of imagining that the Omnipotent can be distressed, or made uneasy by such rivalry. The humility of moderating our claims lest they should come into collision with those of God, is like the humility of bowing our head low lest we should strike it against the sky. The commands God has given us are not for His sake, but for ours; and if He has taught us to condemn self-righteousness, it is not because it is a disparagement to

Him, but because it is an injury to ourselves. The real mischief is that the self-righteous man destroys all hope of his rising above that moral condition with which He is so well contented. There is hope of the slave of sin who groans under his bondage, and longs to break his chains; but what hope is there of him to whom the servile yoke gives no discomfort or uneasiness? How is he to be benefited who, though "wretched, and poor, and miserable, and blind, and naked," imagines he is "rich and increased with goods, and has need of nothing?" The moment we begin to admire ourselves, the moment we are satisfied with the advance we have already made, that moment we cease to aspire after anything higher, that moment our progress is arrested; and in progress our very life consists.

If we clearly understand that self-righteousness consists, not so much in thinking oneself to be good as in thinking oneself to be good enough, we perceive that it is compatible with a great absence of real righteousness. The man who laughs at all professions of piety, who thinks that the sins he has committed are in God's sight trifling frailties, and who gives the name "Pharisee" to those who make a show of living after God's will and in obedience to God's commands, is, if the truth were told, himself the Pharisee. For though he does not assert himself to be good, it is plain he feels confident that he is good enough. He has no idea of higher excellence than his own; for in his heart he believes his character to be much more amiable than that of those whom he pronounces over-righteous people. And so he is as far as any Pharisee from that real conviction of sin which rouses the benumbed conscience, and awakes the first hunger and thirst after real righteousness.

There are, again, men of quite a different stamp, who inveigh against self-righteousness, yet are themselves deeply involved in it. Everything that is good has its counterfeit. That conviction of sin, which is the first step to the prodigal's return to his father, is simulated by a false conviction of sin, which means no more than that they who experience it are for the time frightened at the possibility that they may go to hell. That it is no more than this is evident from the fact, that it commonly does not include consciousness of, nor repentance from, any particular sin; nay, by many, self-examination for such sins or acknowledgment of them is discouraged. And when once they have quelled their fears by the acknowledgment that our Blessed Lord is the only way of salvation, they care not to remember the lessons of self-denial He has taught, and go on living the rest of their lives in as easy satisfaction with themselves as the worldling of whom I spoke just now; or rather easier, inasmuch as the conscience of the latter is seldom quite comfortable, and theirs has received a strong opiate.

But it may be urged with truth that there have been innumerable cases in which a conviction of sin, which probably was no more than terror of judgment to come, has been the turning-point of a transition from a life of careless ungodliness to a life of consistent holiness. Far be it from me to dispute the beneficial effects which the terrors of the law have in some cases produced. It sounds in our ears exceptional arrogance that the Pharisee should say, I am not as other men are. It is in truth what the voice of every one of our hearts whispers to us; and if I were asked to name the chief cause of danger to a young man of taking a course which may wreck his life, I think I should answer, his persuading himself that he is not as other men. For we are each the centre of our own horizon. We know ourselves as we can know no one else: in fact, we guess at others from what we know of ourselves. And in spite of theoretical conviction, it is hard to resist the impression that that one being, whose happiness is all the world to us, and whom we know as we know no other, must be different from any other. And it seems incredible to us that the disaster which has befallen others should overtake us. We cannot bear to think it possible that our own life should be a failure and a wreck. The gamester, though perfectly aware that the chances of the table are against him, fears not to take his risk, trusting that, however others may have been ruined, exceptional good fortune will bring him out a triumphant winner. And similarly, too, a young man is apt to expect that he will be an exception to the law that whatsoever a man soweth he shall reap. He thinks that he can touch pitch without being defiled; the good feelings of which he is conscious will guard his heart from being hardened by the deceitfulness of sin; others have been entangled beyond extrication in the downward path on which he ventures to tread; but it cannot be but that when he pleases there will be a way of return for him. Happy for him if a wholesome fear dispels this delusion, and out of the conviction that the way of sin is a way of real danger, there springs earnest desire to escape from it.

In another sense, it is easy for us to persuade ourselves that we are not as other men. It is not pleasant to be on bad terms with ourselves; and the commonest way of satisfying ourselves is to try ourselves by the standard of other men, the result of which is sure to be favourable, since we can choose our own standard of comparison. The very worst man we know knows others worse than himself; not worse, perhaps, in every respect, but worse in some points, and these are the points which he will consider really important; and so he prides himself that with all his faults he is not such as they. It was a true remark as to the effect of bad example, that for one who is hurt by being led to imitate a bad example, two are hurt by being content with being themselves a little better. It is a common remark, how the tone of a whole party, religious or political, is altered by violent and extreme men, whom the great bulk of the party repudiate. Far be it from them to justify such language or opinions; but still new ideas arise as to the length to which men may go; and men pass now, in comparison, for quiet, moderate men, who would have been counted extreme before. Just in the same way every sinful act lowers the moral standard of those who witness it. Men compare themselves with the flagrant offences or easily marked inconsistencies of others, and flatter themselves that because they have escaped these, all must be well with them. And their heart fills with secret and very ill-founded pride; and if they ventured, in their prayers, to express the true feelings of their hearts, their address to God would also be that of the Pharisee: "God, I thank Thee that I am not as other men are."

Brethren, the best practical rule for avoiding the dangers which arise from comparing ourselves with others, is to strive to keep ever before our minds as our rule of life the character of Him who gave us an example that we should follow in *His* steps. "Be ye holy, even as I am holy," is the charge of Him whom we are bound to follow. If we strive not to walk by His rule, what will it profit us that we have been a little less unfaithful than others? As well might the guest who came into the marriage supper without a wedding garment boast himself that he had not repulsed or slighted the messengers who brought their master's invitation. He had not made light of his summons; much less had he involved himself in the deeper guilt of those who used those servants despitefully, and slew them. There he was in obedience to the master's call. He was not as other men. Yet on him the sentence was pronounced, "Bind him hand and foot, and take him away, and cast him into outer darkness; there shall be weeping and gnashing of teeth." Even so it is that there is no example, but one, which may not mislead us—mislead us even when we have succeeded in arriving at the standard we aim at, or in going beyond it. There is but One in striving to resemble whom we can never be led astray; One whose character the more closely we study, and the more thoroughly we love, the more nearly we approach to be perfect, even as our Father which is in heaven is perfect. The contemplation of such an example, and the contrast with what you know yourselves to be, cannot but deepen your sense of sin, and drive you to the supplication, "God, be merciful to me, a sinner." Remember, then, that it was for sinners Christ died; for sinners He gave His precious blood; to sinners He promised His Holy Spirit. He has revealed God as a loving co-operator in the work of your sanctification. When you need strength to overcome your spiritual enemies, you cannot be so ready to ask it as He to give it. If the sense of sin drive you to Christ, if you feel that it is too great to be hidden by any fig-leaf covering of your own devising, if it force you to cast yourselves unreservedly on Him, then you will know His pure and spotless righteousness as sufficient to cover all your sins, and such that you may present yourselves arrayed in it without reproach in the presence of God. May God then declare to you so much of your true state, that you can never trust that you are righteous, never be content whereunto you have yet attained, but be always straining upward, always aiming at something higher. Then will you not despise others, but love them, help their tottering steps when they fail where you have been strengthened by God's grace to stand, help them, counsel them, pray for them.

And if in your struggles for higher attainments you find yourselves at times baffled, if indwelling corruption is difficult to subdue, if besetting sins imagined to be rooted out revive and endeavour to recover their dominion, let every fresh revelation of your sinfulness, driving you into fresh supplications, " God, be merciful to me, a sinner," urge you to wrap yourselves more closely in the robe of Him who has been made unto you wisdom, and righteousness, and sanctification, and redemption.

XIII

THE SLAVERY OF SIN

> "They answered him, We be Abraham's seed, and were never in bondage to any man: how sayest thou, Ye shall be made free? Jesus answered them, Verily, verily, I say unto you, Whosoever committeth sin is the servant of sin. And the servant abideth not in the house for ever: but the Son abideth ever. If the Son therefore shall make you free, ye shall be free indeed."—ST. JOHN viii. 33-36.

"NEVER in bondage to any man!"—it seems strange to hear so ill-grounded a boast from men whose nation had suffered Egyptian bondage, Babylonish captivity, and was then groaning impatiently under the Roman yoke. But we can well believe that the speakers were thinking rather of personal than of political freedom. The institution of domestic slavery prevalent then in Judea as elsewhere had divided society into the two great classes, bond and free. It was the pride of the children of Abraham that they could not belong to the former class. Their great Lawgiver had permitted slavery, but had ordained that it should not extend to the chosen people. "Thy bond-men and thy bond-maids which thou shalt have, shall be of the heathen that are round about you; of them shall ye buy bond-men and bond-maids. If thy brother that dwelleth by thee be waxen poor, and be sold unto thee, thou shalt not compel him to serve as a bond-servant; but as an hired servant, and as a sojourner, he shall be with thee, and shall serve thee until the year of jubilee." The effect of such a law was, that a Jew prided himself on personal freedom as the prerogative of his birth, and looked on slavery as a state to which he could not be reduced: just as the effect of a legal decision in our own land was to furnish us with a still higher boast, that on the soil of England slavery could not exist.

St. Chrysostom notes it as remarkable, that when our Lord had said, "Ye shall know the truth, and the truth shall make you free," His hearers should have passed unnoticed the implied reproach that they, divinely taught though they had been by Moses and the prophets, did not know the truth; and only resented the imputation that they were not free, which in one sense they undeniably were not. But certainly what has been said shows that it was not likely to be less true in Judea than it is in other places that the word slave conveys an insult, which the word ignorant does not. And justly so, since no defects of intellectual culture can produce such deep degradation as the loss of that distinctive property of manhood, the possession of an independent will. To be but the moving, breathing instrument of another's will—to belong to another as his cattle belong to him—to be not a person, but one of the things which constitute his riches—to have no rights against him, no hopes independently of him, this is a lot inexpressibly miserable, if endured by one who still retains so much of the spirit of a freeman as to chafe under the sense of his degradation ; more pitiable still, if undergone by one into whose soul the iron of slavery has so entered, that he never murmurs that he is not free.

Now this is the condition to which our Saviour, in the discourse from which the text is taken, declares (as heathen moralists also have observed) that sin reduces those who commit it. Our own experience will tell us of slaves of sin of both those kinds which I have described—struggling and reluctant slaves, who groan under their bondage ; and willing slaves, in whom the spirit of freedom is so extinct, that they have no sense of their degradation. Has it never occurred to any of you to mourn the small efficacy of good resolutions ? You became conscious of some evil habit growing upon you, or your eyes were opened to the sinfulness of some old habit, and you saw the necessity of shaking it off. You resolved that that sin should not triumph over you again, and for a time it seemed as if your endeavour would be successful. But a moment came when you were off your guard, temptation suddenly came upon you, and ere you were aware the sin, which you had resolved to forsake, was again committed. You repented, renewed your resolutions with greater firmness only to find them broken again. Ever as you attempted to struggle on to the dry land out of the sea of sin, the resorbent wave sucked you back, and you could describe your experience in the words of the Apostle, " To will is present with me, but how to perform that which is good, I find not ; for the good that I would, I do not ; but the evil that I would not, that I do. I see a law in my members warring against the law of my mind, and bringing me into captivity to the law of sin which is in my members. O wretched man that I am ! who shall deliver me from the body of this death ? " Yet this state of captivity is not so truly wretched as the bondage of that man who has so far lost his freedom as to have ceased to struggle—who, being past feeling, has given himself over to lasciviousness to work all uncleanness with greediness. But no word other than slavery adequately describes either state in which the sinner has lost that distinctive attribute of freedom, the exercise of an independent will.

It may be asked are we but using figurative language when we thus describe the victim of sin as a slave. Is there any real difference between his condition and that of one whom, in our Lord's language, the truth has made free, except that the impulses which the one habitually obeys are, in our judgment, more noble than those followed by the other? Can the one be said more than the other to have, in real truth, an independent will? It would be very unsuitable to this place if I were to entangle you in a metaphysical discussion, still more in a discussion of the metaphysical problem on which, more perhaps than on any other, counsel has been darkened by words without knowledge. Yet one can scarcely speak on this subject without taking some notice of the increasing tendency on the part of the investigators of physical science to obliterate all distinction between human volitions and the phenomena of the material world, and to make one as much as the other the necessary result of antecedent conditions; so that it becomes difficult to say whether we can with more propriety describe a man as acting freely when he obeys the strongest motive which is presented to him, than we might describe a planet as moving freely when it takes the path prescribed by the resultant of the forces which act upon it. All study of physical science impresses us with the universal prevalence of law. Every condition of the material world is the consequent, according to a fixed rule, of the condition immediately preceding. Sometimes those rules are so simple in their application that, as in the case of the motions of the heavenly bodies, we can predict results long beforehand. In other cases the working of the rules is so complicated that we can trace them but a little way, and yet we have no doubt that we are still in the domain of law. In these climates we cannot predict from what direction nor with what strength the wind will blow a week hence. Yet we understand well enough the causes which produce motions of the atmosphere, such as its unequal temperature in different places, combined with the rotation of the earth—causes which enable us to give a sufficient explanation of its movements in those places where the wind will blow in the same direction for weeks together; and we can have no doubt that the same causes are in operation here as there. Again, when a die is thrown out of a box, we speak as if it were absolute chance on what side it will fall; yet we cannot doubt that, notwithstanding our inability to predict the result, the die obeys, according to the strictest physical rules, the impulses communicated to it. One who is imbued with these conceptions is not deterred by the complexity of human actions from ascribing them to the operation of fixed laws. We cannot predict with absolute certainty how a certain man under certain circumstances will act; yet we can, in many cases, tell with tolerable confidence what he will do; and if we cannot speak with certainty of the actions of an individual, we can often be nearly certain what a large majority of a given number will do.

The question then arises—Is the relation between the decisions of the human will, and the motives which act upon it, different in kind from that between the motions of a body, and the forces which act upon it? The theory suggested is that each individual is born into the world inheriting from his parents a constitution endowed with susceptibility to different motives in different degrees. This inherited constitution is daily and hourly insensibly modified by his education and the other influences to which he is subjected. A man's character is thus undergoing insensible change from moment to moment. If we know how he has acted on one occasion, we cannot predict with absolute certainty that he will, on the next occasion, act in the same way under similar circumstances, because we know not the history of the influences which may, in the interval, have modified his character. But still our inability to predict a man's conduct is consistent with the possibility that his conduct at any moment may be the necessary inevitable result of his previous condition. Just as it is theoretically possible, if the exact motions communicated to a dice-box were known, to predict on what side the die would fall, so it is held it would be theoretically possible, if a man's inherited constitution were known, and also the whole history of the influences to which he had been subjected since his birth, to deduce by necessary inference his conduct on any given occasion. I have stated, with all the advantage I can give it, that theory of human actions which seems to leave no room for any to call himself free; since it avails nothing to acknowledge how much a man may do to modify his own character —how, by one act of strenuous resistance to temptation, he gains force to conquer it with more ease in time to come—because these very acts by which character is modified are, on this hypothesis, themselves as little free as any others.

But, looking at the matter from a practical point of view, and it is only thus that I care to treat it, what is really of importance is what we can ourselves do to change our characters for the better. I am addressing a congregation the great majority of whom are at that time of life when most important work in this way can be done; when most important work certainly *is* done, whether for good or for evil—work of which they who are doing it are usually at the time quite unconscious. It is certainly startling to see with what careless hands men scatter the seeds whose fruit they must eventually taste, some sowing to the flesh, certain in the end of the flesh to reap corruption: others sowing to the Spirit who shall, of the Spirit, reap life everlasting—the one, perhaps, little more than the other reflecting on what they are doing, or conscious of its immense importance to them. It seems, then, that there is some practical utility in considering what part of the process of building up our characters is within our own control, and what the promise of freedom through the truth can give us.

Now the mental process of suggestion of thoughts is one over which our will exercises no direct control. It goes on even in sleep; in our waking hours thoughts sometimes flash into our minds unbidden and unexpected: sometimes the thought which would have been most useful to us does not present itself at the right time, the idea or the word which we are in search of refuses to suggest itself. We can and do, however, exercise great influence over this process of suggestion by our knowledge of the laws which regulate it, in particular the law that a thought which has been often before the mind will be likely to present itself again, and that of two thoughts which have been connected before, one will be likely to suggest the other. In this way we are able to make preparation beforehand for any special occasion, and to provide that we shall then be furnished with the thoughts and words which we foresee that we shall require. The process of suggestion of desires is also out of our direct control. Sometimes desires naturally arise on the presence of their object; at other times, even in the absence of their object, when the thought of it presents itself in the ordinary course of mental suggestion; and the more the thought is entertained the stronger the desire, and the more likely that both thought and desire will recur.

Now desire leads to action; we do not act without some motive, but in order to bring about some result which seems to us desirable. And the process of suggestion of desires, we have seen, is not under the immediate control of the will: *but our real freedom consists in our power of resistance to desire.* It is not practically true that our will is irresistibly swayed by the motives which are presented to it, in the same way that a body is constrained to move by the forces which act upon it. Take the most simple case, when we are not in any degree swayed by passion, when we are, let us suppose, playing a game of skill, or when we find it necessary to take action in some practical matter in which our sole object is to take the course which our judgment shall approve as most advantageous. We do not necessarily take the course which our judgment, on a first sight view, recommends as best; we pause on the probability that more mature consideration may show a preferable mode of action. The suggestion of arguments in favour of different courses is a mental process which takes place independently of the will. One mind is naturally more fertile in such suggestions than another, and no effort of will will place the inferior in this respect on a level with the superior. All he can do is by avoiding hasty action, and by patient thought, to get all that his understanding is capable of furnishing. Now this constitutes the main difference between the action of a motive on the mind, and the action of a force on the body, that no material body, when a force is presented to it, and there is no opposing force, can choose not to move, on the chance that a stronger force may act on it hereafter. It cannot say, It is true this is a strong force which is pressing me in such a direction, but it is better to wait, because if I do, it is possible a stronger force may afterwards urge me in another direction. To my purpose, it is immaterial what account a speculative philosopher may, on further analysis, give of this power of resistance to desire, but practically it is in this power of resistance that all our freedom consists. The process of suggestion of thoughts and desires goes on independently of us: our choice is only whether or not we will yield to them. If there were no power of resistance, we must drift like a balloon, which is at the mercy of the current in which it finds itself; but we are rather like the ships which, "though they be driven of fierce winds," yet by means of the resistance which the rudder offers can be guided "whithersoever the governor listeth." This power of resistance is not altogether wanting in the lower animals, but in all of them it is weak, and in some is nearly entirely absent. In man, at times, it disappears under the pressure of strong bodily cravings; but when it does, he ceases to deserve to be called free. And if a man's impulses are altogether uncontrollable, he is counted a maniac, and not held responsible for his actions.

I have heard of such a case as a young man to whom fortune had at an early age given abundant wealth without restraint, boasting of his perfect freedom. Not a wish did he form that he did not immediately gratify. Not a whim seized him that he did not in a moment carry into act. He was settled here to-day; if the idea took him he would be on his way to Italy to-morrow. Such a one might mean to boast himself free, but he, in reality, proclaimed himself a slave—constrained to obey each impulse that moved him, drifting rudderless, as the gusts of passion impelled him. Such a case as I have described may justly be regarded as exceptional; for there are few who are not prevented by external impediments of different kinds from gratifying many of their desires. But can we not recognise the same picture on a smaller scale ofttimes when we are under no restraint from without, and impulses incredibly weak, are as helplessly submitted to? Is this case so very uncommon?—You sit down to some task of study that you have resolved to undertake; scarcely has your work been begun when some other subject of inquiry suggests itself, or the thought of some book of amusement, or something else to divert you from your appointed task. Immediately that impulse is obeyed, and your work abandoned; you return to it after a time, only to be diverted from it anew. At length, the time comes for leaving off, and you find that nothing has been done. When the matter is thought over, it will be seen that the power of concentrating attention, and of repelling diverting impulses, is itself a part of freedom. Need I say how much that power may be gained by the discipline of the studies of this place rightly used ; or, on the other hand, how much of mental tension is lost by habits of frivolous reading. I do not mean to include under the name the study of works of imagination which demand of the reader some effort of his own mind to enter into them ; but I mean that reading in which the reader's mind is completely passive ; for the evil of which Bishop Butler complained has certainly not diminished since his time—namely, " The great number of books and papers of amusement by which time, even in solitude, is happily got rid of without the pain of attention : no part of time being more put to the account of idleness, or spent with less thought, than great part of that which is spent in reading ; so that people habituate themselves to let things pass through their minds rather than to think of them ; review and attention, and even forming a judgment, become a fatigue, and to lay anything before them that requires it is putting them quite out of their way."

Besides that loss of freedom which results from a general weakening of the power of control exercised by the will, a man becomes enslaved when he allows any passion to acquire a tyrannical mastery. Extreme cases, where the power of resistance is almost quite lost, will serve to illustrate the danger and mischief of those sins which tend to weaken it. The dipsomaniac (the word is comparatively a new one to express a terrible fact, the reality of which modern observation has ascertained) may be a man of ability—one in the intervals of its accesses hating his sin, understanding the ruin it is bringing on him, yet when the paroxysm seizes him, sacrificing money, health, fair fame, all his worldly prospects, to gratify cravings which he cannot master. How often has the love of gambling wasted inherited wealth, or blighted the fruits which the possession of brilliant intellect would have insured, while the victim, though conscious of his folly, has involved in his own ruin those whose welfare should be most dear to him. How powerless does the spendthrift often seem to resist the impulse,—I will not say to procure some present gratification, but often—to command the purchase of that whose possession will yield him hardly any pleasure, and which he well knows he cannot afford; he, too, with heartless selfishness, making others pay the penalty of his misconduct; a son pledging the resources of a father who has already made more sacrifices on his behalf than he had any right to claim; a husband and father consigning wife and children to poverty. And it would be false delicacy if I were to speak only of the dangers of intemperance or extravagance, and to omit to speak of the tendency of sins of impurity to acquire a terrible dominion, under the iron yoke of which powers of mind and body wither. I have engaged you to-day in some dry discussions, certainly unsuitable for any other pulpit, and possibly for this, and I should be sorry if I had only wrapped you in a cloud of metaphysics, and not left on you a definite impression. I wished to make you understand that, while what freedom we possess consists in our power of resistance to the impulse of desire, and to the entertainment of thoughts suggested to us, the suggestion of those thoughts and desires is independent of our direct control, obeying laws of its own as real as the law of gravitation—laws which we can only control by complying with them ; for here, as in every other department of nature, we can only command by obeying. And as certainly as in making preparation for an examination, or for speaking in public, by dwelling beforehand on the topics on which we shall have to speak, we can insure that the thoughts we want shall suggest themselves at the proper time, so certainly will the mind which has permitted itself to dwell with pleasure on thoughts polluting and enervating be again invaded by similar suggestions, the frequency of which will amount to a tyranny groaned under, yet most difficult to shake off.

A few words may be said as to the details of the process by which the will loses its power. We have heard much recently of the theory that we are but machines. If we are machines, we are machines the action of which is determined by physical causes utterly disproportionate; for a word, a look, may determine our action at the most important crisis of our lives. It seems a contradiction in terms to speak of a machine which wills, and whatever philosophic theory we form, the fact is certain that we do deliberate and choose. If a magnet be held to iron filings they have no choice whether or not they will join themselves to it. When an attraction is presented to us, we can refuse to obey; we can suspend our action, and allow countervailing motives to operate. Other men are persuaded that we can, for they blame us if we blindly yield to impulse. If a worker at a factory step incautiously within reach of a whirling wheel, we do not blame the machine which reduces his body to an unsightly lump of mangled flesh; it has but acted according to its nature, and done what it could not help doing. But when we blame the sufferer for his want of caution, or the owner of the factory for not having guarded the machinery, by the very act of blame, we express our belief that they were not mere machines, but could have done otherwise if they had pleased. If a man believed himself to be the mere plaything of the motives which act on him, he would yield himself quietly to these irresistible forces, and behave as a wise man or a profligate, according as the better or worse desire chanced to prevail. It would be as unmeaning to say that he ought to be more virtuous than he is, as to say that he ought to be a foot taller than he is. For there is no meaning in saying that anything ought to be that which it has no power to be. But the existence in us of a power to resist impulse is attested to us by the chidings of our own conscience, and by the reproaches of our fellow-men when we fail to use that power rightly.

And yet, though to describe us simply as machines is to use very misleading language, it is indisputable that there are many of our actions that can only be described as mechanical, and that the process of education that we undergo may be described as a transference of a portion of our acts and thoughts from that sphere of our life which is directly controlled by thought and volition to that which proceeds with scarcely any consciousness on our part. You are familiar with what takes place in the education of the skilled musician, how that which he originally learned with attention and toil becomes so easy to him that he can perform it without a thought, and talk of other things the while. This is what is going on in education of all kinds, that actions are becoming instinctive, trains of thought so linked together that they cannot now be disjoined, and the desired word and thought suggests itself spontaneously. And far the larger portion of this education we receive without knowing it at the time. How vast a difference it will make to you hereafter what is the character of that part of your life which has come to be nearly independent of your volition ; whether to do God's will is that which comes naturally to you ; or whether temptation can only be resisted by effort and struggle. There is no time of life too advanced for a sinner to repent and turn to God ; but, surely, there is an immense difference between the condition of him to whom the holy thought is that which first suggests itself, the right action that which presents itself instinctively, and the condition of him whose task is to unwind, if he may, the chains which long habit has wrapped round him, whose mind is beset by hosts of impure imaginations claiming to be welcomed as once they had been, and who needs perpetual vigilance in order that the sinful thought should not pass into sinful act. And it is remarkable how every form of vicious indulgence not only weakens power of resistance to the particular temptation yielded to, but produces a general paralysis of the will, and deprives the sinner of the power to set aside any impediment, and throw himself with all his energy on any desired task.

There will probably be some present but lately come to the University, and who hear me now for the first time. Would that I could impress them with my conviction of the importance of the few years they will spend here, which will probably determine whether for life they are to be freemen or · slaves ; according as by discipline and self-denial they learn to have under full control all the powers of body and mind with which God has endowed them, or as by self-indulgence and yielding to temptation they wind round themselves chains of habit, slight at first, afterwards found to be iron fetters. When one compares all that is given up with the miserable sensual gratification that is received in exchange, one cannot but repeat the Apostle's warning, Beware " lest there be any fornicator or profane person like Esau, who for one morsel of meat, sold his birthright : for ye know how that afterwards when he would have inherited the blessing he was rejected, for he found no place of repentance, though he sought it carefully with tears."

Thanks be to God, brethren, these words which

I have read are but a warning, and not a description of the state into which any of you have fallen. If you have fallen under the dominion of sin in any of its various forms of temptation, first resolve that you will not be one of those willing, contented slaves in whom the spirit of freedom is extinct, but that you will fight and struggle to be free. And if you find your strength small and your strugglings vain, still lift up your heads, for there is a Helper and Deliverer at hand.

You have heard the promise of Him who is the Truth: "Ye shall know the truth, and the truth shall make you free." He whose work it is to save His people from their sins has by His apostle given us the promise — "Sin shall not have dominion over you," and the exhortation, "Walk in the Spirit, and ye shall not fulfil the lusts of the flesh." His own life was one of self-denial, the very opposite to that self-indulgent yielding to desire which I have described as slavery; and He has commanded us to take up our cross and follow in His steps. And, as of old, at the words "Arise and walk," the feet and ankle bones of the lame man received strength, so even now His word is all-powerful; and when He gives a command, He gives also strength to obey the command. He has promised His Holy Spirit to them that ask Him. Make trial of that promise of Him who cannot lie. If worsted in any conflict, be not so faint-hearted and unbelieving as to abandon the struggle as unavailing. Draw near to your Master for fresh supply of the strength which He has promised to give; and relying on His might, not your own, renew the battle. May God be with you all, brethren, to " strengthen such as do stand, and to comfort and help the weakhearted, and to raise up them that fall, and finally to beat down Satan under your feet."

XIV

PROGRESS

"But many that are first shall be last, and the last shall be first."
—St. Matthew xix. 30.

It is a question we hear discussed from time to time, and which has interest for us here, What correspondence is there between a man's university career and his success in after life? Are the honours we bestow here a sure presage of subsequent distinctions? Are those who fail with us, to the end laggards in the race? It is a question on which instances can be produced on both sides. Not to travel out of the list of our own graduates, of the two distinguished men whose statues grace the entrance of our college,[1] one has left on our rolls the records of his undergraduate success; the other, during his residence here, found little of happiness or honour, and when he went away none who had watched his career would have ventured to imagine that he was one to whose

[1] Burke (scholar, 1746) and Goldsmith.

memory his place of education would ever have pleasure in paying honour. So, against the names of Ussher and Berkeley, we have to set that of Swift,[1] who, though far from having misspent his

[1] The facts collected by Mr. Forster enable me to interpret the statement which has puzzled Swift's former biographers, that he obtained his degree *speciali gratia*; for it seems to me that the course of procedure at the Dublin University altered less in the interval between Swift's time and mine than it has done in my own lifetime. A degree examination is a modern invention which did not exist in Swift's time. The qualification for a degree was the performance of a certain scholastic disputation; but before a candidate was admitted to dispute, he must have completed a certain number of terms. In Dublin an examination has always been held at the beginning of each term in the subjects lectured on in the preceding term, and a term did not count towards a candidate's degree until he had attended the corresponding examination. Mr. Forster has recovered the records of one of the examinations of Swift's last college year. He obtained best marks in his Greek and Latin authors, was pronounced to have written his Latin theme carelessly, and in what then went by the name of "Physics," to have failed altogether. This discriminating judgment commends itself to us as very likely to have been a just one. On these marks he could not have passed the examination, and therefore, when the time came for graduation of his class, he probably had credit only for having passed eleven examinations instead of twelve, which I believe to have been the proper number. Rigorous justice, then, would have degraded him to a lower class, and postponed his graduation for a year. Actually, he was allowed to take his degree, but the "grace" for the degree could not be supplicated for in the usual form, "Ut duodecim termini a matriculatione in artium studio, etc.," and it was necessary, therefore, that a "special" grace should be obtained. The entry, *speciali gratia*, disappears from the registry shortly after Swift's time, and, as I imagine, in consequence of the adoption of the plan by which the case of men deficient by a single examination was afterwards met—namely, the holding of a supplemental examination, at which they were given another opportunity of maintaining their position. The evidence, then, would lead us to think of Swift not as an idle under-

time here as much as has sometimes been represented, has given occasion to his latest biographer to contrast his comparative failure with the successes of a class-fellow, whose name has now fallen into complete obscurity.

On the whole, the conclusion we may come to is, that while many of the qualities which insure success in the contests of youth (such as diligence, energy, power of concentrating the attention on the work in hand) are likely to remain improved by exercise, and to insure like success in the contests of later life; and while there are some special gifts, the possession of which manifests itself at a very early age, we must own that cases do, from time to time, occur when it is comparatively late in life that men discover the work congenial to them, and that under the pressure of necessity, or at the promptings of a late-roused ambition, they find energy to prosecute it with success. Even in the course of the three or four years young men spend here, we can constantly see their relative position alter. Some who come up from school far in advance of their class-fellows

graduate, but as one who confined his studies to subjects which interested himself, neglecting some parts of the prescribed *curriculum*. His shortcomings were not very great, and were treated with every indulgence; and no doubt, if he had been an idle man, it would not have hurt his pride so much, as it would seem it did, that any indulgence should have been necessary. He always retained a strong friendship for his college tutor.

win their first triumphs with so little exertion that they expect to gain other victories on as easy terms. Then, thinking themselves able with impunity to give up much of their time to unprofitable pursuits, they find themselves outstripped by despised competitors whose powers had ripened more slowly, or who had been forced to compensate by sheer industry for early disadvantages. So we find that there are first who become last, and last who become first. You will observe that the text does not say that this reversal of position always takes place. But the words, *many* that are first shall be last, assert no more than in our experience of life we constantly witness.

What our Lord taught on more than one occasion in the words of the text, is that it is not merely with regard to the things of this life that this change of relative position occurs, but that even in that race, the prizes of which are eternal, those who at first run well sometimes do not retain their advantage to the end.

I do not think it adequately brings out the meaning of the text to interpret it, as is sometimes done, of merely apparent advantage, as if it only meant that there are some who in man's sight appear to be first, who are discerned by Him who seeth the hearts to deserve to take the lowest place. We need not doubt that even in respect to things spiritual, one man may have not only apparent, but very real, advantages over another, and yet fail to keep these advantages permanently. This may be granted even if it be held that no step made on the heavenly way can ever be lost; for we are for the moment speaking not of actual, but of comparative progress, and it is evidently possible that a man may, without losing any ground himself, be overtaken and passed by others. This is the case presented in the parable which St. Matthew relates to have been spoken by our Lord in order to impress the lesson of the text. We are not given to understand that the labourers who obeyed the call they received early in the morning to work in the vineyard were slack or unfaithful in the performance of the labour they had undertaken; their superiority to those who were standing idle must therefore have been real, and not merely apparent; yet we find that there were some who did not begin to work till the burden and heat of the day were over, who received from Him who judgeth righteously as large a reward as they.

This parable had many applications. Take first the case of the Jewish nation. It had possessed the knowledge of the true God for centuries, while the surrounding peoples were sunk in darkness and superstition. Who can doubt the reality of the advantage over them which it possessed? While their neighbours were striving to win the favour of gods, the patrons of war and lust, by acts corresponding to the supposed character of their divinities—forcing the attention of their Deities, when their prayers were not answered, by cutting themselves with knives and lancets till the blood gushed out upon them; burning their sons with fire for burnt-offerings to Baal (or, as the Psalmist has it, "sacrificing their sons and daughters to devils, shedding innocent blood, even the blood of their sons and daughters, whom they sacrificed to their idols"), and mixing these ensanguined rites with wild orgies of unbridled lasciviousness, in which, also, they thought to offer acceptable worship to their gods—the Jews believed in a God who loved righteousness and hated iniquity, whose favour was to be gained not by thousands of rams or ten thousands of rivers of oil, not by giving their first-born for their transgression, the fruit of their body for the sin of their soul, but by doing justice, loving mercy, and walking humbly before Him. Thus was generation after generation of Israelites trained in the love of truth, and purity, and justice, while the ever-brightening declarations of prophecy gave promise of clearer light on the religious truths which they still but dimly discerned. With truth, then, could that New Testament writer who was charged by his countrymen with striving to annihilate every special prerogative of the sons of Abraham, reply to the questions—What advantage hath the Jew? or what profit is there of circumcision? Much every way. To them were committed the oracles of God. To them pertained the adoption, and the glory, and the covenants, and the giving of the law, and the service of God, and the promises. Theirs were the fathers, and of them, as concerning the flesh, Christ came, who is over all, God blessed for ever.

The Jews have long since lost their superiority. We believe that we have long since learned from them the lessons they were commissioned to teach, and we look on them as having lagged behind in the progress of spiritual enlightenment. Yet their loss of place was due to no actual retrogression on their parts. It was not that they gave up any part of the truth they possessed, but that they refused to open their eyes to the fuller revelations of truth which God disclosed to them. They kept their talent buried, and would not permit it to fructify, as He who had entrusted it to them designed. Never were the Jews more free from idolatry than since their return from Babylon. Their aversion to the prevailing allurements of the surrounding heathendom reached the point of narrowness and bigotry. They held in honour all that their latest prophets had made known to them of the spiritual requirements of their law. They cannot be charged with going back. But when He came who was to be not only the glory of His people Israel, but the light of the Gentiles also, other nations came, and walked and rejoiced in that light; while they who had exulted in the prerogatives of superior knowledge, confident that they must always remain the guide of the blind, the light of them which are in darkness, refused to know anything of the new truths which the despised Gentiles were eager to learn. And so they dropped behind in the race, not because they took any backward step, but because, in indolent and arrogant self-satisfaction with the attainment they had made, they stopped short, and allowed themselves to be overpassed by others.

Take, next, another application which our Lord's words, when they were spoken, were meant to have. Those who, at the time, were most respected in the nation for their morality and their piety were, as a general rule, indifferent to His teaching, and looked down with scorn on the converts who flocked to Him. "Have any of the rulers or of the Pharisees believed on Him?" was their cry; "but this people who knoweth not the law are cursed." For while the Scribes and Pharisees stood aloof, the publicans and harlots were pressing into the kingdom of God, joyfully embracing the glad tidings that their degradation was not hopeless, for that He, who was Himself despised of men, looked on them with loving compassion. He had come to call not the righteous, but sinners to repentance. He had come to seek and to save them which were lost. He had come to wash away their sins, and to give them an inheritance among them who were sanctified through faith in Him. Many of them accepted the message of salvation, which they who deemed themselves their superiors disdained : and thus, in this case, also, it was true that the first were the last, and the last first.

But, surely, it would be untrue to say that those who were once accounted first never had had any real advantage. Shall we say that they to whom the oracles of God had been committed did not do well in striving to acquaint themselves with what those fountains of truth contained, even though, in their diligent searching of the Scriptures, thinking that, in the dead letter, they had life, they failed to find Him of whom all the Scriptures testified, in whom they really might have had life ; and so their boasted knowledge of the law did not profit them. Shall we say that they did not do well in obeying those precepts of the law, the meaning of which was clear, without need of an interpreter, and that they had not a right to look down with disapprobation, and to regard as their moral inferiors those who were living by extortion, and rapine, and unchastity? We might as well deny that the prodigal who left his home, and wasted his father's substance in riotous living sank, for the time, deeply below the brother who was able to say, that many years he had served his father, and had never, at any time, transgressed his commandments.

It might seem that the point on which I am insisting was one on which it is unnecessary to dwell; but I do not think so. At the present day, the Publican is a much more popular character than the Pharisee. It is not uncommon now, in light literature, to have our sympathies enlisted for those who have incurred the disapprobation of society: to paint in bright colours the kindliness and good-nature of these light-hearted Bohemians: to touch tenderly on their faults as if they were but the transgressions of some conventional restrictions: to depict the affronts and rebuffs they have to endure from those who, in the world's eyes, are counted more respectable, and to contrast with their amiability, the selfishness, the rapacity, the untruthfulness, and false seeming, of which persons may be guilty without forfeiting the world's good opinion; and so to present the practical conclusion that the rules by which our judgments have been governed are all wrong; and that vice is, on the whole, more lovely, and not really worse than virtue. I have seen one case in which a writer, endowing a vicious character with some noble qualities (as a writer of fiction out of his boundless store is easily able to do), draws the moral that "different minds have different standards of right and wrong, and that we must not judge one another."

We must not let ourselves be abused by any representations of this kind, or be persuaded to think lightly of the immutable distinction between right and wrong which God has written on our hearts. In this life we meet only with mixed characters. The greatest saint has his human weaknesses: the greatest sinner his redeeming qualities. The ruthless smuggler, who had shed human blood like water, might be able very truly to say that he had been faithful to his employers, and "had always accounted for cargo to the last stiver." Unskilful or prejudiced historians are apt to paint their villains all black; and the result is that some succeeding inquirer, cooler in temper, is able to scrape off some of the darker pigments, and to bring to light some traces of noble or estimable qualities which his predecessors had buried out of sight. In this way there is scarcely one of those whom history has marked for infamy who has not been, in modern days, whitewashed, or to use a better-sounding word, rehabilitated. Yet, in many cases, the original estimate was nearest the truth. It is a common symptom of what Macaulay has called the "lues biographica," to be so blinded by the virtues of a good man as to be unable to censure his faults. It is surely a worse weakness to be so blinded by the virtues of a villain as to have no censure for his villainy. He who rules the world can unravel the tangled skein of which human character is made up; and it is wonderful how, even in this life, the good and the evil receive each their fit recompense of reward. The wickedness of the bad man does not prevent his reaping the natural fruit of whatever good there may be in him. He, for instance, who has outraged every human law may find the meet reward for his courage and his fidelity to his comrades in their trust and admiration. And there are no favourites of heaven who can commit wrong-doing with impunity. He who has served God best, while he is obliged to own that every thing good in him is requited in even fuller measure than he could have dared to claim, finds too that every sin he commits brings with it bitter punishment—punishment which he feels more keenly than a more practised offender, as indeed it is meet he should, since his sins are less excusable as committed against fuller light. Everything in nature, then, teaches us that we are not to think lightly of evil in others, or in ourselves, because of any attractive qualities which may co-exist with it in the sinner. To use an old illustration,[1] it would be as rational, merely because it had been ascertained that a patient was not affected with heart-disease, to pronounce him well, and give him leave to get up. One part of the bodily frame may be attacked with fatal disease, and the brain and other vital organs still perform their work with perfect regularity. Yet, as the disease eats its way, the neighbouring organs are surely at length affected. And such is the sure result of permitted indulgence in sin. At first, no doubt, a man who denies himself no pleasure because the law of God forbids it, may continue to exhibit much kindness and amiability toward others. But the tendency of vice is to "harden all within, and petrify the feeling;" and consideration for others will not be suffered long to stand in the way of the gratification of the desires of a man who has habituated himself to subordinate all to self, and with whom conscience has no restraining power.

[1] Non est cardiacus (Craterum dixisse putato)
Hic aeger. Recte est igitur, surgetque? negabit,
Quod latus aut renes morbo tententur acuto.
—Hor. Sat., ii. 3.

The Gospel does not teach us to think lightly of sin, though it has brought the blessed tidings that the evil is not without remedy. It does not encourage those who are last to deceive themselves with the idea that they are not last, though it reveals to them the possibility that they may one day be the first. So was it with the publicans and sinners who flocked to hear our Lord. Their superiors in morality and in obedience to the precepts of their law counted themselves to be whole men who had no need of the physician, and satisfied with their existing state, they remained in a frozen condition of arrested development. Those, on the contrary, who had been convinced by our Lord that they were sinners, but who also believed His word that they were such as He had come to seek and to save, obeying His call to repentance, restored to life and self-respect, cherishing carefully those seeds of better which He had planted in them and taught them to recognise, made spiritual growth so rapid as to stand soon on a far higher level than they who had lately looked down on them. In short, then, the first may become last, and the last first, whenever that which is now last still has the living principle of growth and development, while that which is now first has arrived at the unprogressive state which is the commencement of decay, and which ends in death.

I have spoken hitherto only of comparative advance, and have been content to accept the assumption that every advance made is absolutely permanent, everything gained incapable of being ever lost. But this is not the teaching of the New Testament. The Gospel tells of some of the good seed which rapidly sprung up, but afterwards was scorched and withered away, either on account of shallowness of soil, or on account of the pressure of other plants. And this is explained of some who receive the word with joy, and believe for a while, but afterwards are offended, and fall away. But it is worth while to consider for a little what we mean when we use the word permanent in speaking of man who fleeth as it were a shadow, and never continueth in one stay. The old man smiles when he hears the young man professing that his feelings can never change. He has seen too many eternal passions blaze out, burn away, and be succeeded by others as transitory. How many old friendships are loosened or dissolved by disputes about money, or rivalries for honour, or from taking of different sides in religion or politics. How many former adversaries, when brought together by common interests, are willing to confess that they had formerly not done each other justice. Often has the experience of the Trojan chieftain been repeated, who found that in his danger safety came from the quarter whence he had least expected it, the help of those whom he had regarded as his deadly foes. Scarcely had we ceased to commemorate the battle of Waterloo by annual festivities, when another 18th June (1855) found the two "natural enemies" fighting side by side. How few of our public men live through a long career without finding themselves at its close surrounded by very different allies from those among whom they had stood at its commencement. Burke and Brougham and Burdett and Peel and Gladstone are a few of the names which rise to illustrate the truth of what I have been saying. An Augustinian monastery trained the overthrower of Romanism in Germany; one of the strictest of High Churchmen founded the most extensive of modern schisms in the Church of England; from one evangelical household in our own time the two Newmans went forth to opposite results, both equally abhorrent to the convictions of their early years. How then is it that with all this experience of mutability we can put so much reliance on one another? How is it that our most valued friendships are those which have subsisted the longest? How is it that two people can pledge themselves to love each other to their lives' end, and that in most cases the pledge is faithfully and happily redeemed?

The explanation of the paradox is got when we examine what the facts really are, when we say that two persons, after long intervals of time, regard each other with the same feelings. The traveller over Californian plains may find them arrayed in the same gay clothing which had charmed him twenty years before. The flowers are not the same, but each which has perished, ere it died has scattered a multitude of seeds abroad, and has renewed and multiplied itself in its descendants. And so it is when we compare the feelings of to-day with the feelings of past years. No human feeling is permanent. What seems to be one continuous muscular strain is but a succession of throbs of effort. The most bitter griefs, the most racking anxieties, come in paroxysms leaving intervals during which the sufferer can, if he will, jest and laugh. And so the feeling with which we regard those we love now cannot be in any strict sense the feeling with which we regarded them in former days, but it is the offspring of it. What we felt then bore its fruit in kindly words, in deeds of love, in mutual services rendered, in counsel given, in practical proofs of affection. And from these, as their natural fruit, fresh love has sprung up, so that though our affection remains unchanged, it is the same only as our bodies remain to outward appearance the same: while there really is going on a continuous process of waste and renewal, resulting in the growth and increase of the healthy frame from infancy to maturity, yet liable to disease and dissolution if what is daily lost is not daily given back.

It is idle to think that our love to God can be maintained on other terms than those on which human love is kept fresh. There are some who would practically reduce their spiritual life to the memory of past feelings, and who put their confidence in having once experienced emotions which, though they cannot be reproduced with the same intensity, were undoubtedly genuine at the time. The memory of a dead friend may be a hallowed recollection, but it is an insult to Him who never dies, if in our thoughts He lives but in the recollection of the past. . Whatever holy feelings He has given us experience of were not intended to be cherished like the withered flowers given us by a hand now no more which we preserve as a sacred treasure, but were meant to renew themselves by sowing their seeds of earnest resolve, of constant striving to do the will of Him we love. When they are so renewed, they result in something which gains far more than an equivalent in strength and power for what it loses in youthful fervour. St. James speaks of a dead faith. We call a seed dead when nothing will spring from it. If this process of transformation of feeling into action, and consequent generation of new feelings does not go on, our emotions have no life, they pass away without leaving successors, and what might have been a fruitful field becomes a wilderness.

It follows from all that I have been saying that we use a very fallacious method when we form an estimate of ourselves by comparing ourselves with others. Supposing that we are entirely free from self-deception, and judge with absolute correctness of our present state, yet our relative position may alter, either on account of their more rapid progress, or because of our actually losing the advance we have made. Our talent may gain but one or two talents, while that entrusted to them gains ten, or we may bury our talent in a napkin, and suffer the penalty of having it taken from us and given to those who show themselves willing faithfully to employ it. It is the existence of these latent possibilities, beyond the power of man's eye to discern, which gives force to the lesson, " Judge not, that ye be not judged." That maxim is grossly abused if it is interpreted to mean that there is no possibility of a fixed standard of moral judgment, that we cannot tell when our fellows are doing wrong, or cannot venture to say that what they are doing is wrong, and will be attended with evil consequences. We may see all this with perfect accuracy; but if we venture on account of what we see faulty in them to exalt ourselves above them, in the first place, we may shut our eyes to sins in ourselves worse and more pregnant with evil than those sins of theirs of which we think so harshly, though it may be quite truly; and secondly, we may overlook the good which may co-exist with their faults, which may be blessed by God's grace to grow so as to expel the evil, and in consequence of which they may attain to heights far above us.

The same truth that those are last who shall be first gives us a lesson of encouragement if we are tempted to despond because we see others who seem far in advance of us: we must look not on them but on the path before us; nay, look not on it, but on Him, the author and finisher of our faith, who has trod that path before us, who gives power to the faint, and will hold up our goings if we stumble. The human models of excellence, intellectual or moral, that we set before us in our youth, disappoint us as we grow older. What had once seemed far beyond our reach we now count easy of attainment, or, perhaps, we regard it as progress made on a wrong road which we care not to follow. Nothing less must content us than to be perfect even as our Master is perfect. Forgetting those things which are behind, and reaching forth to those which are before, let us press toward the mark for the prize of the high calling of God in Christ Jesus.

XV

TRUTHFULNESS

" Putting away lying, speak every man truth with his neighbour, for we are members one of another."—EPHESIANS iv. 25.

IF there be any duty which it might seem unnecessary to enforce by Christian motives, it is that of truthfulness, of which the text speaks. There are some subjects on which the rules of fashionable morality by no means coincide with what we learn from the Bible ; but on this subject, it would appear that men might very safely be trusted to the guidance of the popular code of honour. All agree in counting a lie disgraceful. The strongest insult you can offer a man is to tell him that he lies. We are accustomed to pride ourselves on truth, as a specially English virtue. Different nations are tempted to different kinds of sins ; and lying is not the sin that has attractions for the people of a nation that has long been powerful abroad, and has enjoyed civil and political freedom at home. Falsehood and cunning are the natural weapons of the weak ; but such expedients are disdained as slavish and cowardly by those who feel themselves strong enough boldly to avow what they think, and what they have done, and to take the consequences.

We have been accustomed also to look upon truthfulness, not only as a specially English, but as a specially Protestant virtue. Nor is this altogether without reason ; for, if the standard of morality in this matter is not as high in some foreign countries as in ours, I believe that some share of the blame is fairly chargeable on their religious instructors. It is true that some of the language used by these teachers is so strict that we almost hesitate to go along with them. I quote the words of two who have been most called in question for the laxity of their doctrine. One of them says : "A lie is always a sin, even though it be told in joke, or to benefit our neighbour ; even though, by a lie, a man could save his life, it would not be lawful to tell it." The other says : "So foully venomous is a lie, that even though honour, life, or the salvation of the world were at stake, and could be saved by ever so slight a lie, which would bring injury to none, yet ought that little lie to be rejected, and the world's destruction rather permitted."

This strictness of theoretical teaching may, in a great measure, be ascribed to the influence of St.

Augustine. That great Father had a very honest hatred of deceit. Some of you know the success with which he overthrew the account, accepted in his day, of Paul's reproof of Peter at Antioch, and which represented the dispute as a scene concerted by the Apostles, who were really at one in the matter. Augustine, with so much indignation, rejected a theory which attributed simulation to the Apostles, and made them guilty of acting a lie, that even those who would be best pleased to clear Peter from all charge of error, do not venture now to use for his vindication the solution at one time accepted by some of the highest authorities in the Church. When treating directly on the subject of falsehood, Augustine's morality is almost impracticably severe. He does not allow the smallest deviation from truth, though such might be necessary to save the life of an innocent man from his pursuers, not even though, by such a falsehood, the eternal salvation of another could be gained.

These doctrines passed into the teaching of the Scholastic divines, with whom Augustine was an authority of the highest rank. But the severity of this doctrine was indirectly mitigated by another influence. They had learned from ethical speculations antecedent to Christianity a classification of the moral virtues under four heads—prudence, justice, temperance, and fortitude. In order to make out veracity to be a duty, it was necessary to find a place for it under one of these four heads. It is certainly a curious example how practice may be affected by what seem to be most harmless differences in scientific theory, that the greatest difference has been found to exist between the importance attached to veracity, among those whose ethical teachers made it a duty of primary obligation, and those who treated a lie as a sin only if it could be shown to be a breach of justice, for that was the head under which it was found easiest to class veracity. Many of you will remember how Bishop Butler habitually puts veracity, justice, and goodness all on the same level. But when veracity was regarded merely as a subordinate branch of justice, there were some falsehoods of which it was not, at first sight, easy to establish the sinfulness. It would, no doubt, be clearly a sin to tell a lie calculated to inflict an injury on one's neighbour; but where would be the injustice if the falsehood had no such tendency; nay, if it were even intended to do good. Again, it would, no doubt, be a breach of that virtue which renders to each man his due, if a witness were not to make true answers to a judge lawfully entitled to demand the truth from him; but where is the injustice of withholding truth from one who has no lawful claim to receive it from you? For instance, if an impertinent person ask a question which he has no right to put, is there any injustice in answering with the first ready lie which may suggest itself?

The manner in which these difficulties were settled was, that though, in compliance with St. Augustine's authority, it was acknowledged that every lie was a sin, yet a distinction was made. Three classes of lies were enumerated: the pernicious lie, intended to injure your neighbour; the officious lie, intended to do him a service; and the jocose, told only in sport; and of these the first alone was held to be a mortal sin: the others were accounted to be only venial sins—that is to say, frailties which do not separate him who lapses into them, from the love and favour of God, and which, if not specially repented of or forgiven, are at worst visited by temporal consequences, and, no matter how numerous, do not expose the transgressor to danger of eternal punishment. There were, however, divines who, testing this theory by extreme cases, found it still unreasonably strict, and who contended that, at least, some kinds of officious lies ought to be taken out of the category of sins altogether. For it was owned to be unjustifiable deliberately to commit even a venial sin. "The Church holds it better," says Dr. Newman, "for sun and moon to drop from heaven, for the earth to fail, and for all the many millions who are upon it to die of starvation in extremest agony than that one soul should commit one single venial sin."[1] But sublime as this language sounds, can it be reconciled with reason? In order to avert the destruction, we will not say of the whole human race, but of one innocent fellow-creature, ought a good man to hesitate to commit an act which would not separate himself from the favour of God, and would at worst draw on him some temporal punishment? And then, could an act which Christian charity seems to dictate be properly called, in any sense, a sin? There were divines who drew the consequence in theory, and followed it out in practice, that if it were permissible to tell a lie in order to gain such a temporal end as the saving a fellow-creature's life, still more was it allowable to lie and deceive for the noblest object of all, the good of the Church. Others who maintained that under no circumstances was it lawful for us to deceive our neighbour, held, nevertheless, that it was still quite innocent to allow him to deceive himself. For example, if we were questioned by men whom we knew to be assassins seeking the blood of an innocent man, supposing that we could not, without sin, answer them untruly; yet no one would maintain that it was our business to set them right, if, having given them an ambiguous

[1] *Anglican Difficulties*, Lecture viii.

answer, we perceived that they had misunderstood us, and were prosecuting their search in a wrong direction. From the discussion of these extreme cases were suggested theories of equivocation and mental reservation which have obtained unhappy notoriety. I have no wish, however, to dwell on the lax teaching of individual divines, condemned by others of their own communion; but I did think it necessary to take notice of the injurious effect of the doctrine common to all Roman Catholic divines, that a lie is, in itself, but a venial sin, unless there be some special reason to the contrary. Thus a malicious lie told to injure our neighbour would, no doubt, be a mortal sin; but, then, it is the malice and the intention to injure which gives the sin the graver character. If we were to agree to make the distinction between sins which this theory demands, our study of Scripture would certainly not lead us to class among sins in their own nature having no tendency to hinder eternal salvation, one concerning which we read such threatenings as these: "All liars shall have their part in the lake which burneth with fire and brimstone." "There shall, in no wise, enter into the heavenly city anything that defileth; neither whatsoever worketh abomination, or maketh a lie." "Without are murderers and idolaters, and whosoever loveth and maketh a lie."

But it may plausibly be said on behalf of the Roman Catholic distinction between mortal and venial sins that, so far from springing out of a desire to relax morality, it actually indicates a superiority of strictness to the Protestant standard. It must be understood that we are dealing with the case of a regenerate person, enjoying God's grace, and living in His favour; then, according to the Roman Catholic definition, a venial sin is one compatible with that state of grace; a mortal sin is one which puts him out of God's favour, kills the grace by which he lives, and entails the loss of his salvation, unless he is restored by contrition, confession, and absolution. A venial sin is one which need not be confessed, a mortal sin one which must. Now, Protestants, it is said, do not consider confession in any case to be necessary; and many of them hold that he who has been once justified can never, by any sin, forfeit God's favour; so that, instead of its being the case, as some of them suppose, that they hold all sins to be mortal, while Roman Catholics regard some as venial, it turns out, when the definitions of the terms have been explained, that they regard all a Christian's sins as venial, whereas Roman Catholics look on some of them as mortal.

But with whatever plausibility this argument might be urged, I believe that in real truth the most Antinomian teaching to be found among Protestants does less practical injury to their moral standard than that distinction between mortal and venial sin of which I speak. The Antinomian is not trained to look with special indulgence on any particular sins; his teaching relates to all alike, and even the removal of all fear that sinning will hazard his security of eternal salvation still leaves many motives to well-doing untouched. Very often his errors remain in the region of speculative theology, and do not descend to affect his practice. He who believes that his present conduct will not affect his future condition is in some respects in much the same state as he who does not believe in a future state; and there are many unbelievers, as well as many Antinomians, who live the purest lives. But when men are taught that there are certain sins for which they need fear no eternal punishment, not because God has forgiven them, but because these sins are in their own nature so light as not to entail the consequences which follow from graver sins, it is impossible that the sins thus leniently judged of can be regarded with any very strong detestation. And accordingly Dr. Newman fully acknowledges the different tone of feeling in respect of certain sins which is engendered by the teaching of his communion. And he owns and defends their toleration of the sins which are classified as venial. "The Church," he says, "cannot do everything. She has no warrant, and she has no encouragement, to enforce upon men in general more than those habits of virtue the absence of which would be tantamount to their separation from God; and she thinks she has done a great deal, and exults in her success, does she proceed so far; and she bears as she may what remains still to be done, in the conviction that did she attempt more she might lose all. There are sins which are simply incompatible with contrition and absolution under any circumstances; there are others which are disorders and disfigurements of the soul. She exhorts men against the second, she directs her efforts against the first."[1] There needs no fuller proof of the mischievous practical effect of this distinction between mortal and venial sin; the sins classed under the latter head not only come to be lightly regarded by the people, but even their religious guides content themselves with a formal protest, and think that it would be ill-spent labour to make any serious effort against them.

When I began to write this sermon I by no means intended to occupy so much of it with the faults of the teaching of another communion. My purpose was rather to speak of our own shortcom-

[1] *Anglican Difficulties*, Lecture viii.

ings, and that in a matter on which it might have been supposed that we were above reproach. Yet, enforced though this duty of truthfulness is by all the sanctions of religion and of public opinion, and whatever satisfaction we may feel in comparing the standard prevalent among ourselves with that among other peoples less favourably circumstanced, I fear we come very far short of what Christ's rule requires. In those ranks of life in which temptations to the grosser sins are less strong, sins of the tongue assume greater prominence. I dare say there are very few among such as hear me who would, without some strong temptation, wilfully say what they know to be totally untrue; but it is common enough for persons to say things the truth of which they have taken no pains to ascertain; to say things that are untrue, and which, with ordinary care, they might have found out to be untrue: to say things that, though not actually without foundation, are so coloured and exaggerated as to convey a totally false impression. Too often do we find persons of good character, in order to gain quite trifling objects, descending to petty misrepresentations of facts. And constantly in our daily life may we hear the commandment violated, "Thou shalt not bear false witness against thy neighbour." Things are said to the discredit of others; and a story passes from hand to hand for which even the person who first set it going would be puzzled to give any tolerable proof. Most persons will acknowledge that untruth is blamable when it tends to injure others, but no one will find it easy to avoid untruth of this kind who does not cultivate the habit of truth on all occasions.

I do not think it necessary in this congregation formally to refute the doctrine that a lie is to be regarded as but a venial sin except in the cases where it does harm to some one. There is, for example, one very common form of untruthfulness which has no direct tendency to injure others, and yet which will not be seriously defended. I mean untruthfulness prompted by the desire that we should ourselves be thought more highly of. Any claims that people have on the respect of others are seldom apt to lose on their own showing forth. If they have done wrong, their own version of the story seldom exhibits much cause for censure; if there are claims on them which they have very inadequately satisfied, they find it convenient, first, not to retain in their own memory a very accurate knowledge of exactly how much they have done, and then, when they tell the story, their performance comes out a great deal more than it actually has been. And in this there often is not much conscious falsehood, for it frequently happens that a man tells lies to himself, in order to keep up his own good opinion of himself, before he repeats those lies to others.

The best safeguard, as I have said, against falling into untruthfulness of this kind is to cultivate a habit of accurate truthfulness in ordinary conversation. Shall I be thought over-precise if I say that we ought to aim at being as careful about our statements in ordinary conversation as if we were giving evidence in a court of justice? Yet is not this what follows from our Lord's rule in the Sermon on the Mount, not to use any oath, but let our Yea be Yea, and our Nay Nay,—that the simple affirmation of one of His disciples ought to count for as much with him as if it were given under the sanction of an oath. Yet how many are there who give themselves the habit of embellishing and exaggerating every tale they repeat, sometimes, because they think it amusing, oftener, because through indolence of mind they will not take the trouble to know, or to remember, what the facts exactly are, and then think the best way of hiding their inaccuracy is unmistakable exaggeration. Falsehood of this kind may seem very excusable, inasmuch as it is prompted neither by vanity, nor malevolence, nor any other bad motive. Yet, on the other hand, it may be said that the less the motive, the less the excuse.

And if we give ourselves the habit of deserting truth with scarcely any inducement, how can we be expected to resist if exposed to any strong temptation to depart from it?

If the inattention to strict truth in small matters does no harm to others, it certainly does harm to the person guilty of it. The requirements of modern times have made necessary a degree of minute accuracy far greater than would have sufficed in former days. The first labourers in the fields of literature and science naturally turned to account all the most striking facts. In order to make progress, it has been necessary to take notice of the more minute facts which escaped the attention of the first observers. Persons engaged in any literary inquiry are constantly tempted to complain of the unveracity of their predecessors, as they learn by sad experience the danger of trusting any one's word, or taking a fact or reference on second-hand authority without verification. In short, a higher standard of accuracy is now demanded than would have sufficed in former days; and in every branch of literature and science a daily increasing closeness of observation and accuracy in reporting facts is required. And any one who has become unable to observe correctly and faithfully report what he has observed, may at any time find himself unable to discharge some task in which he will be extremely sorry to have failed.

I may congratulate myself that a very happy revolution of sentiment makes it unnecessary for me to do more than allude to one class of untruths, which in former times could not rightly have been omitted in a discourse on this subject before such an audience as I am addressing. The strange idea prevailed, and within living memory, that the relation between young people and those charged with their instruction was to be regarded as one of warfare, in which deceit was a weapon legitimate for the weaker party; so that a lie was not to be regarded as a sin if told by a schoolboy to his master, or by a college student to his tutor. For the prevalence of the notion that those who aim at making you wiser or better are to be regarded as your natural enemies, the instructors themselves were mainly answerable. It moves one's indignation still to read of the cruelty and tyranny that was practised towards the young. It is enough to quote the story told by Erasmus of an amiable and munificent divine, whose name is still held in deserved honour, how he called up after supper a boy of about ten years old, telling Erasmus that he was fresh from his mother, a pious woman, who had commended the child to his especial care: how he then soundly rated the lad for his insolence,

and had him flogged until he nearly fainted. On
Erasmus asking what had been the offence, the
answer was, " Oh, he had done nothing wrong, but
it is necessary to humble his spirit." What wonder
that in those who were treated as slaves the vices
of slaves should show themselves. We have cause
to rejoice in the practical success of the opposite
system with which the name of Dr. Arnold is so
honourably connected. If proof of that success
were needed this might suffice, that in addressing
an audience, many of whom are still in the pupil-
lary state, they would feel themselves insulted if I
were to assume that their ideas on the subject
of truth differed from those of other gentlemen.
And yet, I hope I may be forgiven for expressing
a doubt whether even yet the same standards of
truthfulness are applied by schoolboys, or even by
college students, where their equals, and where
those placed over them, are concerned: whether
a lie is not apt to count as venial, if only an
instructor is deceived, and if a fellow-student is
not injured, or even benefited; whether, for
example, the discredit attaches to the giving, or
obtaining assistance unfairly, if it can be done at
a mere pass examination, which would attach, if
it were done, at a competition for honours.

Returning to the general subject, it remains for
me to say a little more on those breaches of truth

which are certainly the most blameworthy, namely, those by which other persons are injured. For one such injury which is inflicted by wilful malignity, ten are caused by thoughtlessness and culpable negligence. To concoct a deliberate falsehood is, I am happy to say, not a very common offence; but merely abstaining from such sin as this is not showing regard for truth, if you take no pains to make sure whether what you do say is true or not; and if by repeating without inquiry what you have heard, you induce others to state, with the sanction of your authority, what may be entirely without foundation.

In judging of the character of another, one might suppose the natural order would be, first, to observe some instances of improper conduct on his part, and then to form an unfavourable opinion of him. Too commonly the actual order is the reverse: the unfavourable opinion comes first, and the facts to justify it are sought for afterwards. For some reasons a person is disliked, a prejudice is taken against him, a certain character is attributed to him. In conformity with that character there are certain actions that would be natural for him to perform; certain language that it would be natural for him to use. And nothing is more rapid than the passage from our conceptions of what a person *ought* to do, to a belief that he has actually done it. Let one more reckless than the rest take courage to make the assertion ; then, to all who share the prejudice the story carries its own proof ; and so, every day men have to bear the odium of opinions they do not hold ; of language they have never uttered ; of actions they have not committed. Especially is this apt to happen if any party interest is served by the circulation of the story. The rule that in balancing probabilities belief should be given to the side on which there is a preponderance of evidence is seldom acted on if the interests of a party require that a story should be believed. In that case it seems to be held that party loyalty demands that if there be any evidence whatever in favour of it, no matter how great the evidence against it, we should believe it, or at least assert it. You will remember how confidently bulletins were published, and believed in Ireland, of imaginary French victories in the great war with Germany.

And this is one of the reasons why party spirit in the Christian Church is to be hated, namely, that it tempts us to wish influence to be diminished which is likely to be used against us, and, consequently, not to be sorry when persons are discredited who are on the side opposed to ourselves ; forgetting that we are all really on the same side, fighting against common enemies, brethren in Christ, members of the same body, and that it is impossible that one member of the body can be injured without the whole being weakened. Many offences against truth would have been prevented from taking place had there been more of that charity which thinketh no evil. Did we love one another better, we should be more ready to do each other justice, and it would be less easy to us, as well as less pleasant, to think evil of each other. Once more, suppose what we have heard to the disadvantage of another be true, still, is it necessary for us to repeat it? If it gives us no real pleasure to think evil, or to speak evil, we shall not be fond of telling the tale of another's misconduct unless there be some good object to be gained by it. It would be difficult indeed to circulate a calumnious rumour, if only every one of us were as reluctant to repeat it as he ought to be.

The subject I have taken to-day is so extensive that it is difficult to compress it within reasonable limits, and I should detain you long if I were to attempt to touch on all the current forms of untruthfulness. I will, therefore, only say a few words in conclusion on controversial unveracity. Many who would scorn to misrepresent facts will not scruple to misrepresent their opponents' arguments. I will not inquire how far this is done wilfully; because it is an offence against truth, not only to say what you know to be false, but also to state what with reasonable pains you might have ascertained to be false. Very often the misrepresentation of the opponents is indirect. It is not actually stated that they deny certain truths, but by making a great parade of proving them it is implied that they do. One of the most common fallacies going is the "ignoratio elenchi," in which that is disproved which never had been asserted, and proved which never had been denied. When it is required to make a telling argument in defence of a bad cause, the rule most commonly acted on is this: Select, in order to prove it, a syllogism of which one premiss is true and the other false; silently take the false premiss for granted, and display all your ability in proving the true one. You thus not only gain the credit of having delivered a convincing argument, but you often succeed in casting on your opponents the odium of having denied what you have been at such elaborate pains to establish.

But, indeed, before we complain of disregard of truth, in the manner in which controversy is conducted, there is, with respect to religious controversy at least, a still deeper question: Would there be in theology so much hot and bitter controversy leading to so little result, if men loved truth better than the victory of their party; if they sought for truth with more humility, instead of, in the conceit of fancied knowledge, resenting as an insult every attempt to set them right?

Are we worthy disciples of Him whose name is the Truth, if greater love of truth can be found among others than amongst us? And yet, if any were now to look for examples of the love of truth, it is not in the religious world he would seek them, but rather among men of science. These last have learned by experience the conditions of success in their pursuit. They must make love of truth their one guiding principle. They must sacrifice to this their most rooted prejudice their most favourite theory. If any one points out to them an error in their system they must not be angry at the insult, but be thankful as having received a benefit. They must not be obstinate in defence of the detected error, but at once cast it out of their system, whether their own reputation suffer or not. It is the same God who is the Author of the book of Nature and of that of Revelation. And the knowledge of both is to be attained under the same conditions. If the students of the one are progressing, and those of the other standing still, it can only be that the latter do not equally comply with the conditions which the love of truth imposes.

One caution more the Apostle suggests: Let those who possess, or believe that they possess, the truth, beware, lest through asperity they throw a hindrance in the way of others attaining to it. In another epistle he gives the rule "in meekness instructing them that oppose themselves." In that from which the text is taken, his rule is, "speaking the truth in love." There are hindrances enough to men's reception of the truth without any being added on our part. Can we expect that men will accept at our hands correction of their errors, if we give them reason to regard us as enemies triumphing in their humiliation, rather than as friends lovingly imparting to them such knowledge as Christ may have made known to us, and they not yet attained to? And that duty on which I have insisted, of truth in our daily intercourse with others, might, if not guarded by love, generate a habit of saying disagreeable things under the cloak of sincerity, as little consistent with our duty as members one of another as the falsehood which the Apostle condemns.

May Christ fill our hearts more and more with love to Himself, and love to our brethren in Him; that we may earnestly desire fully to know Him in every way in which He has revealed Himself; that we may submit our minds in all humility to the removal of every error or prejudice which obscures that knowledge, making known to our brethren, in all love, the lessons Christ has taught us, thankfully learning from them in turn wheresoever they know the way of God more perfectly, and careful in our daily life to show ourselves followers of Him, all whose words were truth, all whose actions love.

XVI

THE SIN OF MUTILATING THE GOSPEL MESSAGE

"Therefore leaving the principles of the doctrine of Christ, let us go on unto perfection; not laying again the foundation of repentance from dead works, and of faith towards God, of the doctrine of baptisms, and of laying on of hands, and of resurrection of the dead, and of eternal judgment."—HEBREWS vi. 1, 2.

THE passage that immediately follows the verses which I have read as the text is one which, from its unusual sternness, has been felt to require some explanation, asserting, as it does, the impossibility of renewing again to repentance those who, after having received certain high privileges, have fallen away. What I am concerned with now is the context in which these threatening words occur. What the writer is insisting on is the necessity of progress in the spiritual life—progress in knowledge as well as in holiness; and what he warns his readers of is the danger that if there is not such progress, there will be retrogression, and such retrogression as may prove to be irretrievable. He has rebuked his readers because when, for the time, they ought to have been teachers, there was need to teach them again the first principles of the oracles of God, and because they had come to have need of milk, and not of strong meat. He exhorts them to leave the principles of the doctrine of Christ, and go on unto perfection. The principles which he wishes them to leave behind are no unimportant doctrines, but the very fundamentals of Christianity. He desires not to have occasion to lay again the foundation of repentance from dead works, of faith toward God, of the doctrine of baptisms, and of laying on of hands, and of resurrection of the dead, and of eternal judgment. This progress they must make, *for* it is impossible for those who were once enlightened, if they shall fall away, to renew them again to repentance. Not such, however, he trusts will be the fate of those whom he addresses, if only they show the same diligence which they had already shown to the full assurance of hope to the end, and be not slothful, but followers of them who, through faith and patience, inherit the promises.

It is impossible to conceive a greater contrast than that between the conception of Gospel preaching entertained by the writer of the Epistle to the Hebrews and that prevalent at the present day. He is impatient if baptized Christians need to be taught again the way of salvation. He augurs ill of them, and is filled with awful apprehensions as to their condition if there is occasion to speak to them of such fundamental points as repentance and faith and eternal judgment, and the doctrine of baptism, and the laying on of hands. Now, on the contrary, the restatement of the way of salvation is held to be the only thing that deserves the name of Gospel preaching. No matter how often the people have been told it, and how well they all know it, they must be told it over again every time they are addressed, lest, perchance, some one should come in among them who has not been informed of it. Whatever is more than this is condemned as unedifying. Naturally, when the preacher's range of topics is so much circumscribed, a danger might seem to arise that he might not have materials to occupy his time. But this danger is avoided by the wide range of illustration which is permitted. Lest the hearers should weary at the sameness of the sermon, the preacher may rouse their flagging attention by telling them stories. There is scarcely any anecdote known to him which an ingenious man may not utilise by a suitable application. The only one thing he must not do is to bring his hearers' intellect into action, for if the sermon gives exercise to the reasoning powers, it is held not to belong to the class of evangelistic preaching.

Closely akin to what I have been saying as to the difference between the teaching of the text and common modern opinion is the prevalent approval of undenominational religion. Why, it is asked, should not clergymen of different denominations lay aside their disputes about the unimportant matters on which they disagree, and all join in preaching those fundamental doctrines in which they are united? It is a kind of compact in which members of our own Church of necessity get the worst. Our Church, for instance, attributes a certain importance to the sacraments; some, like the Quakers, think it needless or superstitious to use these rites at all; others think we may lawfully use them, provided we don't think we get any particular good by them. Well, it is proposed we should all sink our disputes, and work together on the terms of saying nothing about the sacraments. So, again, our Church holds that the Christian ministry is of divine institution, and that its threefold order dates from apostolic times. We are asked to work together with men all of whom reject the episcopal order, and many of whom treat as a usurpation the setting apart any order of men to minister in divine things, on the terms that the joint services shall be conducted on an equality by men who have received episcopal orders, or non-episcopal orders, or no orders at all.

I need not speak of such minor matters as the preference we give to forms of prayer. In order to work together with persons who dislike them, we compromise matters by giving them up as long as our joint action continues. In short, without going into details this is evident, that if two persons dispute whether certain things be true, silence on their subjects of difference determines nothing either way; but if their difference be whether certain things are of any importance, then an agreement that nothing shall be said about this controversy, or that the whole subject shall be put out of sight, is really a very decisive determination in favour of the side which lightly esteems the things in question.

However, putting this point aside, what I am now insisting on is the complete contradiction of undenominational preaching to the teaching of the text. If we put out of our Gospel any teaching on the points on which Christians disagree, we leave behind such merely elementary doctrines that the preacher must be perpetually laying the foundation, and never building on it; always feeding his flock with the thinnest of milk, so that their growth is impossible. And without growth, what sign of life is there?

It ought to be well understood that the cry for undenominational religion, that is to say, the cutting out of the Gospel all but a very small number of doctrines supposed to be essential, really implies the rejection of the claims of Christianity to be a revelation from God. If Christianity be of man, we can easily apply our measures to it, and can pick out in it those things which we judge to be really useful and important, throwing aside all that seems to us superfluous or not well calculated to produce good results. If Christianity be a revelation from God, we may not thus deal with it. A message from God in its very conception tells us of something which our natural powers could not reveal to us. It is so absurd as to be inconceivable that any man should in his heart believe that God had sent him a message, but at the same time judge that certain parts of that message were so unimportant as not to be worth his attending to them. Any one who accepts Christianity as a revelation is self-condemned if he do not make it his business to know *all* that it contains, and to practise *all* that it commands. Accordingly the great strength of the cry for undenominational religion is that it exactly expresses the feelings of all who are anti-supernaturalists, and who do not regard Christianity as a revelation. Such men recognise the Christian Church to be what Mr. Matthew Arnold has truly, however inadequately, described it, a great society for the promotion of goodness in the world. Just so far as it fulfils this end they look upon it as deserving of regard; when it proceeds a step beyond they deny its claim to be attended to. That enforcement of the moral law in which Christian sects generally agree they accept; the points on which these sects differ they reject as unprofitable subtleties, as questions on which it cannot be said that there is a right side and a wrong side, the folly being to discuss them at all.

> " For modes of faith let graceless zealots fight ;
> His can't be wrong whose life is in the right."

A body of so-called Christians, who cry out for undenominational religion, naturally finds sympathy and applause from professed or unconscious unbelievers. It may be said, indeed, that it is unfair to class the evangelistic patrons of an undenominational Christianity with the infidel approvers of undogmatic religion: for that the residuum of teaching to which the two parties respectively cut down the Christian doctrine is in the two cases quite different. To the one who looks mainly to the welfare of society, and values the Christian minister chiefly because he helps or supersedes the policeman, the Ten Commandments appear to be the most important part of the message he delivers. But this is exactly the part which is left out of the teaching of the others. "Do this," is the maxim of the one. "Do nothing," the favourite watchword of the other. And it is a curious instance how a Scripture phrase often gets a meaning put upon it quite at variance with the general drift of the passage in which it occurs, that those who seem to give no heed to the lesson taught in the passage I have read as my text have derived from the phrase "dead works" which occurs in this, and in another passage in the same Epistle, the doctrine for which it is not easy to find Scripture warrant, that "doing is a deadly thing." For it need hardly be said that the doctrine that there is something wrong or dangerous in doing good works is very different from the doctrine that we are to trust for salvation only to the merits of our Lord and Saviour Jesus Christ, and not to our own works or deservings. It must be owned, then, that the different parties who would reduce Christian teaching to that part of it which is common to several sects are not agreed among themselves as to the part which they retain; but they are perfectly agreed as to their principle of procedure; and it is the infidel who carries out that principle most consistently. He who regards natural religion as the sole revelation of the Creator's will, justly and consistently dismisses as unworthy of attention the additions by which what he regards the simple truth has been overlaid. But if one holds that what the light of nature had made known has been supplemented by a miraculous revelation, with what consistency can he undertake to pronounce himself to be a competent judge as to what parts of that revelation are important? When those who agree in acknowledging the authority of that revelation differ as to whether this or that doctrine be part of it, that is a question that deserves examination, in order that if the doctrine be found really to belong to the revelation we may embrace it, or if not, we may reject it as a vainly imagined fable. But surely it is arbitrary in the highest degree to say, either that no doctrine as to which any Christian sect has doubted can belong to the divine revelation; or else to say, that though such disputed doctrines may belong to it, they cannot be of any importance.

And even if this principle were true, it is again the infidel who consistently carries it out. For the doctrines which he counts important are held in common by all who call themselves Christians; but according to the others, those truths which they specially regard as the Gospel were buried out of sight almost before the Apostles were in their graves, were scarcely heard of for hundreds of years, and even now are only distinctly proclaimed by a minority of Christians. There is one party now who only acknowledge, as forming part of the Christian Church at all, those bodies which have preserved episcopal organisation—namely, the Roman, the Greek, and the Anglican communions. It is remarkable that these bodies, which in the eyes of some form the entire of the Church, in the view of others are just those who are most completely ignorant of the Gospel; the Romans and the Greeks not preaching it at all, and probably more than half the English clergy being not less remiss in proclaiming it. So it is that the infidel, in his call for undogmatic religion, is far more comprehensive in his sympathies than the bulk of Protestants who desire to sink denominational distinctions. Take the Church in the darkest and most ignorant of times, the one has no eyes for anything but the superstition which prevailed, and regards the whole as possessed by the spirit of evil; the other has frank recognition for the good that was done. An unbeliever of our own day has energetically protested against the doctrine "that the mediæval Church, with the fine reticulation of its common Christian sentiment, penetrating into recesses of the German forests, and into valleys of the Caledonian hills, in which the Roman legions never made good their footing, binding Europe into a unity of Christian brotherhood, finer and deeper than the unity of imperial dominion, should have been a masterpiece of

Satanic organisation; that the Crusaders who shed their blood to rescue the sepulchre of Christ from the infidel; the monks and nuns, whose prayers arose night and day in Alpine valleys, their table spread for the wayfarer by day, and their unquenched taper guiding his steps in the darkness; the bishops and abbots and preaching friars who, amid countless instances of failure and falsity, were, on the whole, the friends of the poor and the teachers of the ignorant, should have been the subtly hoodwinked emissaries of the devil." Thus we see that if we are to understand by undenominational Christianity that portion of Christian doctrine which is common to the various sects, then unless we put a most arbitrary restriction on the name Christian, we are reduced to the system of doctrine which is held by every enlightened Deist.

Once more those fragments of Christianity which the unbeliever values are unquestionable truths which before revelation the Author of our nature had written on our hearts; but the form which our religion takes in the representations of the other is so at variance with the witness of our consciences, that if it truly represented Christianity, the evidence for Christianity would not suffice to prove its truth. God is depicted as selecting certain persons as the objects of special favour denied to others, the favoured persons being not the best, the most virtuous, the most unselfish, but the most self-confident. The favour with which these persons are regarded is not diminished whatever their sins may be; and, on the other hand, if they who are not so favoured strive to their utmost to do God's will, their "doing" is in itself a deadly thing sufficient to insure their condemnation. If it could be proved that this were the doctrine of the Bible, it would follow that the Bible did not come from that God who loves righteousness and does justice.

If it be asked, how is it possible that any could imagine the Gospel to be anything resembling the system I have described, the source of the error may be traced to neglect of the lessons taught in the text, to forgetfulness that the Christian life is one of progress, and, consequently, to the conception that the one important thing is that step which marks the transition from darkness to light. If that step have been once made all fear may be dismissed: the Christian life may be trusted to take care of itself: all will be sure to follow right from a good beginning; he who has started well need thenceforward think of nothing but how to induce others to do as he has done. If this theory were true, there would be no foundation for the rebuke of the text; we could do nothing better than go over again and again what be the first principles of the doctrine of Christ; nothing better than lay over and over again the foundations, the right laying of which involves of necessity the perfection of the building. But the Apostle teaches us to look on our religion rather as a life than as an act; he calls on us to run with patience the race that is set before us, not to make with confidence the jump that is set before us: in other words, the metaphors that are employed, and the general tenor of the language used, not only in the Epistle we are considering, but by all the New Testament writers, teach us to look on religion not as a thing disposed of and settled in one great crisis, but as a long-continued, lifelong series of actions and affections. That in such a life there will be crises and points of transition we need not deny. It is so in nature: continuity is the law that pervades all nature, yet that continuity is not inconsistent with certain points of abrupt change. For instance, there is no change more wonderful, if familiarity had not dulled in us all sense of wonder, than the rising of the sun, which wakes the world from cold and deathlike sleep to heat and life and light. But this passage from darkness to light is but a stage in a continuous process. The darkness that had preceded was not of uniform gloom. Before the sunrise many a premonitory twilight ray had brightened the sky; and after the sunrise the brightening still goes on until it arrives at meridian splendour. So again, our spiritual birth is compared to natural birth: yet that great and wonderful change of state and condition is consistent with a necessity of growth both previous and subsequent. And this is the analogy urged in the text. For if any cut down the Gospel message to, "Ye must be born again," and have nothing more to say, they are reminded that for any one to continue in the state in which he was born, a mere babe, desiring the same nutriment as at first, and making no growth, is a thing impossible, if there have been any real life at all.

Perhaps it may be said that I am combating an imaginary danger. It may be said that they who confine their preaching to the doctrine of conversion fully acknowledge that no man deserves to be owned as a Christian if his life is inconsistent with his profession, and that their own lives sufficiently show that they are as zealous for good works as those who give them a more prominent place in their preaching. If this were even true, the warning of the text would no less deserve to be attended to; for even though we could see no bad consequence to follow from the setting our own measures on God's revelation, and from the neglect of all the parts of it which seemed to us of less importance, we might still be sure that no part of His revealed Word could be useless, and that by neglecting any part of it we must do ourselves an injury. But I think it is plain to see that bad consequences do follow from the maiming of Christ's Gospel, both to the individual who is wrongly taught and to the whole Christian society. In the first place, a prominent feature of this teaching is the disparagement of the means of grace. At the time when the Epistle to the Hebrews was written, there were certain doctrines connected with baptism and the laying on of hands, which the writer counted so fundamental and important, and knew to be habitually taught to Christians so early, that he regarded it as needless to dwell on them to any well-taught Christian as on the doctrines of repentance from dead works and of faith in God. It is on the surface of the New Testament that Christ instituted certain ordinances, and appointed them as means of grace to those who should believe on Him. But the theory that every believer is at once complete and perfect in Christ, wanting nothing, leads immediately to the inference, what need now of baptism or of the Lord's Supper, or of Church attendance, when I have already everything I want? It follows that if these institutions of Christ really confer any benefit, these benefits are lost to those who are instructed lightly to esteem them. Connected with this is the total absence of humility in the new converts. They are taught that they have no need to mourn for sin either past or still present with them. All has been buried out of sight. It is even an insult to God's grace to ask His forgiveness of it. It is clear what must be a man's habitual judgment of himself if even when he comes into the presence of a God of infinite purity no thought suggests itself to him that there is anything in his soul which needs restoration or pardon. But it is said God looks on the believer as he is in Christ, and can see nothing of sin or imperfection in him. But it is forgotten how dangerous it is to press to forced consequences the metaphorical language which we are of necessity forced to employ when we speak of the Divine mind. We are absolutely unable to conceive of God's attributes as they are in themselves, but only as they affect us. The fact that God for Christ's sake does not inflict on Christ's people punishment which their sins deserve, may be briefly expressed in the form, that God does not impute sin to those who believe in Christ. But still it must remain true that things are what they are, and that God must see them as they are. Otherwise we should arrive at the absurd conclusion that men are more clear-sighted than God; that it is possible to deceive God when it is not possible to deceive man. Men can discern plainly that you are full of pride, self-will, unchastened tempers, unholy dispositions; but God can see none of these things. Such is not the doctrine of the real Gospel. That never leads us to forget that we are guilty creatures who have erred and strayed from God's ways; who have done what we ought not to have done, and left undone what we ought to have done: though it does teach us to look on God not as an enemy, but as in Christ an Almighty and most merciful Father, who is able and willing for Christ's sake not merely to remit the punishment of sin, but to give us His Holy Spirit, if we seek it as He has appointed, to help us to fight against sin, and to subdue its power over our souls.

The absence of humility in the new converts does not merely consist in over-confidence in their attainments in holiness, but also in knowledge. All through the Epistles it is assumed that a man is not competent to fill the office of teacher if he be but a novice. A babe, it is said in the context of the passage read as my text, is unskilful in the word of righteousness. Those addressed are reproached because they needed to be taught when for the time they ought to be teachers; implying that it was some standing in the Church which would qualify them to fill the office of teachers. Now all this is reversed. Every one is dealt with as if on the first moment of his conversion he were complete in knowledge and competent to instruct others. I have been told of cases of mere children in an inquiry room, who the moment the terrors that had been raised in them had abated, and they were able to say they had found peace, were directed to get up from their knees, and go and teach others what they had learned. And it really is the case that such children would then know all that their directors themselves counted important to teach, all that they themselves habitually dwelt on. Not merely are the new converts led to acquiesce in their own scanty knowledge, as if it were complete, but they are taught to despise as ignorant of the Gospel those who reject their system, not by any means because they are ignorant of it, but because they know it too well, and are persuaded that this maimed Gospel is a false representation of the real Gospel.

If every new convert is qualified to teach, *a fortiori*, every member of the Church is fit to teach; not only to proclaim Christianity to heathen, as every one admits he may, but to instruct his brother Christians. And, indeed, in the system I am considering, the Gospel has been so mutilated and cut down, that little time is necessary to learn it, and little learning necessary to teach it. Thus the system is at once, practically and theoretically, in flagrant contradiction with what is patent on the surface of the New Testament, that Christ and His Apostles instituted an order of men whose special work it should be, by giving heed to reading and exhortation and doctrine, to make themselves fit to teach—that so rightly dividing the Word of Truth they might by sound doctrine exhort and convince the gainsayers.

From the effects of the teaching I am considering on individual converts, let me pass to its effect on Christians as a body. And here its mischievous effects are even more apparent. For the whole teaching only regards as important the question, how the individual is to obtain pardon of his sins from God, and deliberately ignores anything that may be said in the New Testament as to the relations in which he stands to his brother Christians. Now it is plain from the New Testament that Christ formed His people into a Society; that the Apostles never made a single convert who was taught that his isolated faith in Christ would save him, if he did not show the reality of his faith by public confession of it in visible union with the society which Christ formed. It is certain from history that the triumphs the Church won were greatly due to the perfection of its organisation; and experience tells us now that the dissensions of Christians among themselves are a grave hindrance to the progress of the Gospel among unbelievers. When we see what a power for good the Christian Church has been in the world, we find nothing incredible in the statement that Christ has made it a duty on every believer in His Gospel to join himself to the society which He formed, or in the statement that Christ has made it His ordinary method to bestow through that society certain spiritual blessings.

When, then, I am asked to excuse men's errors in doctrine in consideration of the amount of good they are doing, I find myself unable to recognise them as doing good, or as helping Christ's cause, when I see that what they are really doing is, under the name of unsectarianism, to add a new sect to the many into which Christianity has been broken: when I see that, by pulverising Christians into a number of loosely connected units, they are destroying their power to deal with the vice and ungodliness in the world; when I see that they weaken their disciples' respect and love for all Christians who will not say their shibboleth; when I see that they repel unbelievers by presenting to them the Gospel, as if it were nothing but an ignoble scheme for quieting men's fears of hell;

fears from which the unbeliever thinks he can relieve himself by a shorter process. I do not refuse to recognise that good has been done when men who had been living in habitual forgetfulness of God, and in disobedience to His law, are taught, even with considerable mixture of error, to rule their life by a higher standard. I unfeignedly rejoice, and I count it as good work, whenever irreligious men, who, in no true sense of the word, deserved to be called Christians, are brought, with however defective knowledge, to be in some sense worthy of that name. If only such were the converts made, I should utter no word of blame; but it seems to me that the great majority of them are persons who have been brought up in the fear of God, and in respect for His Word, who have been causelessly disquieted with alarm because they only venture to speak of their future salvation in terms of faith and hope, and not of infallible certainty. And striking a balance as best I can between those who, by the exertions of the so-called Evangelists, are raised to a higher level in the Christian life, and those who are dragged down to a lower, I am unable to give a verdict in their favour.

But our business is not to judge others but to seek our own duty, and it seems plain, not from single texts, but from the whole tenor of the New

Testament, that the Christian life, if it be real, is one of continuous growth and progress; that he who believes in Christ is not complete and perfect in Him in any such sense as to exclude the necessity of continual advance both in holiness and in knowledge; that we are not justified in allowing our estimate of the importance of any one part of the Christian scheme to cause us to lose sight of any other; and that no Christian minister has done his duty to his people if he shun to declare unto them the *whole* counsel of God.

THE END

Printed by R. & R. CLARK *Edinburgh.*